One of America's finest poets and feminist theorists here gathers together her most important prose pieces, writings which investigate literature and politics, women's history and culture, exploring problems of power and the lack of it: the transforming power of literature, illustrated by brilliant essays on the works of Charlotte Brontë, Anne Sexton, Emily Dickinson, Natalya Gorbanevskaya and others; the power of education – its misuse, its hope for the future; the power of language to re-name, re-define, re-shape the world.

This is no mere collection of writings: it is a book by a great poet and thinker, with a movement and force of its own, documenting the development of one individual consciousness and presenting a determined attempt to establish women's work and thinking with a tradition of its own.

Adrienne Rich was born in Baltimore in 1929. She graduated from Radcliffe College in 1951, the year her first volume of poems was published. She has held two Guggenheim Fellowships, and has taught at many American colleges and universities. She has published nine volumes of poetry, one of which, *Diving Into The Wreck* was co-winner of the 1974 National Book Award of America. Her first prose work, *Of Woman Born: Motherhood as Experience and Institution*, is also published by Virago. Professor of English at Douglass College, Rutgers University, Adrienne Rich lives in Massachusetts.

By Adrienne Rich

On Lies, Secrets, and Silence ~

Selected Prose 1966-1978

 ADRIENNE RICH

On Lies, Secrets, and Silence ◠

Selected Prose 1966–1978

Virago
London

Published by VIRAGO Limited 1980
5 Wardour Street, London W1V 3HE

First published in America by
W. W. Norton & Company, Inc. 1979

ISBN 0 86068 155 6 Casebound Edition
ISBN 0 86068 156 4 Paperback Edition

Printed in Great Britain by
Lowe & Brydone Printers Ltd,
Thetford, Norfolk

Acknowledgments

"The Tensions of Anne Bradstreet" originally appeared as "Anne Bradstreet and Her Poetry." Reprinted by permission of the publishers from *The Works of Anne Bradstreet*, edited by Jeannine Hensley, Cambridge, Mass.: The Belknap Press of Harvard University Press, copyright © 1967 by the President and Fellows of Harvard College. "When We Dead Awaken: Writing as Re-Vision" first appeared in *College English*, vol. 34, no. 1 (October 1972). "Teaching Language in Open Admissions" first appeared in *Harvard English Studies*, #4, edited by Monroe Engel (1973). Reprinted by permission of the Editors and the Department of English of Harvard University. "The Antifeminist Woman" first appeared in *The New York Review of Books*. "Woman Observing, Preserving, Conspiring, Surviving: The Poems of Eleanor Ross Taylor," © 1972 by The New York Times Company. Reprinted by permission. "Jane Eyre: The Temptations of a Motherless Woman" first appeared in *Ms.*, vol. 2, no. 4 (October 1973). "Caryatid: Two Columns" first appeared in *The American Poetry Review*. "Vietnam and Sexual Violence," vol. 2, no. 3 (May–June 1973); "Natalya Gorbanevskaya," vol. 2, no. 1 (Jan.–Feb. 1973). "Toward a Woman-Centered University," from *Women and the Power to Change* edited by Florence Howe. Copyright © 1975 by the Carnegie Foundation for the Advancement of Teaching. Reprinted by permission of the Foundation and McGraw-Hill Book Co. "Vesuvius at Home: The Power of Emily Dickinson" first appeared in *Parnassus: Poetry in Review* (Fall–Winter 1976). "Women and Honor: Some Notes on Lying" first appeared in *Heresies*, vol. 1, no. 1. "Motherhood in Bondage," © 1976 by The New York Times Company. Reprinted by permission. "It Is the Lesbian in Us . . ." first appeared in *Sinister Wisdom*, vol. 1, no. 3 (Spring 1977). "Conditions for Work: The Common World of Women" first appeared in *Working It Out*, edited by Sara Ruddick and Pamela Daniels, New York: Pantheon Books, 1977. "Husband-Right and Father-Right" first appeared as the introduction to *Legal Kidnapping* by Anna Demeter, published by Beacon Press, 1977. "The Meaning of Our Love for Women Is What We Have Constantly to Expand" was first published by Out & Out Books, 1977. "Claiming an Education" first appeared in *the common woman*, vol. 1, no. 2 (Autumn 1977). "Power and Danger: Works of a Common Woman" originally appeared as the introduction to *The Work of a Common Woman: The Collected Poetry of Judy Grahn*, 1964–1977, published by and available from Diana Press, 4400 Market St., Oakland, CA 94608. "Disloyal to Civilization: Feminism, Racism, Gynephobia" first appeared in *Chrysalis*, #7 (1979).

Grateful acknowledgment is made for permission to quote from the following: Emily Dickinson, copyright 1914, 1942 by Martha Dickinson Bianchi. Copyright 1929 by Martha Dickinson Bianchi. Copyright © 1957 by Mary L. Hampson. Copyright 1935 by Martha Dickinson Bianchi. Copyright © 1963 by Mary L. Hampson. Reprinted by permission of Little, Brown and Company. Reprinted by permission of the publishers and the Trustees of Amherst College from *The Poems of Emily Dickinson*, edited by Thomas H. Johnson, Cambridge, Mass.: The Belknap Press of Harvard University Press, copyright © 1951, 1955 by the President and Fellows of Harvard College. Judy Grahn, from *The Work of a Common Woman: The Collected Poetry of Judy Grahn*, 1964–1977, Oakland, Calif.: Diana Press, 1977. Reprinted by permission. Richard Hugo, the lines from "Announcement" are reprinted from *What Thou Lovest Well Remains American, Poems by Richard Hugo*, with the permission of W. W. Norton & Company, Inc. Copyright © 1975 by W. W. Norton & Company, Inc. June Jordan, excerpt from "Metarhetoric" from *Things That I Do in the Dark: Selected Poetry by June Jordan*, © 1977 by June Jordan. Reprinted by permission of Random House, Inc. Audre Lorde, excerpt from "Power" from *The Black Unicorn*, New York: W. W. Norton & Company, Inc., 1978. First appeared in *The Village Voice*. Pablo Neruda, from *The Captain's Verses*, translated by Donald D. Walsh. Copyright © 1972 by Pablo Neruda and Donald D. Walsh. Reprinted by permission of New Directions. Adrienne Rich, "Orion," "Aunt Jennifer's Tigers," "Planetarium," "The Loser," and the lines from "Snapshots of a Daughter-in-Law" are reprinted from *Poems Selected and New: 1950–1974*, by Adrienne Rich, with the permission of W. W. Norton & Company, Inc. Copyright © 1975, 1973, 1971, 1969, 1966, by W. W. Norton & Company, Inc. Copyright © 1967, 1963, 1962, 1961, 1960, 1959, 1958, 1957, 1956, 1955, 1954, 1953, 1952, 1951, by Adrienne Rich. Eleanor Ross

Taylor, from *Welcome Eumenides*, © 1972 by Eleanor Ross Taylor. Reprinted by permission of George Braziller, Inc. Virginia Woolf, from a letter to Ethel Smyth, June 8, 1933, in the Henry W. and Albert A. Berg Collection, The New York Public Library, Astor, Lenox and Tilden Foundations; reprinted by permission of Professor Quentin Bell.

Contents

Foreword: On History, Illiteracy, Passivity, Violence, and Women's Culture

In October 1902, Elizabeth Cady Stanton died at the age of eighty-seven. Susan B. Anthony had worked with her for fifty years. Together, they had learned the meaning of activism in the abolitionist movement. Together, over the cradles of Stanton's seven children, they had hammered out political strategy and speeches; together they had traveled from town to town organizing suffrage meetings; together had faced abuse and indignation, caricature and slander; together had argued, disagreed, and persevered through the bonds of an unremitting love and loyalty. Anthony, bereaved both of her most intimate friend and her most trusted colleague, found herself on Stanton's death beset by reporters, whose questions revealed how little they knew and understood of the movement she and Stanton had labored in for half a century. Her cry of impatience could strike a chord of recognition in radical feminists today: *How shall we ever make the world intelligent on our movement?*

As I write this, in North America 1978, the struggle to constitutionalize the equal rights of women finds itself facing many of the same opponents that the fight for the ballot confronted: powerful industrial interests, desiring to keep a cheap labor pool of women or threatened by women's economic independence; the networks of communication which draw advertising revenue from those interests; the erasure of women's political and historic past which makes each new generation of feminists appear as an abnormal excrescence on the face of time; trivialization of the issue itself, sometimes even by its advocates when they fail to connect it with the deeper issues on which twentieth-century women are engaged in our particular moment of feminist history. Susan B. Anthony understood that the demand for the ballot was a radical demand, not simply because she hoped that women voters would use their votes to change the lives of women, but because she sensed a profound symbolism embodied in the denial of suffrage to women: the same kind of symbolism which, in the history of American racism, has surrounded the concept of "separate-but-equal" toilets, drinking fountains, and schools, the symbolism which pervades any arrangement made by a dominant group for the less powerful or the powerless. Anthony has often been represented as a "single-minded," obsessed, narrow-visioned fanatic who could see nothing but the ballot and whose strength was a fanatic's tireless drive. We have only to read her published letters, papers, and speeches, to recognize that she was a remarkable political philosopher, who deeply loved and was loved by women and drew on that love for her strength and persistence; who understood how both middle-class marriage and factory labor enslaved women; who comprehended to the full, and never compromised upon, the radical symbolism of the constitutional amendment for which she and Stanton fought for a lifetime, and whose ratification neither lived to see.

But most twentieth-century feminists have not read the lives and works of Anthony and Stanton, except perhaps as excerpted in anthologies. The six volumes of the *History of Woman Suffrage* and Ida Husted Harper's three-volume life of Anthony, both densely packed sources of knowledge about the real thought and feelings of nineteenth-century feminism, exist in library reprint editions; only Stanton's autobiography has been reprinted in paperback.* So also the work of earlier feminist pamphleteers and theorists like Jane Anger, Rachel Speight, and Elizabeth Carey in sixteenth-century England has been devalued or blotted out. The historian Patricia Gartenberg has noted how little the reign of Elizabeth Tudor—often glorified as

---

The Concise History of Woman Suffrage: Selections from the Classic Work of Stanton, Anthony, Gage, and Harper, edited by Mari Jo and Paul Buhle (University of Illinois Press paperback) was issued as this book went to press.

a feminist heroine—actually affected the possibilities for other women of her time; women writers did *not* flourish during her reign, and the economic and political situation of women was actually in decline. We have been left, however, with Elizabeth I, and have lost the voices and lives of Rachel Speight, Jane Anger, Elizabeth Carey, and Anne Askew, the latter tortured to death and burned as a heretic.*

The entire history of women's struggle for self-determination has been muffled in silence over and over. One serious cultural obstacle encountered by any feminist writer is that each feminist work has tended to be received as if it emerged from nowhere; as if each of us had lived, thought, and worked without any historical past or contextual present. This is one of the ways in which women's work and thinking has been made to seem sporadic, errant, orphaned of any tradition of its own.**

In fact, we do have a long feminist tradition, both oral and written, a tradition which has built on itself over and over, recovering essential elements even when those have been strangled or wiped out. Yet still a Mary Wollstonecraft (labeled "the hyena in petticoats") is viewed without reference to her forebears, not only the sixteenth-century women pamphleteers but the wisewomen and witches, who had been the objects of wholesale persecution and massacre for three centuries. So also Simone de Beauvoir has been read without reference to the destruction of the political women's clubs of the French Revolution, or the writings of Olympe des Gouges and Flora Tristan. So also has the articulate political feminism and socialism of Virginia Woolf been obscured by the notion that she was "Bloomsbury"—individualist, elitist, lacking class-consciousness, and "gay" in the most frivolous sense, without reference to her connections with Margaret Llewelyn Davies, the Women's Cooperative Guild, the antipatriarchal anthropologist Jane Harrison, the lesbian/

---

* Patricia Gartenberg, "Women in the Culture of Renaissance England: 1500–1640." Paper presented at the Berkshire Conference on Women's History, Mount Holyoke College, August 1978.

** For a detailed delineation of the effects of "the phenomenon of interruption" on women's culture, see Michelle Cliff, "The Resonance of Interruption," in *Chrysalis: A Magazine of Women's Culture*, no. 8 (635 South Westlake Avenue, Los Angeles, Ca. 90057).

feminist suffrage activist Ethel Smyth.* So also is each contemporary feminist theorist attacked or dismissed ad feminam, as if her politics were simply an outburst of personal bitterness or rage.

In particular, the women's movement of the late twentieth century is evolving in the face of a culture of manipulated passivity (the mirror-image of which is violence, both random and institutional). The television screen purveys everywhere its loaded messages; but even when and where the message may seem less deadly to the mind, the nature of the medium itself breeds passivity, docility, flickering concentration. The decline in adult literacy means not merely a decline in the capacity to read and write, but a decline in the impulse to puzzle out, brood upon, look up in the dictionary, mutter over, argue about, turn inside-out in verbal euphoria, the "incomparable medium" of language—Tillie Olsen's term. And this decline comes, ironically, at a moment in history when women, the majority of the world's people, have become most aware of our need for real literacy, for our own history, most searchingly aware of the lies and distortions of the culture men have devised, when we are finally prepared to take on the most complex, subtle, and drastic revaluation ever attempted of the condition of the species.**

The television screen has throughout the world replaced, or is fast replacing: oral poetry; old wives' tales; children's story-acting games and verbal lore; lullabies; "playing the sevens"; political argument; the reading of books too difficult for the reader, yet somehow read; tales of "when-I-was-your-age" told by parents and grandparents to children, linking them to their own past; singing in parts; memorization of poetry; the oral transmitting of skills and remedies; reading aloud; recitation; both community and solitude. People grow up who

---

* See Jane Marcus, "No More Horses: Virginia Woolf on Art and Propaganda" in *Women's Studies*, vol. 4, 1977; also Marcus's essay, "Thinking Back Through Our Mothers" in the essay collection of the same name, edited by her, to be published in 1979.

** According to an NBC study, working women watch television much less than women at home (*National NOW Times*, October 1978). The implications for the television industry of a massive withdrawal of women from its audience, particularly from daytime viewing, are interesting to contemplate. It is clearly in the interests of the industry and its advertisers to keep women addicted, not merely to TV but to the social arrangements which isolate us in the home and which reinforce economic dependency and apolitical panaceas for political problems.

not only don't know how to read, a late-acquired skill among the world's majority; they don't know how to talk, to tell stories, to sing, to listen and remember, to argue, to pierce an opponent's argument, to use metaphor and imagery and inspired exaggeration in speech; people are growing up in the slack flicker of a pale light which lacks the concentrated burn of a candle flame or oil wick or the bulb of a gooseneck desk lamp: a pale, wavering, oblong shimmer, emitting incessant noise, which is to real knowledge or discourse what the manic or weepy protestations of a drunk are to responsible speech. Drunks do have a way of holding an audience, though, and so does the shimmery ill-focused oblong screen.*

Women's culture, on the other hand, is active: women have been the truly active people in all cultures, without whom human society would long ago have perished, though our activity has most often been on behalf of men and children.** Today women are talking to each other, recovering an oral culture, telling our life-stories, reading aloud to one another the books that have moved and healed us, analyzing the language that has lied about us, reading our own words aloud to each other. But to name and found a culture of our own means a real break from the passivity of the twentieth-century Western mind. It is the deadly "radical passivity of men" (Daly's phrase) that has given us an essentially passive-voiced dominant culture, whose artifacts are the kind that lead to a deepening passivity and submission: "Pop" art; television; pornography.

To question everything. To remember what it has been forbidden even to mention. To come together telling our stories, to look afresh at, and then to describe for ourselves, the frescoes of the Ice Age, the nudes of "high art," the Minoan seals and figurines, the moon-

---

* To view on television a film of any depth or dimensionality first seen in a theater is to experience directly how the conditions of television dilute and degrade whatever it processes. The difference between television and cinema is vast, and deserves more exploration than I can attempt here.

** The myth of female passivity has been broken, I should hope by now, by writers such as Mary Daly (*Gyn/Ecology: The Metaethics of Radical Feminism*) and Susan Griffin (*Woman and Nature: The Roaring Inside Her*), if not earlier by the Brontës in nineteenth-century England, by Sojourner Truth in her famous pronouncement, or by twentieth-century women novelists like Zora Neale Hurston (*Their Eyes Were Watching God*), Toni Morrison (*Sula*), or Tillie Olsen (*Tell Me a Riddle; Yonnondio*).

landscape embossed with the booted print of a male foot, the micro-
scopic virus, the scarred and tortured body of the planet Earth. To do
this kind of work takes a capacity for constant active presence, a natu-
ralist's attention to minute phenomena, for reading between the
lines, watching closely for symbolic arrangements, decoding difficult
and complex messages left for us by women of the past. It is work, in
short, that is opposed by, and stands in opposition to, the entire
twentieth-century white male capitalist culture.

How shall we ever make the world intelligent on our movement? I
do not think the answer lies in trying to render feminism easy, popular, and instantly gratifying. To conjure with the passive culture and
adapt to its rules is to degrade and deny the fullness of our meaning
and intention. When I thought of publishing these essays, and of
how they might be read, I was faced with a significant effect of cultural passivity: that for many readers the feminist movement is simply whatever the mass media say it is, whether on the television screen
or in the pages of the *New York Times, Psychology Today, Mother
Jones,* or *Ms.* Willful ignorance, reductiveness, caricature, distortion, trivialization—these are familiar utensils, not only in the rhetoric of the organized opposition. We encounter them in the mindless
reviewing of feminist books, and in the fear of feminism prevailing in
the scholarly and academic world. As the film-maker Michelle Cit-
ron remarks, "The culture assumes in general, that male films [read
art, journalism, scholarship, etc.] are objective and female films are
subjective; male subjectivity is still perceived as *the objective point of
view* on all things, in particular women."*

This culture of manipulated passivity, nourishing violence at its
core, has every stake in opposing women actively laying claim to our
own lives. Of all issues on which women around the world are currently moving, the demand for abortion rights has most often been
used to distort and distemper the meaning of our movement. Abortion, like sterilization abuse, is a concrete issue; hardly *the* issue
women would have chosen to symbolize our struggle for self-determination, but one which has been perhaps more mystified, more in-

---

* "Women and Film: A Discussion of Feminist Aesthetics," in *New German Critique,*
no. 13, winter 1978, p. 104.

tellectualized and emotionalized, than any other, and which glares out from the complex spectrum of issues surrounding women's claim to bodily—and hence spiritual—integrity. Sexual harassment on the job; women-beating; rape; genital mutilation; pornography; psychosurgery; the use of dangerous and/or pacifying drugs on women; equal pay for equal work; the rights of lesbian mothers; the erasure of women in the history of the species—these are some of those issues; and most certainly the violent seizure of poor and Third World women's uteruses by the agents of enforced sterilization. I think it is no accident that for all the issues our movement has been addressing, abortion has become the most visible and emotionally charged of all our efforts to speak for ourselves and to defend our own lives. This process, named murder, has been selected to represent the radical feminist struggle as antilife, irresponsible, or ruthless, and as leading to other antilife acts.* A pornography of antiabortion literature and imagery exists: the fetus who will never disturb a mother's sleep; the fetishism of tiny fingers and toes; the image of the callously death-dealing mother. Feminists have responded to this obscene campaign by demonstrations with coat-hangers, reminding the public of the thousands of women—mostly poor women and women of color— who have died and will die of self-abortion or botched illegal abortion. But the imagery of violence persists, whether as inflicted by a woman on a fetus or on herself. The institutional and physical violences against women which lead to an abortion decision, which force us to exert our moral and political energies on this issue at all instead of on ways to create a world more livable for the living, remain unnamed and invisible in the rhetoric of the opposition.

Philosophical, juridical, and Jesuitical debates over the morality of abortion have long filled the legal and theological casebooks, the texts of medical ethics. Meanwhile, in churches and on the steps of legislatures the issue is aired with the self-righteous emotionalism which once marked the casting-out of the unwed mother from the community. Both these forms of the debate are framed in terms of a morality, an ethic, a social conscience which is manmade and

---

*For a discussion of male parasitism on women and identification with the fetus, see Marilyn Frye, "Some Thoughts on Separatism and Power," in *Sinister Wisdom*, no. 6, summer 1978. Available from *Sinister Wisdom*, Box 30541, Lincoln, Nebraska.

male-defined. The questions raised thereby (At what point is a ferti-
lized egg a person? When does the soul start to exist? Shall abortion,
if legal, be federally funded?) are inevitably male questions, posed in
a worldview and an ethical system which has persistently denied
moral and ethical value to women, viewing us always as marginal,
dubious, or dangerous, and in need of special controls. It is time that
we frame our own questions on this as on every other issue, and that
we do so with a full recognition of the weight of the language,
theodicy, and politics that would obstruct our doing so.*

In a world dominated by violent and passive-aggressive men, and
by male institutions dispensing violence, it is extraordinary to note
how often women are represented as the perpetrators of violence,
most of all when we are simply fighting in self-defense or for our
children, or when we collectively attempt to change the institutions
that are making war on us and on our children. In reality, the
feminist movement could be said to be trying to visualize and make
way for a world in which abortion would not be necessary; a world
free from poverty and rape, in which young girls would grow up with
intelligent regard for and knowledge of their bodies and respect for
their minds, in which the socialization of women into heterosexual
romance and marriage would no longer be the primary lesson of culture; in which single women could raise children with a less crushing
cost to themselves, in which female creativity might or might not
choose to express itself in motherhood. Yet, when radical feminists
and lesbian/feminists begin to speak of such a world, when we begin
to sketch the conditions of a life we have collectively envisioned, the
first charge we are likely to hear is a charge of violence: that we are
"man-haters." We hear that the women's movement is provoking
men to rape; that it has caused an increase in violent crimes by
women; and when we demand the right to rear our children in circumstances where they have a chance for more than mere physical
survival, we are called fetus-killers. The beating of women in homes
across this country, the rape of daughters by fathers and brothers, the
fear of rape that keeps old—as well as young—women off the streets,
the casual male violence that can use a car to run two jogging
women off a country road, the sadistic exploitation of women's bod-

* I attempt to frame some of these questions at the end of the essay, "Motherhood: The
Contemporary Emergency and the Quantum Leap" on p. 259.

ies to furnish a multibillion-dollar empire of pornography, the decision taken by powerful white males that one-quarter of the world's women shall be sterilized or that certain selected women—poor and Third World—shall be used as subjects for psychosurgery and contraceptive experiments—these ordinary, everyday events inevitably must lead us to ask: who indeed hates whom, who is killing whom, whose interest is served, and whose fantasies expressed, by representing abortion as the selfish, wilful, morally contagious expression of *woman's* predilection for violence?

The question finally, from a radical feminist and lesbian/feminist perspective, is whether women's bodies are to be viewed as essentially at the service of men; and to what extent the institution of heterosexuality promotes and fosters the belief that they are. Both abortion and lesbianism have been and still are defined as perverse and criminal behavior, by the same culture which endorses sado-masochistic male homosexual and heterosexual behavior, violent pornography, and forcible sterilization. The Marxist-feminist historian Linda Gordon observes in her book *Woman's Body, Woman's Right: A Social History of Birth Control in America*, that heterosexual relations are charged with extreme risk for women, and that the entire balance of power between the sexes must change if birth control and abortion are to be genuinely effective in changing women's lives. She is one of the few heterosexual feminists to have confronted so clearly the institution of heterosexuality as a major buttress of male power. It is high time that that institution receive the same searching scrutiny that class and race have received and are receiving, and that the indoctrination of women toward heterosexuality be challenged just as feminists have challenged women's indoctrination into "feminine" roles and behavior.

It is also crucial that we understand lesbian/feminism in the deepest, most radical sense: as that love for ourselves and other women, that commitment to the freedom of all of us, which transcends the category of "sexual preference" and the issue of civil rights, to become a politics of *asking women's questions*, demanding a world in which the integrity of all women—not a chosen few—shall be honored and validated in every aspect of culture.

The essays in this book represent the journey of my own thought toward the paragraph I have just written. A journey of this kind is not linear. I would feel sorry if I thought that anyone reading this collection of writings would imagine that I had arrived smoothly from that point to this. Rather, I trust the contradictions and repetitions in this book to speak for themselves. I disagree with myself in this book, and I find in myself both severe and tender feelings toward the women I have been, whose thoughts I find here.

Of course a collection like this has involved choice, weeding-out. I have chosen not to include book reviews, for instance, except for "The Antifeminist Woman" and a review of a book by Eleanor Ross Taylor, and I've included the latter both because her remarkable poetry is so little known, and because in the review I touched on themes that run through this volume as a whole. I have not published here anything I do not think is still to some degree usable: that is, part of the effort to define a female consciousness which is political, aesthetic, and erotic, and which refuses to be included or contained in the culture of passivity.

On Lies, Secrets, and Silence ∾

Selected Prose 1966–1978

The Tensions of Anne Bradstreet
(1966)

I wrote this essay at the request of the Harvard University Press, for their edition of *The Works of Anne Bradstreet*, edited by Jeanine Hensley (1967). Reading and writing about Bradstreet, I began to feel that furtive, almost guilty spark of identification so often kindled in me, in those days, by the life of another woman writer. There were real parallels between her life and mine. Like her, I had learned to read and write in my father's library; like her, I had known the ambiguities of patronizing compliments from male critics; like her, I suffered from chronic lameness; but above all, she was one of the few women writers I knew anything about who had also been a mother. The tension between creative work and motherhood had occupied a decade of my life, although it is barely visible in the essay I wrote in 1966. This essay, in fact, shows the limitations of a point of view which took masculine history and literature as its center (e.g., the condescending references to "Women's Archives" on pp. 26 and 29) and which tried from that perspective to view a woman's life and work.

Ten years later, lecturing at Douglass College on American women poets, I could raise questions which were unavailable to me when I wrote the Bradstreet essay: What did it really mean for women to come to a "new world"; in what sense and to what extent *was* it "new" for them? Do the lives of the women of a community change simply because that community migrates to another continent? (The question would have to be asked differently for the poet Phyllis Wheatley, brought to the "new world" as a slave.) What has been the woman poet's relationship to nature, in a land where both women and nature have, from the first, been raped and exploited? Much has been written, by white American male writers, of the difficulties of creating "great literature" at the edge of wilderness, in a society without customs and tradi-

tions. Were the difficulties the same for women? Could women attempt the
same solutions? To what strategies have women poets resorted in order to
handle dangerous and denigrated female themes and experiences? What did
the warning of the midwife heretic Anne Hutchinson's fate mean for Anne
Bradstreet? To what extent is Bradstreet's marriage poetry an expression of
individual feeling, and where does it echo the Puritan ideology of marriage,
including married love as the "duty" of every god-fearing couple? Where are
the stress-marks of anger, the strains of self-division, in her work?

If such questions were unavailable to me in 1966, it was partly because of
the silence surrounding the lives of women—not only our creative work, but
the very terms on which that work has been created; and partly for lack of any
intellectual community which would take those questions seriously. Yet
they were there; unformed. I believe any woman for whom the feminist
breaking of silence has been a transforming force can also look back to a time
when the faint, improbable outlines of unaskable questions, curling in her
brain cells, triggered a shock of recognition at certain lines, phrases, images,
in the work of this or that woman, long dead, whose life and experience she
could only dimly try to imagine.

〜〜〜〜〜〜〜

1630: the expected sea-voyage with its alternations of danger and
boredom, three months of close quarters and raw nerves, sickness
and hysteria and salt meats; finally the wild coast of Massachusetts
Bay, the blazing heat of an American June, the half-dying, famine-
ridden frontier village of Salem, clinging to the edge of an incalculable land-mass.

"*I found a new world and new manners, at which my heart rose.
But after I was convinced it was the way of God, I submitted to it and
joined to the church at Boston.*" Sixty years later she was to write that.
Other hearts had hesitated, at the first view of the same world and its
manners. Anne Bradstreet's heart rose against much that lay before
her, much too that had come along with her in the *Arbella*. She was
eighteen, two years married, out of a civilized and humane background. Her father, Thomas Dudley, a man of education and
worldly experience, had been steward to an earl; her mother, by Cotton Mather's account, "a gentlewoman whose extraction and estates
were considerable." Her own education had been that of the clever
girl in the cultivated seventeenth-century house: an excellent library,

worldly talk, the encouragement of a literate father who loved history. Her husband was a Cambridge man, a Nonconformist minis-
ter's son. Her father, her husband, each was to serve as governor of
Massachusetts; she came to the wilderness as a woman of rank.

Younger, Anne Bradstreet had struggled with a "carnall heart."
Self-scrutiny, precisianism, were in any event expected of Puritan
young people. But her doubts, her "sitting loose from God," were
underscored by uncommon intelligence and curiosity. Once in Massachusetts, in a society coarsened by hardship and meager in conso-
lations, any religious doubt must at times have made everything
seem dubious. Her father wrote back to England a year after their arrival:

> If there be any endued with grace . . . let them come over. . . . For
> others, I conceive they are not yet fitted for this business.
>
> . . . There is not a house where is not one dead, and some houses
> many . . . the natural causes seem to be in the want of warm lodging
> and good diet, to which Englishmen are habituated at home, and the
> sudden increase of heat which they endure that are landed here in sum-
> mer . . . for those only these two last years died of fevers who landed in
> June or July, as those of Plymouth, who landed in winter, died of the
> scurvy.[1]

To read and accept God's will, not only in the deaths of friends, but
in one's own frequent illness, chronic lameness, political tension between one's father and Governor Winthrop, four changes of house
in eight years, difficulty in conceiving a child, private and public
anxiety and hardship, placed a peculiar burden of belief and in-
trospection on an intellectually active, sensually quick spirit.

Seventeenth-century Puritan life was perhaps the most self-conscious ever lived in its requirements of the individual understanding:
no event so trivial that it could not speak a divine message, no disappointment so heavy that it could not serve as a "correction," a
disguised blessing. Faith underwent its hourly testing, the domestic
mundanities were episodes in the drama; the piecemeal thought of a

---

[1] Augustine Jones, *Thomas Dudley, Second Governor of Massachusetts* (Boston,
1899), p. 449.

woman stirring a pot, clues to her "justification" in Christ. A modern consciousness looks almost enviously upon the intense light of significance under which those lives were lived out: "everything had a meaning then," we say, as if that had ever held alert and curious minds back from perverse journeys:

> When I have got over this Block, then have I another put in my way. That admitt this be the true God whom we worship, and that be his word, yet why may not the Popish religion be the right? They have the same God, the same Christ, the same word: they only interpret it one way, we another.

Thus Anne Bradstreet described in her old age, for her children, what the substance of doubt had been. And if Archbishop Laud and the Hierarchists back in England were right, what was one doing, after all, on that stretch of intemperate coast, hoarding fuel, hoarding corn, dragging one's half-sick self to the bedsides of the dying? What was the meaning of it all? One's heart rose in rebellion.

Still, she was devotedly, even passionately married, and through husband and father stood close to the vital life of the community. (Her father was a magistrate at the trial of Anne Hutchinson, the other, heretical, Anne, who threatened the foundations of the colony and "gloried" in her excommunication.) And her mind was alive. Thomas Dudley's library had passed to the New World, and the early childless years, for all their struggles with theology and primitive surroundings, left time, energy to go on reading and thinking. The Bible was the air she and everyone else breathed; but she also knew Raleigh's *History of the World*, Camden's *Annals of Queen Elizabeth*, *Piers Plowman*, Sidney's poems; and she was deeply impressed by Joshua Sylvester's translation of Guillaume Du Bartas's *La Sepmaine du Creation*. [2]

The Divine Weekes and Works, as this elephantine poem was called in English, was an acknowledged popular masterpiece. Du Bartas, the leading French Calvinist poet, was admired as a peer of Ronsard. Sylvester was not his only English translator: Philip Sidney

[2] See Jones, *Thomas Dudley*, p. 260, for a partial listing of books in Dudley's library.

among others had been moved to undertake a version. Sylvester's own poetry had been praised—in verse blurbs—by Samuel Daniel and Ben Jonson.[3] Milton had pillaged *The Divine Weekes* in composing *Paradise Lost*. Anne Bradstreet was thus showing no provinciality of taste in her response to Du Bartas. His poem was, in fact, as one scholar has exhaustively shown, a perfect flea market of ideas, techniques, and allusions for the Puritan poet.[4] Crammed with popular science, catalogues of diseases, gems, fauna, and flora, groaning with hypotheses on the free will of angels, or God's occupation before the First Day, quivering with excesses, laborious and fascinating as some enormous serpent winding endlessly along and forever earthbound, *The Divine Weekes* has, yet, a vitality of sheer conviction about it; one can understand its mesmeric attraction for an age unglutted by trivial or pseudomomentous information. And this poem, sublime at least in its conception, was directly concerned with the most gripping drama recognized by the seventeenth-century mind.

One thing is clear, when one actually reads Anne Bradstreet's early verse by the side of Du Bartas: however much she may have admired his "haughty Stile and rapted wit sublime," she almost never lapsed into his voice. Her admiration was in large measure that of a neophyte bluestocking for a man of wide intellectual attainments; in emulating him she emulated above all:

> Thy Art in natural Philosophy,
> Thy Saint-like mind in grave Divinity.
> Thy piercing skill in high Astronomy,
> And curious insight in Anatomy: . . .
> Thy Physick, musick and state policy . . .

She was influenced more by Du Bartas's range and his encyclopedic conception of poetry, than by his stylistic qualities. That early verse of hers, most often pedestrian, abstract, mechanical, rarely becomes elaborately baroque; at its best her style, even in these apprentice pieces, has a plain modesty and directness which owe nothing to Du

[3] *The Complete Works of Joshua Sylvester* (Edinburgh, 1880), I, xxxvi ff., 13 ff.

[4] See George Coffin Taylor, *Milton's Use of Du Bartas* (Cambridge, Mass.: Harvard University, 1934).

Bartas.[5] She feels herself in his shadow, constantly disclaims the ability to write like him, even if she would; but she seems further to have had reservations about mere imitation of even so stylish a model: "My goods are true (though poor) I love no stealth."

Versifying was not an exceptional pursuit in that society; poetry, if edifying in theme, was highly recommended to the Puritan reader. (A century later Cotton Mather was finding it necessary to caution the orthodox against "a Boundless and Sickly Appetite, for the Reading of Poems, which now the Rickety Nation swarms withal.")[6] Unpublished verse manuscripts circulated in New England before the first printing press began operation. By her own admission, Anne Bradstreet began her verse-making almost accidentally:

> My subject's bare, my brain is bad,
> Or better lines you should have had:
> The first fell in so naturally,
> I knew not how to pass it by . . .

Thus ends her *Quaternion*, or four poems of four books each, written somewhere between 1630 and 1642. Her expositions of "The Humours," "The Ages of Man," "The Seasons," and "The Elements," and above all her long historical poem, "The Four Monarchies," read like a commonplace book put into iambic couplets, the historical, scientific journal of a young woman with a taste for study. Had she stopped writing after the publication of these verses, or had she simply continued in the same vein, Anne Bradstreet would survive in the catalogues of Women's Archives, a social curiosity or at best a literary fossil. The talent exhibited in them was of a kind acceptable to her time and place, but to a later eye indistinct from masses of English verse of the period.

The seventeenth-century Puritan reader was not, however, in search of "new voices" in poetry. If its theme was the individual in his experience of God, the final value of a poem lay in its revelation

[5] To judge from its "Dedication," her *Quaternion* may have owed its inception as much to a poem written by her father on "The Four Parts of the World" as to *The Divine Weekes*.

[6] Kenneth Murdock quotes this in his *Literature and Theology in Colonial New England* (Cambridge, Mass.: Harvard University, 1949) from Mather's *Manductio ad Ministerium*, 1726.

of God and not the individual. Least of all in a woman poet would radical powers be encouraged. Intellectual intensity among women gave cause for uneasiness: the unnerving performance of Anne Hutchinson had disordered the colony in 1636, and John Winthrop wrote feelingly in 1645 of

> a godly young woman, and of special parts, who was fallen into a sad infirmity, the loss of her understanding, and reason, which had been growing upon her divers years, by occasion of her giving herself wholly to reading and writing, and written many books.

Anne Bradstreet's early work may be read, or skimmed, against this background. Apart from its technical amateurishness, it is remarkably impersonal even by Puritan standards. She was receiving indelible impressions during those years between her arrival in New England and the publication of her verses in 1650. But she appears to have written by way of escaping from the conditions of her experience, rather than as an expression of what she felt and knew. New England never enters her book except as the rather featureless speaker in a "Dialogue Between Old and New England"; the landscape, the emotional weather of the New World are totally absent; the natural description in her "Four Seasons" woodenly reproduce England, like snow-scenes on Australian Christmas cards. Theology, a subject with which her prose memoir tells us she was painfully grappling, is touched on in passing. Personal history—marriage, childbearing, death—is similarly excluded from the book which gave her her contemporary reputation. These long, rather listless pieces seem to have been composed in a last compulsive effort to stay in contact with the history, traditions, and values of her former world; nostalgia for English culture, surely, kept her scribbling at those academic pages, long after her conviction had run out. Present experience was still too raw, one sought relief from its daily impact in turning Raleigh and Camden into rhymed couplets, recalling a scenery and a culture denied by the wilderness. Yet it is arguable that the verse which gained her serious acceptance in her own time was a psychological stepping-stone to the later poems which have kept her alive for us.

When, in 1650, Anne Bradstreet's brother-in-law returned to

England, he carried along without her knowledge a manuscript containing the verses she had copied out for family circulation. This he had published in London under the title, *The Tenth Muse, Lately Sprung Up in America*. There was considerable plotting among friends and family to launch the book. Nathaniel Ward, the "Simple Cobbler of Agawam" and former neighbor of the Bradstreets, wrote a blurb in verse, rather avuncular and condescending. Woodbridge, the brother-in-law, himself undertook to explain in a foreword that the book

> is the Work of a Woman, honoured, and esteemed where she lives, for her gracious demeanour, her eminent parts, her pious conversation, her courteous disposition, her exact diligence in her place, and discreet managing of her Family occasions, and more than so, these Poems are but the fruit of some few houres, curtailed from her sleepe and other refreshments.

Mixed feelings entered the woman's proud and self-critical soul when the printed volume was laid, with due mystery and congratulation, in her lap. "The Author to Her Book" makes this abundantly clear. *She* had not given the "rambling brat" leave to stray beyond the family circle. Fond relatives, "less wise than true," had connived under her nose to spread abroad what they knew she had "resolved in such a manner should never see the Sun." The seductions of print, the first glamor of success, were paid for by the exposure of weakness, by irritation at the printer's errors which only compounded her own. Ward's jocular praise—"a right Du Bartas Girle . . . I muse whither at length these Girles would go"—surely stung the woman who wrote:

> If what I do prove well, it won't advance.
> They'l say it's stoln, or else it was by chance.

But she was a spirited woman with a strong grasp on reality; and temperament, experience, and the fact of having reached a wider audience converged at this period to give Anne Bradstreet a new assurance. Her poems were being read seriously by strangers, though not in the form she would have chosen to send them out. Her intellectual delight was no longer vulnerable to carping ("Theyl say my hand a needle better fits"); it was a symptom neither of vanity nor infirmity; she had carried on her woman's life conscientiously while composing her book. It is probable that some tension of self-distrust was relaxed, some inner vocation confirmed, by the publication and praise of *The Tenth Muse*. But the word "vocation" must be read in a special sense. Not once in her prose memoir does she allude to her poems, or to the publication of her book; her story, as written out for her children, is the familiar Puritan drama of temptation by Satan and correction by God. She would not have defined herself, even by aspiration, as an artist. But she had crossed the line between the amateur and the artist, where private dissatisfaction begins and public approval, though gratifying, is no longer of the essence. For the poet of her time and place, poetry might be merely a means to a greater end; but the spirit in which she wrote was not that of a dilettante.

Her revisions to *The Tenth Muse* are of little aesthetic interest. Many were made on political grounds, although a reading of North's Plutarch is supposed to have prompted insertions in "The Four Monarchies." What followed, however, were the poems which rescue Anne Bradstreet from the Women's Archives and place her conclusively in literature. A glance at the titles of her later poems reveals to what extent a real change in her active sensibility had taken place after 1650. No more Ages of Man, no more Assyrian monarchs; but poems in response to the simple events in a woman's life: a fit of sickness; her son's departure for England; the arrival of letters from her absent husband; the burning of their Andover house; a child's or grandchild's death; a walk in the woods and fields near the Merrimac River. At moments her heart still rises, the lines give back a suppressed note of outrage:

> By nature Trees do rot when they are grown,
> And Plumbs and Apples thoroughly ripe do fall,
> And Corn and grass are in their season mown,
> And time brings down what is both strong and tall.
> But plants new set to be eradicate,
> And buds new blown, to have so short a date,
> Is by his hand alone that guides nature and fate.

The delicacy and reticence of her expression at its best are seen in her poem, "Before the Birth of One of Her Children," which voices woman's age-old fear of death in childbirth, in the seventeenth century a thoroughly realistic apprehension. The poem is consequently a practical document, a little testament. Neither bathos nor self-indulgence cloud the economy of these lines; they are honest, tender, and homely as a letter out of a marriage in which the lovers are also friends. The emotional interest of the poem lies in the human present and future; only in its conclusion does it gesture toward a hoped-for immortality. And the writer's pangs arise, not from dread of what lies after death, but from the thought of leaving a husband she loves and children half-reared.

> That there is a God my reason would soon tell me by the wondrous works that I see, the vast frame of the heaven and the earth, the order of all things, night and day, summer and winter, spring and autumn, the daily providing for this great household upon the earth, the preserving and directing of all to its proper end.

This theme, from her prose memoir, might be a text for the first part of her "Contemplations," the most skilled and appealing of her long poems. In its stanzas the poet wanders through a landscape of clarity and detail, exalting God's glory in nature; she becomes mindful, however, of the passing of temporal pleasure and the adversity that lies the other side of ease and sweetness. The landscape is more American than literary; it is clearly a sensuous resource and solace for the poet; but her art remains consistent in its intentions: "not to set forth myself, but the glory of God." It is of importance to bear this in mind, in any evaluation of Anne Bradstreet; it gives a peculiar poignancy to her more personal verse, and suggests an organic impulse toward economy and modesty of tone. Her several poems on recovery from illness (each with its little prose gloss recounting God's "correction" of her soul through bodily fevers and faintings) are in fact curiously impersonal as poetry; their four-foot-three-foot hymn-book meters, their sedulous meekness, their Biblical allusions, are the pure fruit of convention. Yet other occasional poems, such as "Upon the Burning of Our House," which spring from a similar motif, are heightened and individualized by references to things intimately known, life-giving strokes of personal fact:

> When by the ruins oft I past
> My sorrowing eyes aside did cast,
> And here and there the places spy
> Where oft I sat and long did lie:
> Here stood that trunk, and there that chest,
> There lay that store I counted best.
> My pleasant things in ashes lie,
> And them behold no more shall I.
> Under thy roof no guest shall sit,
> Nor at thy table eat a bit.
> No pleasant tale shall e'er be told,
> Nor things recounted done of old.
> No candle e'er shall shine in thee,
> Nor bridegroom's voice e'er heard shall be.

Upon the grounds of a Puritan aesthetic either kind of poem won its merit solely through doctrinal effectiveness; and it was within a Puritan aesthetic that Anne Bradstreet aspired and wrote. What is remarkable is that so many of her verses satisfy a larger aesthetic, to the extent of being genuine, delicate minor poems.

Until Edward Taylor, in the second half of the century, these were the only poems of more than historical interest to be written in the New World. Anne Bradstreet was the first nondidactic American poet, the first to give an embodiment to American nature, the first in whom personal intention appears to precede Puritan dogma as an impulse to verse. Not that she could be construed as a Romantic writing out of her time. The web of her sensibility stretches almost invisibly within the framework of Puritan literary convention; its texture is essentially both Puritan and feminine. Compared with her great successor, Taylor, her voice is direct and touching, rather than electrifying in its tensions or highly colored in its values. Her verses have at every point a transparency which precludes the metaphysical image; her eye is on the realities before her, or on images from the Bible. Her individualism lies in her choice of material rather than in her style.

The difficulty displaced, the heroic energy diffused in merely living a life, is an incalculable quantity. It is pointless, finally, to say that Poe or Hart Crane might have survived longer or written dif-

ferently had either been born under a better star or lived in more encouraging circumstances.[7] America has from the first levied peculiarly harsh taxes on its poets—physical, social, moral, through
absorption as much as through rejection. John Berryman admits that
in coming to write his long poem, *Homage to Mistress Bradstreet*, "I
did not choose her—somehow she chose me—one point of connection being the almost insuperable difficulty of writing high verse at
all in a land that cared and cares so little for it."[8] Still, with all stoic
recognition of the common problem in each succeeding century
including the last half-hour, it is worth observing that Anne Bradstreet happened to be one of the first American women, inhabiting a
time and place in which heroism was a necessity of life, and men
and women were fighting for survival both as individuals and as a
community. To find room in that life for any mental activity which
did not directly serve certain spiritual ends, was an act of great self-
assertion and vitality. To have written poems, the first good poems in
America, while rearing eight children, lying frequently sick, keeping
house at the edge of wilderness, was to have managed a poet's range
and extension within confines as severe as any American poet has
confronted. If the severity of these confines left its mark on the poetry
of Anne Bradstreet, it also forced into concentration and perma-
nence a gifted energy that might, in another context, have spent itself in other, less enduring directions.

[7] A. R., 1978: Of course, circumstances (gender, color, education, the sense of
belonging to a literary tradition) did make it possible for both Poe and Hart Crane to
create work which has not only survived, but has remained part of literary history. The
question is really, not what else "might have" happened to Poe or Crane, but what
did happen to the numberless poets who were born as women, or black slaves, or into
other economic and intellectual deprivation?—all those circumstances which Tillie
Olsen relentlessly depicts in her *Silences* (New York: Seymour Lawrence/Delacorte,
1978).

[8] From an interview in *Shenandoah*, Autumn 1965.

When We Dead Awaken: Writing as Re-Vision (1971)

The Modern Language Association is both marketplace and funeral parlor for the professional study of Western literature in North America. Like all gatherings of the professions, it has been and remains a "procession of the sons of educated men" (Virginia Woolf): a congeries of old-boys' networks, academicians rehearsing their numb canons in sessions dedicated to the literature of white males, junior scholars under the lash of "publish or perish" delivering papers in the bizarrely lit drawing-rooms of immense hotels: a ritual competition veering between cynicism and desperation.

However, in the interstices of these gentlemanly rites (or, in Mary Daly's words, on the boundaries of this patriarchal space),* some feminist scholars, teachers, and graduate students, joined by feminist writers, editors, and publishers, have for a decade been creating more subversive occasions, challenging the sacredness of the gentlemanly canon, sharing the rediscovery of buried works by women, asking women's questions, bringing literary history and criticism back to life in both senses. The Commission on the Status of Women in the Profession was formed in 1969, and held its first public event in 1970. In 1971 the Commission asked Ellen Peck Killoh, Tillie Olsen, Elaine Reuben, and myself, with Elaine Hedges as moderator, to talk on "The Woman Writer in the Twentieth Century." The essay that follows was written for that forum, and later published, along with the other papers from the forum and workshops, in an issue of *College English* edited by Elaine Hedges ("Women Writing and Teaching," vol. 34, no. 1, October 1972.) With a few revisions, mainly updating, it was reprinted in *American Poets in 1976*, edited by William Heyen (New York: Bobbs-Merrill, 1976). That later text is the one published here.

* Mary Daly, *Beyond God the Father* (Boston: Beacon, 1971), pp. 40–41.

The challenge flung by feminists at the accepted literary canon, at the methods of teaching it, and at the biased and astigmatic view of male "literary scholarship," has not diminished in the decade since the first Women's Forum; it has become broadened and intensified more recently by the challenges of black and lesbian feminists pointing out that feminist literary criticism itself has overlooked or held back from examining the work of black women and lesbians. The dynamic between a political vision and the demand for a fresh vision of literature is clear: without a growing feminist movement, the first inroads of feminist scholarship could not have been made; without the sharpening of a black feminist consciousness, black women's writing would have been left in limbo between misogynist black male critics and white feminists still struggling to unearth a white women's tradition; without an articulate lesbian/feminist movement, lesbian writing would still be lying in that closet where many of us used to sit reading forbidden books "in a bad light."

Much, much more is yet to be done; and university curricula have of course changed very little as a result of all this. What *is* changing is the availability of knowledge, of vital texts, the visible effects on women's lives of seeing, hearing our wordless or negated experience affirmed and pursued further in language.

〜〜〜〜〜〜〜

Ibsen's **When We Dead Awaken** is a play about the use that the male artist and thinker—in the process of creating culture as we know it—has made of women, in his life and in his work; and about a woman's slow struggling awakening to the use to which her life has been put. Bernard Shaw wrote in 1900 of this play:

> [Ibsen] shows us that no degradation ever devized or permitted is as disastrous as this degradation; that through it women can die into luxuries for men and yet can kill them; that men and women are becoming conscious of this; and that what remains to be seen as perhaps the most interesting of all imminent social developments is what will happen "when we dead awaken."[1]

It's exhilarating to be alive in a time of awakening consciousness; it can also be confusing, disorienting, and plainful. This awakening of

[1] G. B. Shaw, *The Quintessence of Ibsenism* (New York: Hill & Wang, 1922), p. 139.

dead or sleeping consciousness has already affected the lives of millions of women, even those who don't know it yet. It is also affecting the lives of men, even those who deny its claims upon them. The argument will go on whether an oppressive economic class system is responsible for the oppressive nature of male/female relations, or whether, in fact, patriarchy—the domination of males—is the original model of oppression on which all others are based. But in the last few years the women's movement has drawn inescapable and illuminating connections between our sexual lives and our political institutions. The sleepwalkers are coming awake, and for the first time this awakening has a collective reality; it is no longer such a lonely thing to open one's eyes.

Re-vision—the act of looking back, of seeing with fresh eyes, of entering an old text from a new critical direction—is for women more than a chapter in cultural history: it is an act of survival. Until we can understand the assumptions in which we are drenched we cannot know ourselves. And this drive to self-knowledge, for women, is more than a search for identity: it is part of our refusal of the self-destructiveness of male-dominated society. A radical critique of literature, feminist in its impulse, would take the work first of all as a clue to how we live, how we have been living, how we have been led to imagine ourselves, how our language has trapped as well as liberated us, how the very act of naming has been till now a male prerogative, and how we can begin to see and name—and therefore live—afresh. A change in the concept of sexual identity is essential if we are not going to see the old political order reassert itself in every new revolution. We need to know the writing of the past, and know it differently than we have ever known it; not to pass on a tradition but to break its hold over us.

For writers, and at this moment for women writers in particular, there is the challenge and promise of a whole new psychic geography to be explored. But there is also a difficult and dangerous walking on the ice, as we try to find language and images for a consciousness we are just coming into, and with little in the past to support us. I want to talk about some aspects of this difficulty and this danger.

Jane Harrison, the great classical anthropologist, wrote in 1914 in a letter to her friend Gilbert Murray:

> By the by, about "Women," it has bothered me often—why do women
> never want to write poetry about Man as a sex—why is Woman a dream
> and a terror to man and not the other way around? . . . Is it mere con-
> vention and propriety, or something deeper?[2]

I think Jane Harrison's question cuts deep into the myth-making
tradition, the romantic tradition; deep into what women and men
have been to each other; and deep into the psyche of the woman
writer. Thinking about that question, I began thinking of the work of
two twentieth-century women poets, Sylvia Plath and Diane Wa-
koski. It strikes me that in the work of both Man appears as, if not a
dream, a fascination and a terror; and that the source of the fascination and the terror is, simply, Man's power—to dominate, tyrannize,
choose, or reject the woman. The charisma of Man seems to come
purely from his power over her and his control of the world by force,
not from anything fertile or life-giving in him. And, in the work of
both these poets, it is finally the woman's sense of *herself*—em-
battled, possessed—that gives the poetry its dynamic charge, its
rhythms of struggle, need, will, and female energy. Until recently
this female anger and this furious awareness of the Man's power over
her were not available materials to the female poet, who tended to
write of Love as the source of her suffering, and to view that victimization by Love as an almost inevitable fate. Or, like Marianne
Moore and Elizabeth Bishop, she kept sexuality at a measured and
chiseled distance in her poems.

One answer to Jane Harrison's question has to be that historically
men and women have played very different parts in each others'
lives. Where woman has been a luxury for man, and has served as
the painter's model and the poet's muse, but also as comforter,
nurse, cook, bearer of his seed, secretarial assistant, and copyist of
manuscripts, man has played a quite different role for the female artist. Henry James repeats an incident which the writer Prosper Méri-
mée described, of how, while he was living with George Sand,

> he once opened his eyes, in the raw winter dawn, to see his companion,
> in a dressing-gown, on her knees before the domestic hearth, a candle-
> stick beside her and a red *madras* round her head, making bravely, with

[2] J. G. Stewart, *Jane Ellen Harrison: A Portrait from Letters* (London: Merlin,
1959), p. 140.

her own hands the fire that was to enable her to sit down betimes to urgent pen and paper. The story represents him as having felt that the spectacle chilled his ardor and tried his taste; her appearance was unfortunate, her occupation an inconsequence, and her industry a reproof— the result of all which was a lively irritation and an early rupture.[3]

The specter of this kind of male judgment, along with the misnaming and thwarting of her needs by a culture controlled by males, has created problems for the woman writer: problems of contact with herself, problems of language and style, problems of energy and survival.

In rereading Virginia Woolf's A *Room of One's Own* (1929) for the first time in some years, I was astonished at the sense of effort, of pains taken, of dogged tentativeness, in the tone of that essay. And I recognized that tone. I had heard it often enough, in myself and in other women. It is the tone of a woman almost in touch with her anger, who is determined not to appear angry, who is *willing* herself to be calm, detached, and even charming in a roomful of men where things have been said which are attacks on her very integrity. Virginia Woolf is addressing an audience of women, but she is acutely conscious—as she always was—of being overheard by men: by Morgan and Lytton and Maynard Keynes and for that matter by her father, Leslie Stephen.[4] She drew the language out into an exacerbated thread in her determination to have her own sensibility yet protect it from those masculine presences. Only at rare moments in that essay do you hear the passion in her voice; she was trying to sound as cool as Jane Austen, as Olympian as Shakespeare, because that is the way the men of the culture thought a writer should sound.

No male writer has written primarily or even largely for women, or with the sense of women's criticism as a consideration when he

[3] Henry James, "Notes on Novelists," in *Selected Literary Criticism of Henry James*, Morris Shapira, ed. (London: Heinemann, 1963), pp. 157–58.

[4] A. R., 1978: This intuition of mine was corroborated when, early in 1978, I read the correspondence between Woolf and Dame Ethel Smyth (Henry W. and Albert A. Berg Collection, The New York Public Library, Astor, Lenox and Tilden Foundations); in a letter dated June 8, 1933, Woolf speaks of having kept her own personality out of A *Room of One's Own* lest she not be taken seriously: ". . . how personal, so will they say, rubbing their hands with glee, women always are; *I even hear them as I write*." (Italics mine.)

chooses his materials, his theme, his language. But to a lesser or greater extent, every woman writer has written for men even when, like Virginia Woolf, she was supposed to be addressing women. If we have come to the point when this balance might begin to change, when women can stop being haunted, not only by "convention and propriety" but by internalized fears of being and saying themselves, then it is an extraordinary moment for the woman writer—and reader.

I have hesitated to do what I am going to do now, which is to use myself as an illustration. For one thing, it's a lot easier and less dangerous to talk about other women writers. But there is something else. Like Virginia Woolf, I am aware of the women who are not with us here because they are washing the dishes and looking after the children. Nearly fifty years after she spoke, that fact remains largely unchanged. And I am thinking also of women whom she left out of the picture altogether—women who are washing other people's dishes and caring for other people's children, not to mention women who went on the streets last night in order to feed their children. We seem to be special women here, we have liked to think of ourselves as special, and we have known that men would tolerate, even romanticize us as special, as long as our words and actions didn't threaten their privilege of tolerating or rejecting us and our work according to *their* ideas of what a special woman ought to be. An important insight of the radical women's movement has been how divisive and how ultimately destructive is this myth of the special woman, who is also the token woman. Every one of us here in this room has had great luck—we are teachers, writers, academicians; our own gifts could not have been enough, for we all know women whose gifts are buried or aborted. Our struggles can have meaning and our privileges—however precarious under patriarchy—can be justified only if they can help to change the lives of women whose gifts—and whose very being—continue to be thwarted and silenced.

My own luck was being born white and middle-class into a house full of books, with a father who encouraged me to read and write. So for about twenty years I wrote for a particular man, who criticized and praised me and made me feel I was indeed "special." The obverse side of this, of course, was that I tried for a long time to please him, or rather, not to displease him. And then of course there were other men—writers, teachers—the Man, who was not a terror or a dream but a literary master and a master in other ways less easy to acknowledge. And there were all those poems about women, written by men: it seemed to be a given that men wrote poems and women frequently inhabited them. These women were almost always beautiful, but threatened with the loss of beauty, the loss of youth—the fate worse than death. Or, they were beautiful and died young, like Lucy and Lenore. Or, the woman was like Maud Gonne, cruel and disastrously mistaken, and the poem reproached her because she had refused to become a luxury for the poet.

A lot is being said today about the influence that the myths and images of women have on all of us who are products of culture. I think it has been a peculiar confusion to the girl or woman who tries to write because she is peculiarly susceptible to language. She goes to poetry or fiction looking for *her* way of being in the world, since she too has been putting words and images together; she is looking eagerly for guides, maps, possibilities; and over and over in the "words' masculine persuasive force" of literature she comes up against something that negates everything she is about: she meets the image of Woman in books written by men. She finds a terror and a dream, she finds a beautiful pale face, she finds La Belle Dame Sans Merci, she finds Juliet or Tess or Salomé, but precisely what she does not find is that absorbed, drudging, puzzled, sometimes inspired creature, herself, who sits at a desk trying to put words together.

So what does she do? What did I do? I read the older women poets with their peculiar keenness and ambivalence: Sappho, Christina Rossetti, Emily Dickinson, Elinor Wylie, Edna Millay, H. D. I discovered that the woman poet most admired at the time (by men) was Marianne Moore, who was maidenly, elegant, intellectual, discreet. But even in reading these women I was looking in them for the same things I had found in the poetry of men, because I wanted women poets to be the equals of men, and to be equal was still confused with sounding the same.

I know that my style was formed first by male poets: by the men I was reading as an undergraduate—Frost, Dylan Thomas, Donne, Auden, MacNiece, Stevens, Yeats. What I chiefly learned from them was craft.[5] But poems are like dreams: in them you put what you don't know you know. Looking back at poems I wrote before I was twenty-one, I'm startled because beneath the conscious craft are glimpses of the split I even then experienced between the girl who wrote poems, who defined herself in writing poems, and the girl who was to define herself by her relationships with men. "Aunt Jennifer's Tigers" (1951), written while I was a student, looks with deliberate detachment at this split.[6]

> Aunt Jennifer's tigers stride across a screen,
> Bright topaz denizens of a world of green.
> They do not fear the men beneath the tree;
> They pace in sleek chivalric certainty.
>
> Aunt Jennifer's fingers fluttering through her wool
> Find even the ivory needle hard to pull.
> The massive weight of Uncle's wedding band
> Sits heavily upon Aunt Jennifer's hand.
>
> When Aunt is dead, her terrified hands will lie
> Still ringed with ordeals she was mastered by.
> The tigers in the panel that she made
> Will go on striding, proud and unafraid.

In writing this poem, composed and apparently cool as it is, I thought I was creating a portrait of an imaginary woman. But this woman suffers from the opposition of her imagination, worked out in tapestry, and her life-style, "ringed with ordeals she was mastered by." It was important to me that Aunt Jennifer was a person as distinct from myself as possible—distanced by the formalism of the poem, by its objective, observant tone—even by putting the woman in a different generation.

In those years formalism was part of the strategy—like asbestos gloves, it allowed me to handle materials I couldn't pick up bare-

[5] A. R., 1978: Yet I spent months, at sixteen, memorizing and writing imitations of Millay's sonnets; and in notebooks of that period I find what are obviously attempts to imitate Dickinson's metrics and verbal compression. I knew H. D. only through anthologized lyrics; her epic poetry was not then available to me.

[6] A. R., 1978: Texts of poetry quoted herein can be found in A. R., *Poems Selected and New: 1950–1974* (New York: Norton, 1975).

handed. A later strategy was to use the persona of a man, as I did in "The Loser" (1958):

> *A man thinks of the woman he once loved: first, after her*
> *wedding, and then nearly a decade later.*

I

I kissed you, bride and lost, and went
home from that bourgeois sacrament,
your cheek still tasting cold upon
my lips that gave you benison
with all the swagger that they knew—
as losers somehow learn to do.

Your wedding made my eyes ache; soon
the world would be worse off for one
more golden apple dropped to ground
without the least protesting sound,
and you would windfall lie, and we
forget your shimmer on the tree.

Beauty is always wasted: if
not Mignon's song sung to the deaf,
at all events to the unmoved.
A face like yours cannot be loved
long or seriously enough.
Almost, we seem to hold it off.

II

Well, you are tougher than I thought.
Now when the wash with ice hangs taut
this morning of St. Valentine,
I see you strip the squeaking line,
your body weighed against the load,
and all my groans can do no good.

Because you are still beautiful,
though squared and stiffened by the pull
of what nine windy years have done.
You have three daughters, lost a son.
I see all your intelligence
flung into that unwearied stance.

My envy is of no avail.
I turn my head and wish him well
who chafed your beauty into use
and lives forever in a house
lit by the friction of your mind.
You stagger in against the wind.

I finished college, published my first book by a fluke, as it seemed to me, and broke off a love affair. I took a job, lived alone, went on writing, fell in love. I was young, full of energy, and the book seemed to mean that others agreed I was a poet. Because I was also determined to prove that as a woman poet I could also have what was then defined as a "full" woman's life, I plunged in my early twenties into marriage and had three children before I was thirty. There was nothing overt in the environment to warn me: these were the fifties, and in reaction to the earlier wave of feminism, middle-class women were making careers of domestic perfection, working to send their husbands through professional schools, then retiring to raise large families. People were moving out to the suburbs, technology was going to be the answer to everything, even sex; the family was in its glory. Life was extremely private; women were isolated from each other by the loyalties of marriage. I have a sense that women didn't talk to each other much in the fifties—not about their secret emptinesses, their frustrations. I went on trying to write; my second book and first child appeared in the same month. But by the time that book came out I was already dissatisfied with those poems, which seemed to me mere exercises for poems I hadn't written. The book was praised, however, for its "gracefulness"; I had a marriage and a child. If there were doubts, if there were periods of null depression or active despairing, these could only mean that I was ungrateful, insatiable, perhaps a monster.

About the time my third child was born, I felt that I had either to consider myself a failed woman and a failed poet, or to try to find some synthesis by which to understand what was happening to me. What frightened me most was the sense of drift, of being pulled along on a current which called itself my destiny, but in which I seemed to be losing touch with whoever I had been, with the girl who had experienced her own will and energy almost ecstatically at times, walking around a city or riding a train at night or typing in a

student room. In a poem about my grandmother I wrote (of myself):
"A young girl, thought sleeping, is certified dead" ("Halfway"). I was
writing very little, partly from fatigue, that female fatigue of suppressed anger and loss of contact with my own being; partly from the
discontinuity of female life with its attention to small chores, er-
rands, work that others constantly undo, small children's constant
needs. What I did write was unconvincing to me; my anger and frustration were hard to acknowledge in or out of poems because in fact I
cared a great deal about my husband and my children. Trying to
look back and understand that time I have tried to analyze the real
nature of the conflict. Most, if not all, human lives are full of
fantasy—passive day-dreaming which need not be acted on. But to
write poetry or fiction, or even to think well, is not to fantasize, or to
put fantasies on paper. For a poem to coalesce, for a character or an
action to take shape, there has to be an imaginative transformation of
reality which is in no way passive. And a certain freedom of the mind
is needed—freedom to press on, to enter the currents of your thought
like a glider pilot, knowing that your motion can be sustained, that
the buoyancy of your attention will not be suddenly snatched away.
Moreover, if the imagination is to transcend and transform experience it has to question, to challenge, to conceive of alternatives,
perhaps to the very life you are living at that moment. You have to
be free to play around with the notion that day might be night, love
might be hate; nothing can be too sacred for the imagination to turn
into its opposite or to call experimentally by another name. For writing is re-naming. Now, to be maternally with small children all day
in the old way, to be with a man in the old way of marriage, requires
a holding-back, a putting-aside of that imaginative activity, and demands instead a kind of conservatism. I want to make it clear that I
am *not* saying that in order to write well, or think well, it is necessary
to become unavailable to others, or to become a devouring ego. This
has been the myth of the masculine artist and thinker; and I do not
accept it. But to be a female human being trying to fulfill traditional
female functions in a traditional way *is* in direct conflict with the
subversive function of the imagination. The word traditional is important here. There must be ways, and we will be finding out more
and more about them, in which the energy of creation and the
energy of relation can be united. But in those years I always felt the

conflict as a failure of love in myself. I had thought I was choosing a
full life: the life available to most men, in which sexuality, work, and
parenthood could coexist. But I felt, at twenty-nine, guilt toward the
people closest to me, and guilty toward my own being.

I wanted, then, more than anything, the one thing of which there
was never enough: time to think, time to write. The fifties and early
sixties were years of rapid revelations: the sit-ins and marches in the
South, the Bay of Pigs, the early antiwar movement, raised large
questions—questions for which the masculine world of the academy
around me seemed to have expert and fluent answers. But I needed
to think for myself—about pacifism and dissent and violence, about
poetry and society, and about my own relationship to all these
things. For about ten years I was reading in fierce snatches, scribbling in notebooks, writing poetry in fragments; I was looking desper-
ately for clues, because if there were no clues then I thought I might
be insane. I wrote in a notebook about this time:

> Paralyzed by the sense that there exists a mesh of relationships—e.g.,
> between my anger at the children, my sensual life, pacifism, sex (I
> mean sex in its broadest significance, not merely sexual desire)—an in-
> terconnectedness which, if I could see it, make it valid, would give me
> back myself, make it possible to function lucidly and passionately. Yet I
> grope in and out among these dark webs.

I think I began at this point to feel that politics was not something
"out there" but something "in here" and of the essence of my condition.

In the late fifties I was able to write, for the first time, directly
about experiencing myself as a woman. The poem was jotted in fragments during children's naps, brief hours in a library, or at 3:00 A.M.
after rising with a wakeful child. I despaired of doing any continuous
work at this time. Yet I began to feel that my fragments and scraps
had a common consciousness and a common theme, one which I
would have been very unwilling to put on paper at an earlier time
because I had been taught that poetry should be "universal," which
meant, of course, nonfemale. Until then I had tried very much *not*
to identify myself as a female poet. Over two years I wrote a ten-part
poem called "Snapshots of a Daughter-in-Law" (1958–1960), in a
longer looser mode than I'd ever trusted myself with before. It was an

extraordinary relief to write that poem. It strikes me now as too literary, too dependent on allusion; I hadn't found the courage yet to do
without authorities, or even to use the pronoun "I"—the woman in
the poem is always "she." One section of it, No. 2, concerns a
woman who thinks she is going mad; she is haunted by voices telling
her to resist and rebel, voices which she can hear but not obey.

> 2.
> Banging the coffee-pot into the sink
> she hears the angels chiding, and looks out
> past the raked gardens to the sloppy sky.
> Only a week since They said: *Have no patience.*
>
> The next time it was: *Be insatiable.*
> Then: *Save yourself; others you cannot save.*
> Sometimes she's let the tapstream scald her arm,
> a match burn to her thumbnail,
>
> or held her hand above the kettle's snout
> right in the woolly steam. They are probably angels,
> since nothing hurts her anymore, except
> each morning's grit blowing into her eyes.

The poem "Orion," written five years later, is a poem of recon-
nection with a part of myself I had felt I was losing—the active principle, the energetic imagination, the "half-brother" whom I projected, as I had for many years, into the constellation Orion. It's no
accident that the words "cold and egotistical" appear in this poem,
and are applied to myself.

> Far back when I went zig-zagging
> through tamarack pastures
> you were my genius, you
> my cast-iron Viking, my helmed
> lion-heart king in prison.
> Years later now you're young
>
> my fierce half-brother, staring
> down from that simplified west
> your breast open, your belt dragged down
> by an oldfashioned thing, a sword

the last bravado you won't give over
though it weighs you down as you stride

and the stars in it are dim
and maybe have stopped burning.
But you burn, and I know it;
as I throw back my head to take you in
an old transfusion happens again:
divine astronomy is nothing to it.

Indoors I bruise and blunder,
break faith, leave ill enough
alone, a dead child born in the dark.
Night cracks up over the chimney,
pieces of time, frozen geodes
come showering down in the grate.

A man reaches behind my eyes
and finds them empty
a woman's head turns away
from my head in the mirror
children are dying my death
and eating crumbs of my life.

Pity is not your forte.
Calmly you ache up there
pinned aloft in your crow's nest,
my speechless pirate!
You take it all for granted
and when I look you back

it's with a starlike eye
shooting its cold and egotistical spear
where it can do least damage.
Breathe deep! No hurt, no pardon
out here in the cold with you
you with your back to the wall.

The choice still seemed to be between "love"—womanly, maternal
love, altruistic love—a love defined and ruled by the weight of an entire culture; and egotism—a force directed by men into creation,
achievement, ambition, often at the expense of others, but justifiably
so. For weren't they men, and wasn't that their destiny as womanly,

selfless love was ours? We know now that the alternatives are false ones—that the word "love" is itself in need of re-vision.

There is a companion poem to "Orion," written three years later, in which at last the woman in the poem and the woman writing the poem become the same person. It is called "Planetarium," and it was written after a visit to a real planetarium, where I read an account of the work of Caroline Herschel, the astronomer, who worked with her brother William, but whose name remained obscure, as his did not.

> *Thinking of Caroline Herschel, 1750–1848, astronomer, sister of William; and others*
>
> A woman in the shape of a monster
> a monster in the shape of a woman
> the skies are full of them
>
> a woman   "in the snow
> among the Clocks and instruments
> or measuring the ground with poles"
>
> in her 98 years to discover
> 8 comets
>
> she whom the moon ruled
> like us
> levitating into the night sky
> riding the polished lenses
>
> Galaxies of women, there
> doing penance for impetuousness
> ribs chilled
> in those spaces   of the mind
>
> An eye,
>   "virile, precise and absolutely certain"
>   from the mad webs of Uranisborg
>
>   encountering the NOVA
>
> every impulse of light exploding
> from the core
> as life flies out of us

Tycho whispering at last
"Let me not seem to have lived in vain"

What we see, we see
and seeing is changing

the light that shrivels a mountain
and leaves a man alive

Heartbeat of the pulsar
heart sweating through my body

The radio impulse
pouring in from Taurus

      I am bombarded yet   I stand

I have been standing all my life in the
direct path of a battery of signals
the most accurately transmitted most
untranslateable language in the universe
I am a galactic cloud so deep   so invo-
luted that a light wave could take 15
years to travel through me   And has
taken   I am an instrument in the shape
of a woman trying to translate pulsations
into images   for the relief of the body
and the reconstruction of the mind.

In closing I want to tell you about a dream I had last summer. I
dreamed I was asked to read my poetry at a mass women's meeting,
but when I began to read, what came out were the lyrics of a blues
song. I share this dream with you because it seemed to me to say
something about the problems and the future of the woman writer,
and probably of women in general. The awakening of consciousness
is not like the crossing of a frontier—one step and you are in another
country. Much of woman's poetry has been of the nature of the blues
song: a cry of pain, of victimization, or a lyric of seduction.[7] And
today, much poetry by women—and prose for that matter—is
charged with anger. I think we need to go through that anger, and we

[7] A. R., 1978: When I dreamed that dream, was I wholly ignorant of the tradition of
Bessie Smith and other women's blues lyrics which transcended victimization to sing
of resistance and independence?

will betray our own reality if we try, as Virginia Woolf was trying, for an objectivity, a detachment, that would make us sound more like Jane Austen or Shakespeare. We know more than Jane Austen or Shakespeare knew: more than Jane Austen because our lives are more complex, more than Shakespeare because we know more about the lives of women—Jane Austen and Virginia Woolf included.

Both the victimization and the anger experienced by women are real, and have real sources, everywhere in the environment, built into society, language, the structures of thought. They will go on being tapped and explored by poets, among others. We can neither deny them, nor will we rest there. A new generation of women poets is already working out of the psychic energy released when women begin to move out towards what the feminist philosopher Mary Daly has described as the "new space" on the boundaries of patriarchy.[8] Women are speaking to and of women in these poems, out of a newly released courage to name, to love each other, to share risk and grief and celebration.

To the eye of a feminist, the work of Western male poets now writing reveals a deep, fatalistic pessimism as to the possibilities of change, whether societal or personal, along with a familiar and threadbare use of women (and nature) as redemptive on the one hand, threatening on the other; and a new tide of phallocentric sadism and overt woman-hating which matches the sexual brutality of recent films. "Political" poetry by men remains stranded amid the struggles for power among male groups; in condemning U.S. imperialism or the Chilean junta the poet can claim to speak for the oppressed while remaining, as male, part of a system of sexual oppression. The enemy is always outside the self, the struggle somewhere else. The mood of isolation, self-pity, and self-imitation that pervades "nonpolitical" poetry suggests that a profound change in masculine consciousness will have to precede any new male poetic—or other—inspiration. The creative energy of patriarchy is fast running out; what remains is its self-generating energy for destruction. As women, we have our work cut out for us.

[8] Mary Daly, *Beyond God the Father: Towards a Philosophy of Women's Liberation* (Boston: Beacon, 1973).

Teaching Language in Open Admissions (1972)

To the memory of Mina Shaughnessy, 1924–1978

I stand to this day behind the major ideas about literature, writing, and teaching that I expressed in this essay. Several things strike me in rereading it, however. Given the free rein allowed by the SEEK program (described in the text of the essay) when I first began teaching at the City College of New York, it is interesting to me to note the books I was choosing for classes: Orwell, Wright, LeRoi Jones, Lawrence, Baldwin, Plato's *Republic*. It is true that few books by black women writers were available; the bookstores of the late sixties were crowded with paperbacks by Frederick Douglass, Malcolm X, Frantz Fanon, Langston Hughes, Eldridge Cleaver, W. E. B. DuBois, and by anthologies of mostly male black writers. Ann Petry, Gwendolyn Brooks, June Jordan, Audre Lorde, I came to know and put on my reading lists or copied for classes; but the real crescendo of black women's writing was yet to come, and writers like Zora Neale Hurston and Margaret Walker were out of print. It is obvious now, as it was not yet then (except to black women writers, undoubtedly) that integral to the struggle against racism in the literary canon there was another, as yet unarticulated, struggle, against the sexism of black and white male editors, anthologists, critics, and publishers.

For awhile I have thought of going back to City College to ask some of my former colleagues, still teaching there, what could be said of the past decade, what is left there of what was, for a brief time, a profound if often naively optimistic experiment in education. (Naively optimistic because I think the white faculty at least, those of us even who were most committed to the students, vastly underestimated the psychic depth and economic function of racism in the city and the nation, the power of the political machinery that could be "permissive" for a handful of years only to retrench, break promises, and betray, pitting black youth against Puerto Rican and Asian, poor ethnic students against students of color, in an absurd and tragic competition for resources which should have been open to all.) But it has seemed to me that such interviews could be fragmentary at best. I lived through some of that history, the enlarging of classes, the heavy increase of teaching loads, the firing of junior faculty and of many of the best and most dedicated teachers I had known, the efforts of City College to reclaim its "prestige" in the media; I know also that dedicated teachers still remain, who teach Basic Writing not as a white man's—or woman's—burden but because they choose to do so. And, on the corner of Broadway near where I live, I see young people whose like I knew ten years ago as college students "hanging-out", brown-bagging, standing in short skirts and high-heeled boots in doorways waiting for a trick, or being dragged into the car of a plumed and sequined pimp.

   Finally: in reprinting this essay I would like to acknowledge my debt to Mina Shaughnessy, who was director of the Basic Writing Program at City when I taught there, and from whom, in many direct and indirect ways, I learned—in a time and place where pedagogic romanticism and histrionics were not uncommon—a great deal about the ethics and integrity of teaching.

   This essay was first published in *The Uses of Literature*, edited by Monroe Engel (Cambridge, Mass.: Harvard University, 1973).

~~~~~~~~~

My first romantic notion of teaching came, I think, from reading Emlyn Williams's play *The Corn Is Green*, sometime in my teens. As I reconstruct it now, a schoolteacher in a Welsh mining village is reading her pupils' essays one night and comes upon a paper which, for all its misspellings and dialect constructions, seems to be the work of a nascent poet. Turning up in the midst of the undistinguished efforts of her other pupils, this essay startles the teacher. She calls in the boy who wrote it, goes over it with him, talks with him about his life, his hopes, and offers to tutor him privately, without fees. Together, as the play goes on, they work their way through rhetoric, mathematics, Shakespeare, Latin, Greek. The boy gets turned on by the classics, is clearly intended to be, if not a poet, at least a scholar. Birth and family background had destined him for a life in the coal mines; but now another path opens up. Toward the end of the play we see him being coached for the entrance examinations for Oxford. I believe crisis strikes when it looks as if he has gotten one of the village girls pregnant and may have to marry her, thus cutting short a career of dazzling promise before it has begun. I don't recall the outcome, but I suspect that the unwed mother is hushed up and packed away (I would be more interested to see the play rewritten today as *her* story) and the boy goes off to Oxford, with every hope of making it to donhood within the decade.

Perhaps this represents a secret fantasy of many teachers: the ill-scrawled essay, turned up among so many others, which has the mark of genius. And looking at the first batch of freshman papers every semester can be like a trip to the mailbox—there is always the possibility of something turning up that will illuminate the weeks ahead. But behind the larger fantasy lie assumptions which I have only gradually come to recognize; and the recognition has to do with a profound change in my conceptions of teaching and learning.

Before I started teaching at City College I had known only elitist institutions: Harvard and Radcliffe as an undergraduate, Swarthmore as a visiting poet, Columbia as teacher in a graduate poetry workshop that included some of the best young poets in the city. I applied for the job at City in 1968 because Robert Cumming had described the SEEK program to me after Martin Luther King was shot, and my motivation was complex. It had to do with white liberal guilt, of course; and a political decision to use my energies in work with "disadvantaged" (black and Puerto Rican) students. But it also had to do with a need to involve myself with the real life of the city, which had arrested me from the first weeks I began living here.

In 1966 Mayor John Lindsay had been able, however obtusely, to coin the phrase "Fun City" without actually intending it as a sick joke. By 1968, the uncollected garbage lay bulging in plastic sacks on the north side of Washington Square, as it had lain longer north of 110th Street; the city had learned to endure subway strikes, sanitation strikes, cab strikes, power and water shortages; the policeman on the corner had become a threatening figure to many whites as he had long been to blacks; the public school teachers and the parents of their pupils had been in pitched battle. On the Upper West Side poor people were being evicted from tenements which were then tinned-up and left empty, awaiting unscheduled demolition to make room for middle-income housing, for which funds were as yet una-

vailable; and a squatter movement of considerable political consciousness was emerging in defiance of this uprooting.

There seemed to be three ways in which the white middle class
could live in New York: the paranoiac, the solipsistic, and a third,
which I am more hesitant to define. By the mid-sixties paranoia was
visible and audible: streets of brownstones whose occupants had
hired an armed guard for the block and posted notices accordingly;
conversations on park benches in which public safety had replaced
private health as a topic of concern; conversion of all personal anxie-
ties into fear of the mugger (and the mugger was real, no doubt about
it). Paranoia could become a life-style, a science, an art, with the active collaboration of reality. Solipsism I encountered first and most
concretely in a conversation with an older European intellectual
who told me he liked living in New York (on the East Side) because
Madison Avenue reminded him of Paris. It was, and still is, possible
to live, if you can afford it, on one of those small islands where the
streets are kept clean and the pushers and nodders invisible, to travel
by cab, deplore the state of the rest of the city, but remain essentially
aloof from its causes and effects. It seems about as boring as most
forms of solipsism, since to maintain itself it must remain thick-
skinned and ignorant.

But there was, and is, another relationship with the city which I
can only begin by calling love. The city as object of love, a love not
unmixed with horror and anger, the city as Baudelaire and Rilke had
previsioned it, or William Blake for that matter, death in life, but a
death emblematic of the death that is epidemic in modern society,
and a life more edged, more costly, more charged with knowledge,
than life elsewhere. Love as one knows it sometimes with a person
with whom one is locked in struggle, energy draining but also energy
replenishing, as when one is fighting for life, in oneself or someone
else. Here was this damaged, self-destructive organism, preying and
preyed upon. The streets were rich with human possibility and vicious with human denial (it is breathtaking to walk through a street
in East Harlem, passing among the lithe, alert, childish bodies and
attuned, observant, childish faces, playing in the spray of a hydrant,
and to know that addiction awaits every brain and body in that block
as a potential killer). In all its historic, overcrowded, and sweated
poverty, the Lower East Side at the turn of the century had never

known this: the odds for the poor, today, are weighted by heroin, a fact which the middle classes ignored until it breathed on their own children's lives as well.

In order to live in the city, I needed to ally myself, in some concrete, practical, if limited way, with the possibilities. So I went up to Convent Avenue and 133rd Street and was interviewed for a teaching job, hired as a poet-teacher. At that time a number of writers, including Toni Cade Bambara, the late Paul Blackburn, Robert Cumming, David Henderson, June Jordan, were being hired to teach writing in the SEEK program to black and Puerto Rican freshmen entering from substandard ghetto high schools, where the prevailing assumption had been that they were of inferior intelligence. (More of these schools later.) Many dropped out (a lower percentage than the national college dropout rate, however); many stuck it out through several semesters of remedial English, math, reading, to enter the mainstream of the college. (As of 1972, 208 SEEK students—or 35 to 40 percent—have since graduated from City College; 24 are now in graduate school. *None* of these students would have come near higher education under the regular admissions programs of the City University; high-school guidance counselors have traditionally written off such students as incapable of academic work. Most could not survive economically in college without the stipends which the SEEK program provides.)

My job, that first year, was to "turn the students on" to writing by whatever means I wanted—poetry, free association, music, politics, drama, fiction—to acclimate them to the act of writing, while a grammar teacher, with whom I worked closely outside of class, taught sentence structure, the necessary mechanics. A year later this course was given up as too expensive, since it involved two teachers. My choice was to enlarge my scope to include grammar and mechanics or to find a niche elsewhere and teach verse writing. I stayed on to teach, and learn, grammar—among other things.

The early experience in SEEK was, as I look back on it, both unnerving and seductive. Even those who were (unlike me) experienced teachers of remedial English were working on new frontiers, trying new methods. Some of the most rudimentary questions we confronted were: How do you make standard English verb endings available to a dialect-speaker? How do you teach English preposi-

tional forms to a Spanish-language student? What are the arguments
for and against "Black English"? The English of academic papers
and theses? Is standard English simply a weapon of colonization?
Many of our students wrote in the vernacular with force and wit;
others were unable to say what they wanted on paper in or out of the
vernacular. We were dealing not simply with dialect and syntax but
with the imagery of lives, the anger and flare of urban youth—how
could this be *used*, strengthened, without the lies of artificial polish?
How does one teach order, coherence, the structure of ideas while
respecting the student's experience of his or her thinking and perceiving? Some students who could barely sweat out a paragraph delivered (and sometimes conned us with) dazzling raps in the
classroom: How could we help this oral gift transfer itself onto paper?
The classes were small—fifteen at most; the staff, at that time, likewise; we spent hours in conference with individual students, hours
meeting together and with counselors, trying to teach ourselves how
to teach and asking ourselves what we ought to be teaching.

So these were classes, not simply in writing, not simply in literature, certainly not just in the correction of sentence fragments or the
redemptive power of the semicolon; though we did, and do, work on
all these. One teacher gave a minicourse in genres; one in drama as
literature; teachers have used their favorite books from *Alice in Won-
derland* to Martin Buber's *The Knowledge of Man*; I myself have
wandered all over the map of my own reading: D. H. Lawrence,
W. E. B. DuBois, LeRoi Jones, Plato, Orwell, Ibsen, poets from
W. C. Williams to Audre Lorde. Sometimes books are used as a
way of learning to look at literature, sometimes as a provocation for
the students' own writing, sometimes both. At City College all Basic
Writing teachers have been free to choose the books they would assign (always keeping within the limits of the SEEK book allowance
and considering the fact that non-SEEK students have no book allowance at all, though their financial need may be as acute.) There
has never been a set curriculum or a required reading list; we have
poached off each others' booklists, methods, essay topics, grammar-
teaching exercises, and anything else that we hoped would "work"
for us.[1]

[1] What I have found deadly and defeating is the anthology designed for multiethnic
classes in freshman English. I once ordered one because the book stipends had been

Most of us felt that students learn to write by discovering the validity and variety of their own experience; and in the late 1960s, as the black classics began to flood the bookstores, we drew on the black novelists, poets, and polemicists as the natural path to this discovery for SEEK students. Black teachers were, of course, a path; and there were some who combined the work of consciousness-raising with the study of Sophocles, Kafka, and other pillars of the discipline oddly enough known as "English." For many white teachers, the black writers were a relatively new discovery: the clear, translucent prose of Douglass, the sonorities of *The Souls of Black Folk*, the melancholy sensuousness of Toomer's poem-novel *Cane*. In this discovery of a previously submerged culture we were learning from and with our students as rarely happens in the university, though it is happening anew in the area of women's studies. We were not merely exploring a literature and a history which had gone virtually unmentioned in our white educations (particularly true for those over thirty); we were not merely having to confront in talk with our students and in their writings, as well as the books we read, the bitter reality of Western racism: we also found ourselves reading almost any piece of Western literature through our students' eyes, imagining how this voice, these assumptions, would sound to us if we were they. "We learned from the students"—banal cliché, one that sounds pious and patronizing by now; yet the fact remains that our white liberal assumptions *were* shaken, our vision of both the city and the university changed, our relationship to language itself made both deeper and more painful.

Of course the students responded to black literature; I heard searching and acute discussions of Jones's poem "The Liar" or Wright's "The Man Who Lived Underground" from young men and women who were in college on sufferance in the eyes of the educational establishment; I've heard similar discussions of *Sons and Lovers* or the *Republic*. Writing this, I am conscious of how obvious it all seems and how unnecessary it now might appear to demonstrate

cut out and I was trying to save the students money. I ended up using one Allen Ginsberg poem, two by LeRoi Jones, and asking the students to write essays provoked by the photographs in the anthology. The college anthology, in general, as nonbook, with its exhaustive and painfully literal notes, directives, questions, and "guides for study," is like TV showing of a film—cut, chopped up, and interspersed with commercials: a flagrant mutilation by mass technological culture.

by little anecdotes that ghetto students can handle sophisticated literature and ideas. But in 1968, 1969, we were still trying to prove
this—we and our students felt that the burden of proof was on us.
When the Black and Puerto Rican Student Community seized the
South Campus of C.C.N.Y. in April 1969, and a team of students
sat down with the president of the college and a team of faculty
members to negotiate, one heard much about the faculty group's
surprised respect for the students' articulateness, reasoning power,
and skill in handling statistics—for the students were negotiating in
exchange for withdrawal from South Campus an admissions policy
which would go far beyond SEEK in its inclusiveness.

Those of us who had been involved earlier with ghetto students
felt that we had known their strength all along: an impatient cutting
through of the phony, a capacity for tenacious struggle with language
and syntax and difficult ideas, a growing capacity for political analysis which helped counter the low expectations their teachers had
always had of them and which many had had of themselves; and
more, their knowledge of the naked facts of society, which academia
has always, even in its public urban form, managed to veil in ivy or
fantasy. Some were indeed chronologically older than the average
college student; many, though eighteen or twenty years old, had had
responsibility for themselves and their families for years. They came
to college with a greater insight into the actual workings of the city
and of American racial oppression than most of their teachers or
their elite contemporaries. They had held dirty jobs, borne children,
negotiated for Spanish-speaking parents with an English-speaking
world of clinics, agencies, lawyers, and landlords, had their sixth
senses nurtured in the streets, or had made the transition from southern sharehold or Puerto Rican countryside to Bedford-Stuyvesant or
the *barrio* and knew the ways of two worlds. And they were becoming, each new wave of them, more lucidly conscious of the politics
of their situation, the context within which their lives were being
led.

It is tempting to romanticize, at the distance of midsummer 1972,
what the experience of SEEK—and by extension, of all remedial
freshman programs under Open Admissions—was (and is) for the
students themselves. The Coleman Report and the Moynihan Re-

port have left echoes and vibrations of stereotypical thinking which perhaps only a first-hand knowledge of the New York City schools can really silence. Teaching at City I came to know the intellectual poverty and human waste of the public school system through the marks it had left on students—and not on black and Puerto Rican students only, as the advent of Open Admissions was to show. For a plain look at the politics and practices of this system, I recommend Ellen Lurie's *How to Change the Schools*, a handbook for parent activists which enumerates the conditions she and other parents, black, Puerto Rican, and white, came to know intimately in their struggles to secure their children's right to learn and to be treated with dignity. The book is a photograph of the decay, racism, and abusiveness they confronted, written not as muckraking journalism but as a practical tool for others like themselves. I have read little else, including the most lyrically indignant prose of radical educators, that gives so precise and devastating a picture of the life that New York's children are expected to lead in the name of schooling. She writes of "bewildered angry teen-agers, who have discovered that they are in classes for mentally retarded students, simply because they cannot speak English," of teachers and principals who "behaved as though every white middle-class child was gifted and was college material, and every black and Puerto Rican (and sometimes Irish and Italian) working-class child was slow, disadvantaged, and unable to learn anything but the most rudimentary facts." She notes that "81 elementary schools in the state (out of a total of 3,634) had more than 70 per cent of their students below minimum competence, and 65 *of these were New York City public schools!*" Her findings and statistics make it clear that tracking begins at kindergarten (chiefly on the basis of skin color and language) and that nonwhite and working-class children are assumed to have a maximum potential which fits them only for the so-called general diploma, hence are not taught, as are their middle-class contemporaries, the math or languages or writing skills needed to pass college entrance examinations or even to do academic-diploma high-school work.[2] I have singled out these particular points for citation because they have to do directly with our

---

[2] Ellen Lurie, *How to Change the Schools* (New York: Random House, 1970). See pp. 31, 32, 40–48.

students' self-expectations and the enforced limitation of their horizons years before they come to college. But much else has colored
their educational past: the drug pushers at the school gates, the
obsolete texts, the punitive conception of the teacher's role, the ugli-
ness, filth, and decay of the buildings, the demoralization even of
good teachers working under such conditions. (Add to this the use of
tranquilizing drugs on children who are considered hyperactive or
who present "behavior problems" at an early age.)

To come out of scenes like these schools and be offered "a
chance" to compete as an equal in the world of academic creden-
tials, the white-collar world, the world beyond the minimum wage
or welfare, is less romantic for the student than for those who view
the process from a distance. The student who leaves the campus at
three or four o'clock after a day of classes, goes to work as a waitress,
or clerk, or hash-slinger, or guard, comes home at ten or eleven
o'clock to a crowded apartment with TV audible in every corner—
what does it feel like to this student to be reading, say, Byron's "Don
Juan" or Jane Austen for a class the next day? Our students may
spend two or three hours in the subway going to and from college
and jobs, longer if the subway system is more deplorable than usual.
To read in the New York subway at rush hour is impossible; it is virtually impossible to think.

How does one compare this experience of college with that of the
Columbia students down at 116th Street in their quadrangle of gray
stone dormitories, marble steps, flowered borders, wide spaces of
time and architecture in which to talk and think? Or that of Berkeley
students with their eucalyptus grove and tree-lined streets of bookstores and cafés? The Princeton or Vassar students devoting four
years to the life of the mind in Gothic serenity? Do "motivation" and
"intellectual competency" mean the same for those students as for
City College undergraduates on that overcrowded campus where in
winter there is often no place to sit between classes, with two inadequate bookstores largely filled with required texts, two cafeterias and
a snack bar that are overpriced, dreary, and unconducive to lingering, with the incessant pressure of time and money driving at them
to rush, to get through, to amass the needed credits somehow, to
drop out, to stay on with gritted teeth? Out of a graduating class at
Swarthmore or Oberlin and one at C.C.N.Y., which students have

demonstrated their ability and commitment, and how do we assume we can measure such things?

Sometimes as I walk up 133rd Street, past the glass-strewn doorways of P.S. 161, the graffiti-sprayed walls of tenements, the uncollected garbage, through the iron gates of South Campus and up the driveway to the prefab hut which houses the English department, I think wryly of John Donne's pronouncement that "the University is a Paradise; rivers of Knowledge are there; Arts and Sciences flow from thence." I think that few of our students have this Athenian notion of what college is going to be for them; their first introduction to it is a many hours' wait in line at registration, which only reveals that the courses they have been advised or wanted to take are filled, or conflict in hours with a needed job; then more hours at the cramped, heavily guarded bookstore; then perhaps, a semester in courses which they never chose, or in which the pace and allusions of a lecturer are daunting or which may meet at opposite ends of an elongated campus stretching for six city blocks and spilling over into a former warehouse on Broadway. Many have written of their first days at C.C.N.Y.: "I only knew it was different from high school." What was different, perhaps, was the green grass of early September with groups of young people in dashikis and gelés, jeans and tie-dye, moving about with the unquenchable animation of the first days of the fall semester; the encounter with some teachers who seem to respect them as individuals; something at any rate less bleak, less violent, less mean-spirited, than the halls of Benjamin Franklin or Evander Childs or some other school with the line painted down the center of the corridor and a penalty for taking the short-cut across that line. In all that my students have written about their high schools, I have found bitterness, resentment, satire, black humor; never any word of nostalgia for the school, though sometimes a word of affection for a teacher "who really tried."

The point is that, as Mina Shaughnessy, the director of the Basic Writing Program at City, has written: "the first stage of Open Admissions involves *openly admitting* that education has failed for too many students."[3] Professor Shaughnessy writes in her most recent

[3] Mina P. Shaughnessy, "Open Admissions—A Second Report," in *The City College Department of English Newsletter*, vol. II, no. 1., January 1972. A. R., 1978: See

report of the increase in remedial courses of white, ethnic students (about two-thirds of the Open Admissions freshmen who have below-80 high school averages) and of the discernible fact, a revelation to many, that these white students "have experienced the failure of the public schools in different ways from the black and Puerto Rican students." Another City College colleague, Leonard Kriegel, writes of this newest population: "Like most blue-collar children, they had lived within the confines of an educational system without ever having questioned that system. They were used to being stamped and categorized. Rating systems, grades, obligations to improve, these had beset them all their lives. . . . They had few expectations from the world-at-large. When they were depressed, they had no real idea of what was getting them down, and they would have dismissed as absurd the idea that they could make demands. They accepted the myths of America as those myths had been presented to them."[4]

Meeting some of the so-called ethnic students in class for the first time in September 1970, I began to realize that: there *are* still poor Jews in New York City; they teach English better to native speakers of Greek on the island of Cyprus than they do to native speakers of Spanish on the island of Manhattan; the Chinese student with acute English-language difficulties is stereotyped as "nonexpressive" and channeled into the physical sciences before anyone has a chance to find out whether he or she is a potential historian, political theorist, or psychologist; and (an intuition, more difficult to prove) white, ethnic working-class young women seem to have problems of self-reliance and of taking their lives seriously that young black women students as a group do not seem to share.

There is also a danger that, paradoxically or not, the white middle-class teacher may find it easier to identify with the strongly

also Shaughnessy's *Errors and Expectations: A Guide for the Teacher of Basic Writing* (New York: Oxford, 1977), a remarkable study in the methodology of teaching language.

[4] "When Blue-Collar Students Go to College," in *Saturday Review*, July 22, 1972. The article is excerpted from the book, *Working Through: A Teacher's Journal in the Urban University* (New York: Saturday Review Press, 1972). Kriegel is describing students at Long Island University of a decade ago; but much that he says is descriptive of students who are now entering colleges like C.C.N.Y. under Open Admissions.

motivated, obviously oppressed, politically conscious black student
than with the students of whom Kriegel has written. Perhaps a different set of prejudices exists: if you're white, why aren't you more
hip, more achieving, why are you bored and alienated, why don't
you *care* more? Again, one has to keep clearly in mind the real lessons of the schools—both public and parochial—which reward con-
formity, passivity, and correct answers and penalize, as Ellen Lurie
says, the troublesome question "as trouble-making," the lively, independent, active child as "disruptive," curiosity as misbehavior.
(Because of the reinforcement in passivity received all around them
in society and at home, white women students seem particularly vulnerable to these judgments.) In many ways the damage is more insidious because the white students have as yet no real political analysis
going for them; only the knowledge that they have not been as successful in school as white students are supposed to be.

Confronted with these individuals, this city, these life situations,
these strengths, these damages, there are some harsh questions that
have to be raised about the uses of literature. I think of myself as a
teacher of language: that is, as someone for whom language has
implied freedom, who is trying to aid others to free themselves
through the written word, and above all through learning to write it
for themselves. I cannot know for them what it is they need to free,
or what words they need to write; I can only try with them to get an
approximation of the story they want to tell. I have always assumed,
and I do still assume, that people come into the freedom of language
through reading, before writing; that the differences of tone, rhythm,
vocabulary, intention, encountered over years of reading are, whatever else they may be, suggestive of many different possible of modes
of being. But my daily life as a teacher confronts me with young men
and women who have had language and literature *used against*
them, to keep them in their place, to mystify, to bully, to make them
feel powerless. Courses in great books or speed-reading are not an
answer when it is the meaning of literature itself that is in question.
Sartre says: "the literary object has no other substance than the reader's subjectivity; Raskolnikov's waiting is *my* waiting which I lend
him. . . . His hatred of the police magistrate who questions him is
my hatred, which has been solicited and wheedled out of me by

signs. . . . Thus, the writer appeals to the reader's freedom to collaborate in the production of his work."[5] But what if it is these very
signs, or ones like them, that have been used to limit the reader's
freedom or to convince the reader of his or her unworthiness to "collaborate in the production of the work"?

I have no illuminating answers to such questions. I am sure we
must revise, and are revising, our notion of the "classic," which has
come to be used as a term of unquestioning idolatry instead of in the
meaning which Sartre gives it: a book written by someone who "did
not have to decide with each work what the meaning and value of literature were, since its meaning and value were fixed by tradition."[6]
And I know that the action from the other side, of becoming that
person who puts signs on paper and invokes the collaboration of a
reader, encounters a corresponding check: in order to write I have to
believe that there is someone willing to collaborate subjectively, as
opposed to a grading machine out to get me for mistakes in spelling
and grammar. (Perhaps for this reason, many students first show the
writing they are actually capable of in an uncorrected journal rather
than in a "theme" written "for class.") The whole question of *trust* as
a basis for the act of reading or writing has only opened up since we
began trying to educate those who have every reason to mistrust literary culture. For young adults trying to write seriously for the first
time in their lives, the question "Whom can I trust?" must be an underlying boundary to be crossed before real writing can occur. We
who are part of literary culture come up against such a question only
when we find ourselves writing on some frontier of self-determination, as when writers from an oppressed group *within* literary culture, such as black intellectuals, or, most recently, women, begin to
describe and analyze themselves as they cease to identify with the
dominant culture. Those who fall into this category ought to be able
to draw on it in entering into the experience of the young adult for
whom writing itself—as reading—has been part of the not-me rather
than one of the natural activities of the self.

[5] Jean-Paul Sartre, *What Is Literature?* (New York: Harper Colophon Books, 1965),
pp. 39–40.

[6] Ibid., p. 85.

At this point the question of method legitimately arises: How to do it? How to develop a working situation in the classroom where trust becomes a reality, where the students are writing with belief in their own validity, and reading with belief that what they read has validity for them? The question is legitimate—How to do it?—but I am not sure that a description of strategies and exercises, readings, and writing topics can be, however successful they have proven for one teacher. When I read such material, I may find it stimulating and heartening as it indicates the varieties of concern and struggle going on in other classrooms, but I end by feeling it is useless to me. X is not myself and X's students are not my students, nor are my students of this fall the same as my students of last spring. A couple of years ago I decided to teach *Sons and Lovers*, because of my sense that the novel touched on facts of existence crucial to people in their late teens, and my belief that it dealt with certain aspects of family life, sexuality, work, anger, and jealousy which carried over to many cultures. Before the students began to read, I started talking about the time and place of the novel, the life of the mines, the process of industrialization and pollution visible in the slag heaps; and I gave the students (this was an almost all-black class) a few examples of the dialect they would encounter in the early chapters. Several students challenged the novel sight unseen: it had nothing to do with them, it was about English people in another era, why should they expect to find it meaningful to them, and so forth. I told them I had asked them to read it because I believed it was meaningful for them; if it was not, we could talk and write about why not and how not. The following week I reached the classroom door to find several students already there, energetically arguing about the Morels, who was to blame in the marriage, Mrs. Morel's snobbery, Morel's drinking and violence—taking sides, justifying, attacking. The class never began; it simply continued as other students arrived. Many had not yet read the novel, or had barely looked at it; these became curious and interested in the conversation and did go back and read it because they felt it must have something to have generated so much heat. That time, I felt some essential connections had been made, which carried us through several weeks of talking and writing about and out of *Sons and Lovers*, trying to define our relationships to its people and theirs to each other. A year or so later I enthusiastically started working with *Sons and Lovers* again, with a class of largely ethnic students—Jewish, Greek, Chinese, Italian, German, with a few Puerto Ricans and blacks. No one initially challenged the novel, but no one was particularly interested—or, perhaps, as I told myself, it impinged too dangerously on materials that this group was not about to deal with, such as violence in the family, nascent sexual feelings, conflicting feelings about a parent. Was this really true? I don't know; it is easy to play sociologist and make generalizations. Perhaps, simply, a different chemistry was at work, in me and in the students. The point is that for the first class, or for many of them, I think a trust came to be established in the novel genre as a possible means of finding out more about themselves; for the second class, the novel was an assignment, to be done under duress, read superficially, its connections with themselves avoided wherever possible.

Finally, as to trust: I think that, simple as it may seem, it is worth saying: a fundamental belief in the students is more important than anything else. We all know of those studies in education where the teacher's previously induced expectations dramatically affect the learning that goes on during the semester. This fundamental belief is not a sentimental matter: it is a very demanding matter of realistically conceiving the student where he or she is, and at the same time never losing sight of where he or she *can* be. Conditions at a huge, urban, overcrowded, noisy, and pollution-soaked institution can become almost physically overwhelming at times, for the students and for the staff: sometimes apathy, accidia, anomie seem to stare from the faces in an overheated basement classroom, like the faces in a subway car, and I sympathize with the rush to get out the moment the bell rings. This, too, is our context—not merely the students' past and my past, but this present moment we share. I (and I don't think I am alone in this) become angry with myself for my ineffectualness, angry at the students for their apparent resistance or their acceptance of mediocrity, angriest at the political conditions which dictate that we have to try to repair and extend the fabric of language under conditions which tend to coarsen our apprehensions of everything. Often, however, this anger, if not driven in on ourselves, or converted to despair, can become an illuminating force: the terms of the struggle for equal opportunity are chalked on the blackboard: this is what the students have been up against all their lives.

I wrote at the beginning of this article that my early assumptions about teaching had changed. I think that what has held me at City is not the one or two students in a class whose eyes meet mine with a look of knowing they were born for this struggle with words and meanings; not the poet who has turned up more than once; though such encounters are a privilege in the classroom as anywhere. What has held me, and what I think holds many who teach basic writing, are the hidden veins of possibility running through students who don't know (and strongly doubt) that this is what they were born for, but who may find it out to their own amazement, students who, grim with self-depreciation and prophecies of their own failure or tight with a fear they cannot express, can be lured into sticking it out to some moment of breakthrough, when they discover that they have ideas that are valuable, even original, and can express those ideas on ·paper. What fascinates and gives hope in a time of slashed budgets, enlarging class size, and national depression is the possibility that many of these young men and women may be gaining the kind of critical perspective on their lives and the skill to bear witness that they have never before had in our country's history.

At the bedrock level of my thinking about this is the sense that language is power, and that, as Simone Weil says, those who suffer from injustice most are the least able to articulate their suffering; and that the silent majority, if released into language, would not be content with a perpetuation of the conditions which have betrayed them. But this notion hangs on a special conception of what it means to be released into language: not simply learning the jargon of an elite, fitting unexceptionably into the status quo, but learning that language can be used as a means of changing reality.[7] What interests me in teaching is less the emergence of the occasional genius than the overall finding of language by those who did not have it and by

---

[7] Compare Paolo Freire: "Only beings who can reflect upon the fact that they are determined are capable of freeing themselves." *Cultural Action for Freedom*, Monograph Series No. 1 (Cambridge, Mass.: Harvard Educational Review and Center for the Study of Development and Social Change, 1970).

those who have been used and abused to the extent that they lacked it.

The question can be validly raised: Is the existing public (or private) educational system, school, or university the place where such a relationship to language can be developed? Aren't those structures already too determined, haven't they too great a stake in keeping things as they are? My response would be, yes, but this is where the *students* are. On the one hand, we need alternate education; on the other, we need to reach those students for whom unorthodox education simply means too much risk. In a disintegrating society, the orthodox educational system reflects disintegration. However, I believe it is more than simply reformist to try to use that system—while it still exists in all its flagrant deficiencies—to use it to provide essential tools and weapons for those who may live on into a new integration. Language is such a weapon, and what goes with language: reflection, criticism, renaming, creation. The fact that our language itself is tainted by the quality of our society means that in teaching we need to be acutely conscious of the kind of tool we want our students to have available, to understand how it has been used against them, and to do all we can to insure that language will not someday be used by them to keep others silent and powerless.

The Antifeminist Woman
(1972)

This article was written at the request of the *New York Review of Books*, as a review of Midge Decter's *The New Chastity, and Other Arguments Against Women's Liberation*. Decter had charged feminists with laziness, egocentricity, and self-indulgence, with a lack of concern for men and children, and a "puritanical" rejection of the claims of marriage, family, and (by implication) heterosexuality.* I ended by writing a critique of patriarchy and an analysis of what I saw as the real motivating and sustaining forces behind the new wave of feminism.

Rereading this text in 1978 I find opinions which I now question (*Is* there a "ghostly woman" in all men? What did I mean by this anyway?); passages which seem to me superficial (for example, my discussion of the family; wife-battering, conjugal rape, father-daughter incest had not yet been documented as feminist issues, and I underrated the role of male violence in keeping all women subordinate); and statements which I know now to be simply untrue ("Most early feminists did not question the patriarchal family as such"—many did, certainly in the suffrage movement). I find too an awkwardness of style, a confinement of language, which I ascribe to the fact that I was writing for a journal which had not really asked me to contribute a feminist article, and which I had no reason to feel would welcome feminist views. Within these constraints, I was trying to articulate that intense process of self-education, of reading and thinking, and of collective experience and perceptions, which marked the turn of the new decade for me as for so many

* The label of "puritanism" or "neo-puritanism" is frequently leveled at feminists and lesbian/feminists, as if any revaluation or critique of heterosexual relations were by definition asexual, antipleasure, and repressive. All of Decter's charges have more recently been heard from antichoice and anti-ERA spokespeople.

women. It was, of course, only the beginning of a process still continuing and which I conceive as endless.

But writing the article led to something else: it impelled me to think about motherhood in patriarchy, not as each mother's personal dilemma, or in terms of isolated issues of contraception, abortion, and childcare, but as a central social and political issue, radiating outward into all women's lives, whether as daughters or as mothers; and into every aspect of male supremacism. Out of this, four years later, came my book, *Of Woman Born: Motherhood as Experience and Institution*.

~~~~~~~~~~

This book is harmless, predictable, and sad. Like much ad hoc journalism, it is shallow, because the writer has set out to label and destroy a developing phenomenon, the women's movement, rather than to reflect on the needs and conflicts that generated it. Midge Decter's writing lacks any sense of the past and of the ways it continues to haunt, illuminate, and seduce us. She finds that the women's movement is the product of emotional and intellectual laziness masquerading as a "passion for social justice" and that its effect, if it is allowed to pursue its course, will be that "we shall all of us, men, women and babes in arms, live to reap the whirlwind."

What whirlwind, or how our lives might be changed, she does not trouble to say. The book is a sermon, addressed to some presumptive band of the faithful. I cannot imagine it being read—really read—all the way through: it contains no fresh perceptions of women's stake in this society that might revive their faith in it. I can imagine psychiatrists recommending it to their women patients, middle-class husbands presenting it to their wives on their anniversary or Mother's Day, suitably inscribed. I expect its existence will be temporarily soothing to some people, chiefly men (the admiring comments on the jacket are all masculine)—but also perhaps to some women who imagine that feminism is denying the value of their past lives, is accusing them of having literally let their powers, their resourcefulness, their bravery, their intelligence run down the drain of the kitchen sink. I am more concerned with these women and their lives than with anything else that may surround the publication of Decter's book.

Still, I find this a sad book, although its appearance was to be ex-

pected. Decter is an admirer of American society and I am not; this is
one difference between us. She finds all dissenting movements both
counterproductive and phony; she has praised the stability of the
American system in the face of efforts to subvert it by "glamorous
swashbucklers among the heralds of racial revolution; students;
women."[1] She reveals, in her social criticism a strange lack of information about the unfilled needs, let alone the enormous destructiveness, of the social order which she so admires, and which has
brought forth the movements she so dislikes.

But her politics do not, in and of themselves, explain the nature of
her book. I can easily imagine that, as a political conservative, she
feels estranged from the radical left out of which the early women's
movement of our time in part emerged. But she does not tell us this.
I could understand it if she declared that some aspects of the women's movement with which she has come in contact seem to have
nothing to do with *her* life. Black women have said this, and have
been creating a black women's consciousness of their own. What I
wonder at is her failure to suggest, in all the literature she cites, any
reflection of her own experience, any affection for other women, any
sense of what she herself as a woman is uniquely feeling or has ever
felt. Her writing is lifeless because she attempts to stand outside
something which, like it or not, is about and within her; and in so
doing she manages to sound not like a woman but like a priest lecturing his flock on the newest temptation.

But it is pointless to write off the antifeminist woman as brainwashed, or self-hating, or the like. I believe that feminism must
imply an imaginative identification with all women (and with the
ghostly woman in all men) and that the feminist must, because she
can, extend this act of the imagination as far as possible.

I meet, as it happens, very few antifeminist women. I do meet
women who are not feminists: working-class women who identify
strongly with their men and who at the same time know that men
have often used them badly. I meet many middle-class women who

[1] "Success of Our Social Order Depends on a Strong Labor Movement," address to
the League for Industrial Dmocracy, April 1972, published in Albert Shanker's column in the *New York Times*.

feel that they have solved "all these problems" for themselves, have managed motherhood and career, or achieved some other sort of personal solution. Most do, however, at least acknowledge that "these problems" existed and involved much conflict and required unusual luck—chiefly money—to solve; they are sympathetic, even enthusiastic, about efforts to make the process less wasteful for other women. I also meet women, black and white, who still feel, as Simone de Beauvoir did when she wrote *The Second Sex*, that "it is for man to establish the reign of liberty in the world of the given" and that an equal comradeship between man and woman will naturally follow on the heels of socialist or Third World revolution. (Mme. de Beauvoir has since carried her feminism further, as a recent interview in *Ms.* attests.[2]) I know other political women who feel that stopping the annihilation in Vietnam or preventing ecological suicide must take precedence over other politics—women with long and honorable records of opposition to authoritarianism.

I have also known nonfeminist women who have looked long and hard at masculine society and its competitive, paranoiac rules and who say, "There's something wrong here. Better to stay at home, where at least some semblance of emotional life remains, than go out there and become another emotionless flunky." For them the choice is based on the old assumptions. Either you stay at home where you can hope to express tenderness, give and receive warmth, behave spontaneously and generously, or you enter the male world and play the game like a man: the game being control, impassivity, ends above means, exploitation.

[2] "At the end of *The Second Sex*, I said I wasn't a feminist because I thought that the solution to women's problems must depend on the socialist evolution of society. By feminist, I mean fighting for specifically feminist demands, independent of the class struggle. Today . . . I have come to realize that we must fight for an improvement in woman's actual situation before achieving the socialism we hope for. . . . I realize that even in the socialist countries, women's equality has not been won." Interview with Alice Schwartzer, *Ms.*, vol. 1, no. 2, July 1972. A.R., 1978: See also de Beauvoir's message to the 1976 International Tribunal on Crimes Against Women: "I hold this meeting to be a great historic event. . . . Strengthened by your solidarity, you will develop defensive tactics, the first being precisely the one you will be using during these five days: talk to one another, talk to the world, bring to light the shameful truths that half of humanity is trying to cover up. . . . I salute this Tribunal as being the start of a radical decolonization of women."

I also meet women who are trying to rethink their lives, in small and large ways, painfully and fruitfully, as a consequence of the women's movement, and who share an awareness that has affected popular consciousness, not simply in the form of TV clichés and barbed jokes, but as serious thinking and study and self-questioning—a process Decter's book is not likely to scare them from. Her book is irrelevant to all this, because what is really "in the air" is not only the politics of housework or new marriage contracts or even, more seriously, equal pay for equal work, but a sense, on the part of men as well as women, that the way we live in a patriarchal society is dangerous for humanity.

In popular culture, *The Godfather* is of interest here. Again and again it shows men who, while ruling patriarchal families with the most benign authority toward their own women and children are capable at the same time of ruthless intimidation and murder; the efficiency of their violent operations depends on their maintaining an artificial and theoretical wall between fatherhood and godfatherhood. When "business" is discussed at the family table, the Family is already in trouble. Women, with their tendency to ask uncomfortable questions and make uncomfortable connections, are to be excluded from all decision-making, as the final shot somewhat heavily portrays. It is interesting that Marcel Ophuls's *The Sorrow and the Pity*—a film of far more serious poetic and political intentions—provides, again I believe unconsciously, similar images: those women who hover at the edge of things, in doorways, while the men reminisce about their acts of resistance; the medal-heavy Luftwaffe paterfamilias, blandly recounting his Occupation experiences at the wedding banquet of his daughter, while his wife listens and watches with a nervous smile.

Patriarchal organization and culture have been under question for some time; and until recently the best-known questioners have been men.[3] Erich Neumann, a disciple of Jung, wrote in 1952 (in his introduction to *The Great Mother*):

[3] A. R., 1978: Women theorists had, of course, criticized and challenged the institutions of marriage, patriarchal family, and religion for at least three centuries: e.g., Elizabeth Carey, Mary Wollstonecraft, Charlotte Perkins Gilman, Matilda Joslyn Gage, Elizabeth Cady Stanton, Susan B. Anthony, Emma Goldman, Crystal Eastman, Virginia Woolf . . . to name a few.

> . . . this problem of the Feminine has equal importance for the psy-
> chologist of culture, who realizes that the peril of present-day mankind
> springs in large part from the one-sidedly patriarchal development of
> the male intellectual consciousness, which is no longer kept in balance
> by the matriarchal world of the psyche.

Engels had earlier connected the advent of the patriarchal family
with the beginnings of property-hunger, slavery, war as acquisitive
pillage, and ultimately the State itself with its sanction and encouragement of human exploitation. Engels had, of course, as little
regard for religion and mythology as Neumann has interest in the
labor theory of value. Neumann is concerned not with the liberation
of actual women, or even with the political organization of men, but
with the collective loss and fragmentation suffered by human beings
in the denial and suppression of the feminine. He is not interested in
establishing that any actual historical "matriarchal stage" existed but
he insists that it does exist in the human unconscious and that "the
health and creativity of every man depend very largely on whether
his unconscious can live at peace with this stratum of the unconscious or consumes itself in strife with it."

But the patriarchy has come into question in another way: as the
natural order of things. There is a line of speculative inquiry reaching back for over a century that suggests that a matriarchal social
order preceded the patriarchal: for example, J. J. Bachofen's *Das
Mutterrecht* (1861) and Robert Briffault's *The Mothers*, a three-
volume study first published in 1927 and reprinted in an abridged
edition in 1969. Bachofen maintained that civilizations such as the
pre-Hellenic were not simply matrilineal but were based on "the
religious and civic primacy of womanhood" and that many of their
scientific and cultural achievements were lost when the matriarchies
were crushed, some to be recovered only centuries later.

More recently, in a fascinating if problematical book, *The First
Sex*,[4] Elizabeth Gould Davis has attempted to bring together evidence of this primacy—anthropological, archaeological, mythologi-
cal, historical—and to draw connections which have long been left
undrawn, or which if drawn, as by Bachofen and in our century by

[4] Elizabeth Gould Davis, *The First Sex* (New York: Putnam's, 1971). A. R., 1978:
See also Merlin Stone, *When God Was a Woman* (New York: Harcourt Brace, 1978).

Mary Beard (*Woman as Force in History*, 1945), have been largely
ignored or dismissed as unhistorical. While Beard was concerned to
point out that much has been swept under the rug, Davis tries to as-
semble evidence that matriarchies existed, that these may have been
the "lost" cultures later remembered and mythologized as the
Golden Age, and that there was a deliberate effort to obliterate their
memory by the patriarchy—as in the case of mother-goddesses who
were later transformed into paternalistic and judgmental gods like
Yahweh. (Santayana's remark that "there is no God and Mary is his
mother" becomes more than a quip in this context.)

Long before Davis, in the 1930s, Otto Rank was writing that Jewish "monotheism appears as the result of a long struggle against
foreign gods who still betrayed the earmarks of an earlier mother-
goddess";[5] and that "the Torah which guided the nomadic Jews
through the desert represented an original female symbol, a relic of
the great Asiatic Mother-Goddess."[6] Theodor Reik, in his *Pagan
Rites in Judaism* (1964), remarks of the Torah that "*She* is considered
older than the world and is assigned a cosmic role. . . . Even in this
diluted form we recognize the primal female goddess." Rank points
out that the Golden Calf itself was not the proverbial symbol of materialism but a mother symbol.

Implicit in the notion of a matriarchal origin of civilization, or of
"gynocentric" or "gynocratic" societies, of course, is the assumption
that woman is and need be in no way hampered—rather the opposite—by childbearing and nurturing, in governing, inventing, establishing religion, creating works of art, enacting laws, healing the
sick, designing cities. Bachofen suggests that "matriarchal states were
particularly famed for their freedom from intestine strife and conflict. . . . Matriarchal peoples . . . assigned special culpability to
the physical injury of one's fellow men or even of animals."[7] If this
seemed wishful conjecture in 1861, recent archaeological discover-
ies may force us to credit him at least with intuition.

Davis, for example, draws attention to the excavations at Çatal

[5] Otto Rank, *Beyond Psychology* (New York: Dover, 1958), p. 240.

[6] Ibid.; cf. Davis, p. 60.

[7] J. J. Bachofen, *Myth, Religion and Mother Right*, Ralph Manheim, trans.
(Princeton, N.J.: Princeton University, 1967), pp. 80–81.

Hüyük in Anatolia in the 1960s as revealing a Neolithic civilization in which males played a clearly subordinate role, women were heads of households and worshiped as deities, and "there is no evidence of violent deaths." This is borne out by the archaeologist James Mellaart, one of the excavators, in his *Çatal Hüyük: A Neolithic Town in Anatolia:*

> Somewhere during the 58th century B.C. agriculture finally triumphed over the age old occupation of hunting and with it the power of woman increased. . . . The divine family . . . was patterned on that of man; and the four aspects are in order of importance: mother, daughter, son and father.

According to Mellaart the majority of skeletons given sacred burial in shrines are those of women, and "there are no individuals . . . that showed signs of violent death." Although Mellaart cautions against drawing conclusions about Neolithic social structure, he writes,

> In the new economy a great number of tasks were undertaken by women . . . and this probably accounts for her social pre-eminence. . . . Hence a religion which aimed at . . . conservation of life in all its forms, its propagation and the mysteries of its rites connected with life and death, birth and resurrection, were evidently part of her sphere rather than that of man.

Davis's book, while it throws out a wide and potentially illuminating spray of sparks, is not, like Beard's, critical of its sources nor does the author attempt to deal with the special problems of controversy within the fields she draws on. What she does provide is the *idea* of a historical alternative to a society characterized by dominant, aggressive men and passive, victimized, acquiescent women. Even were only half the scholarship she cites accurate, the idea would remain enormously valuable. Davis's book also suggests the necessity for a new and demanding kind of critical scholarship—a searching reevaluation of the "respectable" sources as well as of neglected ones, undertaken in the light of feminist perceptions.[8]

---

[8] A. R., 1978: Mary Daly's *Gyn/Ecology: The Metaethics of Radical Feminism* (Boston: Beacon, 1978) is the most recent and courageous critique of male scholarship.

There are certain difficulties which adhere to any discussion of patriarchal society and feminist consciousness, and which I had better delineate here, though I cannot resolve them. Kate Millett suggests the larger problem when she writes:

> Perhaps patriarchy's greatest psychological weapon is simply its universality and longevity. A referent scarcely exists with which it might be contrasted [here the concept of the gynocracies becomes indeed compelling] or by which it might be refuted. While the same might be said of class, patriarchy has a still more tenacious or powerful hold through its successful habit of passing itself off as nature. . . . When a system of power is thoroughly in command, it has scarcely need to speak itself aloud. . . .[9]

Biological motherhood has long been used as a reason for condemning women to a role of powerlessness and subservience in the social order. Therefore it is hardly surprising that feminist thinking has had to begin by rejecting physiology as a basis for consideration of ability and by exploring whatever else woman is and might be besides a body with uterus and breasts. However, I believe that a radical reinterpretation of the concept of motherhood is required which would tell us, among many other things, more about the physical capacity for gestation and nourishment of infants and how it relates to psychological gestation and nurture as an intellectual and creative force. Until now, the two aspects of creation have been held in artificial isolation from each other, while responsibilities of men and women have largely been determined not by anatomy but by laws, education, politics, and social pressures claiming anatomy as their justification.

Again and again, as I read the literature of the women's movement, I am struck by courageous imaginations that are now trying to go further than feminism has gone before: to grapple with immediate political necessities; with the emotional imprintings of the culture; with the great weight of patriarchal scholarship in need of reevaluation; with much lost and blotted-out history and biography, archae-

---

Patriarchal science is also exposed and parodied in Susan Griffin's *Woman and Nature: The Roaring Inside Her* (New York: Harper & Row, 1978).

[9] Kate Millett, *Sexual Politics* (New York: Doubleday, 1970), p. 58.

ology and anthropology; and with a sense that time, in the sense of human survival, is running out. To think as a feminist means trying to think connectedly about, for example, the science of embryology as it may connect with sexuality (what does it mean, for example, that in the fetus male differentiation occurs only after several weeks);[10] about human body-rhythms and their relation to natural cycles (the menses and the lunar month, the connections between woman, darkness, sleep, and death in the male unconscious; the connections of these with male attitudes and political decisions affecting women); about the uses and criteria of psychology. It is easy to say that we cannot ever know what is truly male or truly female. There is much we can know. We do know that these principles have been split apart and set in antagonism within each of us by a male-dominated intellectual and political heritage. That is at least a starting point.

I would like to clarify here the way in which I am using the term patriarchy. By it I mean to imply not simply the tracing of descent through the father, which anthropologists seem to agree is a relatively late phenomenon, but any kind of group organization in which males hold dominant power and determine what part females shall and shall not play, and in which capabilities assigned to women are relegated generally to the mystical and aesthetic and excluded from the practical and political realms. (It is characteristic of patriarchal thinking that these realms are regarded as separate and mutually exclusive.) Such group organization has existed so long that almost all written history, theology, psychology, and cultural anthropology are founded on its premises and contribute to its survival. Based as it is on genital difference, its concept of sex is genitally centered; entire zones of the body (and soul) are to be used simply as means to a genital end.

At the core of patriarchy is the individual family unit with its division of roles, its values of private ownership, monogamous marriage, emotional possessiveness, the "illegitimacy" of a child born outside legal marriage, the unpaid domestic services of the wife,

[10] Mary Jane Sherfey, *The Nature and Evolution of Female Sexuality* (New York: Random House, 1972), pp. 38 and 141.

obedience to authority, judgment, and punishment for disobedi-
ence. Within this family children learn the characters, sexual and
otherwise, that they are to assume, in their turn, as adults. The
parents are expected to deliver the child up to the educational system, which will carry it further in this acculturation process; the
parents reinforce the values of school and discourage the child from
rebelling against authority, even the most corrupt, lest he or she fail
to enter the mainstream of the society. Throughout, authority
derives from a person's status—father, teacher, boss, law-giver—
rather than from his personal qualities. We all know variations on
this pattern and most of us can cite instances of unusual mutuality
and liberality in families we know or have been part of; but the fact
remains that they do not represent the overruling pattern. The sacredness of the family in the patriarchy—sacred in the sense that it is
heresy to question its ultimate value—relieves the titular head of it
from any real necessity to justify his behavior.

Within this institution, and largely through maternal influence,
have existed tenderness, emotional responsiveness, protectiveness
toward nascent states of being, respect for the process of growing,
along with mutual vulnerability and, though rarely, nonpossessive
love. (Yet Phyllis Chesler suggests that mothers tend to nurture their
sons more readily than their daughters, at least in the sense that they
confirm their sons as potentially strong and active beings, while they
encourage their daughters to become good candidates for marriage,
confirmers of men rather than of one another.)[11] There have been
cells of matriarchy within the patriarchal system everywhere.[12]

[11] Phyllis Chesler, *Women and Madness* (New York: Doubleday, 1972), pp. 17–21.

[12] The black family, for instance, long treated by white observers as no real family at
all but a social disaster area, has under the crushing pressure of slavery and racism not
only survived but carried within it the seeds of black pride, solidarity, and rebellion, as
Pauli Murray points out. Joyce Ladner notes, in her study of young black women, distinct traditional African matrilineal elements in black family life, while Angela Davis
argues the crucial role of the black woman as an agent of resistance to the white patriarchy. (See Pauli Murray, "The Liberation of Black Women," in M. L. Thompson,
ed., *Voices of the New Feminism* [Boston: Beacon, 1970], p. 88; Joyce A. Ladner, *Tomorrow's Tomorrow* [New York: Doubleday, 1971], pp. 18–21; Angela Davis, "Reflec-
tions on the Black Woman's Role, in the *Black Scholar*, vol. 3, no. 1.) A. R., 1978:
But "Matriarchy" as numerous black women have been at pains to point out, is a
dangerously misleading term for the situation of the black woman head of household;

Within the patriarchal family, the maternal element has also been variously misread, distorted, and corrupted. We all know the ways in which maternal care and concern can turn into authoritarian control. It is a truism to say that the channeling of female energy into domesticity can produce overprotectiveness, overscrupulosity, martyrdom, possessiveness disguised as sacrifice, and much repressed and displaced anger. We can expect such distortions when nurturance is a tiny enclave in a harsh and often violent society.

The patriarchy looks to women to embody and impersonate the qualities lacking in its institutions—concern for the quality of life, for means rather than for pure goal, a connection with the natural and the extrasensory order. These attributes have been classified as "female" in part because the patriarchy relegates them to women and tends to deny them—with a certain fatalism—to men. The encouragement of such qualities as intuition, sympathy, and access to feeling by a mother in her sons is deplored because this is supposed to make them unfit for the struggle that awaits them in a masculine world. Thus the "masculinity" of that world is perpetuated.

Most early feminists did not question the patriarchal family structure as such. They wanted education, changes in the marriage laws, birth control, suffrage; the struggle to prove that women could be entrusted with such dangerous tools was energy-consuming—and physically dangerous—enough without taking on the patriarchy en bloc. But recently, as a few, mostly white middle-class, women have obtained token "equality" in the form of permission to attend professional schools, to be pediatricians or psychoanalysts or to argue cases in court, their relationship to the patriarchy has become confusing. When the professor who directs your thesis, the second professor who interviews you for a grant, the editor who hires you for the staff of his magazine, the government official who offers you a position on his committee, the chief surgeon with whom you work as an anesthesiologist, the reviewer who praises you for "logical thinking," the analyst who approves your method of dealing with patients in training, the members of the law firm in which you are the first woman partner, are all male, it is difficult to be sure when and where your "success" begins to build itself on a series of denials, small

and the label of "matriarch" has been used to defame black women as "castrators" of black men.

enough in themselves, perhaps, yet accruing through the invisible process such things follow into acquiescence in a system of values which distrusts and degrades women.

I am not talking here about the loss of some fragile "feminine" quality jeopardized by excellence in reasoning and analysis, or by the desire to have original ideas. I am talking about the consciousness of self as Other which Simone de Beauvoir has described, as that being toward whom man often feels fear, guilt, and hostility, and about whom he weaves his least defensible theories. Few women have grown up without this knowledge, lodged as it may be in some collective unconscious, disguised as it may be under codes of chivalry, domestic sentiment, biological reduction, or as it is revealed in poetry, law, theology, popular songs, pornography, or dirty jokes. Such knowledge—so long as women are not pressured into denying it— makes them [sic] potentially the deepest of all questions of the social order created by men, and the most genuinely radical of thinkers.

It goes without saying that for "successful" women, male hostility usually takes forms less physical and literal than it does in the lives of their "unliberated" sisters. In Bangladesh during the revolution, it has been estimated that 200,000 women were raped by Pakistani soldiers.[13] Many were victims, according to Joyce Goldman in the August 1972 issue of *Ms.*, of highly organized, almost mechanized gang rape. Some were children as young as eight. The husbands, fathers, brothers, fiancés of these women immediately disowned them, made them outcasts of that allegedly revolutionary new society. Many of these women committed suicide, others gave birth to children whom they later murdered. Every one of these women was raped twice: first physically by the enemy soldier, then psychically by the enemy in her own household. I wonder how many women there are, however free and fortunate they consider themselves, who would not respond to that double jeopardy with intense and painful recognition.

[13] A. R., 1978: In *Against Our Will: Men, Women and Rape* (New York: Simon and Schuster, 1975) Susan Brownmiller reports that statistics between 200,000 and 400,000 have been quoted; that the range of ages of the women went from eight to seventy-five years; and that pornographic films were shown in some of the military barracks "to work the men up," according to one of her sources.

The "liberated" woman encounters male hostility in the form of psychic rape, often masked as psychic or physical seduction. It occurs overtly in the classroom where a male teacher denigrates female intellect; more subtly in the committee where she sits as token woman and where her intelligence is treated with benign neglect; in the magnanimous assumption that she is "not like other women" and for this reason is so desirable a colleague, figurehead, or adornment to the establishment (the pitting of woman against woman, woman against herself). At the same time that she is told about her "specialness" she is expected to be flattered, like all women, by flirtation. She is also expected to be flattered by man's sexual self-hatred and sexual confusion, his avowal that "I can talk to women, but not to men," his romanticizing of his sexual dishonesty: "I can't talk to my wife, but I can talk to you."

When she is not flattered, she is accused of causing his impotence. When she responds with strong feeling to any or all of the above, she is charged with emotionalism, hysteria, frigidity, lack of objectivity. The token woman may come to believe that her personal solution has not been bought, but awarded her as a prize for her special qualities. And she may—indeed, must—have special qualities. But her personal solution has been bought at a political price; her "liberation" becomes another small confirmation of the patriarchal order and its principle of division.

The great loss that the "special" woman suffers is her separation from other women, and thus from herself. As soon as she is lulled by that blandishment about being "different," more intelligent, more beautiful, more human, more committed to rational thinking, more humorous, more able to "write like a man," a true daughter of the father-principle, she loses touch with her own innate strength. Underlying the "successful" antifeminist woman's thought is surely the illusion that "if I can be a special woman, I can be free"—even though this freedom requires a masculine approach to social dynamics, to competition with others, to the very existence of other human beings and their needs (which are seen as threatening). She may let herself become concerned with the "status" of other "special" women, while she ignores the women typing in the office or serving in the cafeteria. Even within the women's movement this fragmentation can be seen, and is hailed with satisfaction by its critics: See, those women are fighting each other! But there is a difference between diversity and fragmentation. Fragmentation is endemic in patriarchal society and is in no way unique to the women's movement. But many women of our time, having different experiences to bring the movement, are in serious, affectionate, and difficult struggle with each other as they attempt to sort out the new materials and the long-buried feelings in which the women's movement is so rich.

The nuclear family is a principal form of social fragmentation. It fosters the sense of biologically determined alliance against an outer world which is perceived (in Decter's words) as "a polymorphous mass" rather than as a potential community which might be available for mutual help and generosity and mutual transfusions of psychic energy. But this tiny unit, presumed as a sheltering environment, a safe harbor from the violent and aggressive world of the Strangers, is in fact often also dangerous for the psyche. Freud's own work suggested (though not to him) that the patriarchal family was a source of psychic disorder.

Yet it remains true that within the family the maternal principle has survived in its least damaged form, though drained off from society and channeled into the narrowest possible vessel. Much of the fear that men, and antifeminist women, express at the possible disappearance of the family may be dread that if women decline to become mothers physically we are robbing our culture of all motherly possibilities. And there are passages in Midge Decter's book that make me think that for her, too, this dread exists. Her real whirlwind, her fear that dares not speak its name, may be that all that she knows is most hopeful in herself and most hopeful to society—however the patriarchy may have taught her to diminish it or to keep it in its place—will vanish with the "end of motherhood."

One of the devastating effects of technological capitalism has been its numbing of the powers of the imagination—specifically, the power to envision new human and communal relationships. I am a feminist because I feel endangered, psychically and physically, by this society, and because I believe that the women's movement is saying that we have come to an edge of history when men—insofar as they are embodiments of the patriarchal idea—have become dangerous to children and other living things, themselves included; and that we can no longer afford to keep the female principle enclosed within the confines of the tight little postindustrial family, or within any male-induced notion of where the female principle is valid and where it is not.

In *The Elementary Structures of Kinship*, Lévi-Strauss wrote that "the first problem of mythic thought is that women must be domesticated. I would go so far as to say that even before slavery or class domination existed, men built an approach to women *that would serve one day to introduce differences among us all*." (Italics mine.) There are men, dangerous to us all, who have a personal and collective stake in keeping those imposed differences between man and woman and between man and man. To look freshly at, and to revolt against, the sexuality, the family structure, and the politics that have evolved from that patriarchal "approach" is imperative not only for feminists but for our general survival.

One passage in Decter's book which breaks through her tone of detachment is her description of the loneliness of the pregnant woman. I think here Decter is right: However much the "expectant mother" is told that she is melting into the great stream of being, the Life Force, she suffers from a sense of fear and isolation in this most unmotherly of societies. I wish Midge Decter could sense that in a genuine alliance of women with women, and of women with non-masculinist men, the pregnant woman or the woman in labor would not feel alone; that the women's movement is struggling to imagine and recreate a more natural environment for the process of becoming a mother, an artist, an originator, a human being. The loneliness of the pregnant woman is an archetype of the loneliness of all life-expanding impulses in a society created out of the triumph of force and will.

Woman Observing, Preserving, Conspiring, Surviving: The Poems of Eleanor Ross Taylor (1972)

Eleanor Ross Taylor's first book, *Wilderness of Ladies*, published in 1960, recognized by a handful of people including the late Randall Jarrell, has remained an underground book, fierce, rich, and difficult, though it seems less "difficult" with every passing year, just as Emily Dickinson does. In that book are two poems I've carried about with me for a decade as a kind of secret knowledge and reinforcement: "Woman as Artist" and "Sister." They, like many of Eleanor Taylor's poems, speak of the underground life of women, the southern white Protestant woman in particular, the woman writer, the woman in the family, coping, hoarding, preserving, observing, keeping up appearances, seeing through the myths and hypocrisies, nursing the sick, conspiring with sister-women, possessed of a will to survive and to see others survive. (The southern black woman and the southern white woman share a history and a knowledge that we are barely on the edge of exploring.)

Welcome Eumenides reaches out from this scene yet has its roots there. The South is the only part of the United States to have lost a war and suffered the physical and psychic trauma of military defeat; this is another kind of knowledge that Eleanor Taylor, as a southern woman, possesses. The book ends with a long poem, "A Few Days

Review of *Welcome, Eumenides*, poems by Eleanor Ross Taylor (New York: George Braziller), in the *New York Times Book Review*, July 2, 1972.

in the South in February," which is the monologue or diary of a
Yankee father going down to North Carolina at the end of the Civil
War to find the grave of his son, exhume the body, coffin it, and
bring it home for burial. The father's broodings are entirely personal
yet they reveal the horror of war seen through the victor's eye devoid
of machismo: The war is lost, for this father and for the others like
him. In his forenote to the book, Richard Howard calls this "the best
poem since Whitman about the War Between the States," and the
father Eleanor Taylor has recreated "from family papers" is Whit-
manesque in his compassion, determination and grief-stricken dignity.

"After Twenty Years," another monologue on the aftermath of
another war, uses the voice of a woman in church; her son was killed
and buried in Normandy during World War II; her husband has
since committed suicide.

> My glove's rouge, with lipstick
> Or with teeth. . . . Curse *men*, curse *free*—
> God vault your freedom!
> Oh the acres of undistinguished
> Crosses make me sick.
> Mother could mark Papa's grave
> In the churchyard a mile from home,
> By its firs and shaft. . . .
> Your nothing grave . . .
>   Shame! . . .
> Give my son another life—
> A Norwood ugliness, a bourgeois rot,
> Dust and concrete, Falcons and Mustangs, not . . .

And there the poem ends. This mother does not pray, as the
Yankee father does, "I believe that the bounds of our lives/Are fixed
by our Creator . . . /Blessed be the name of the Lord." Her grief is
anger, a rebellious gnawing at gloved fingers; better her son should
live in the mean material postwar world than be dead in one of those
wars which men have rationalized to her, to themselves.

But the truly remarkable poem in the book, one for which it
should be read even if it did not contain other strong poems, is the
title poem, "Welcome Eumenides." Out of the world and the wars
that men have made she conjures the voice of Florence Nightingale,

reliving her days and nights at Scutari, the death-ward of the Crimean War, with glimpses back into the family-centered, trivializing life of nineteenth-century English women of the leisure class. (Many lines and phrases of the poem are directly quoted from actual notes Florence Nightingale left behind her.) In this heroic, oral poem, densely woven and refrained, Eleanor Taylor has brought together the waste of women in society and the waste of men in wars and twisted them inseparably.

> Who calls?
> Not my child.
> (*O God no more love*
> *No more marriage*)
>   Only my British Army. . . .
>
> (Where did I yawn
> in the face of the gilt clock
> Defying it to reach 10?)
> Stuff straw for deathbeds, for deathbeds,
> For deathbeds.
> Not one shall die alone.
> I die with each.
> Now hurry to the next lax hand, loose tongue,
> Quick messages for forever.
> Mr. Osborne knelt down for dictation.
> His pencil skirmished among lice.
> At last, the chance for a rich and true life. . . .
>
> I dreamed . . .
> Compulsive dreaming of the victim.
> The rich play in God's garden.
> Can they be forgiven?
> Their errors gamble scintillating
> Under the chandeliers like razors honed.
> I murder their heaven,
> *I, starving, desperate, diseased.* . . .
>   ("You'll catch something and bring it home.")
> *Mother, you were willing enough*
> *To part with me to marriage.*
> No, I must take some things;
> They will not be given. . . .

Florence Nightingale, well-born, beautiful, courted, living out the rituals of society and the oppressions of the Victorian family which held its daughters in a clutch of duty and hysteria; becoming neurasthenic; battling her relations and her class to enter a profession considered demeaning and immoral; preparing herself with heroic patience and in secret for the great occasion which Victorian imperialism was eventually to provide her—Eleanor Taylor has compressed what might be the materials for a play or a film into eight intense pages of verse. The materials are ideally suited to her style, a style born of tension, in which whispered undertones are in dialogue with the givens of social existence, with the sudden explosive burst of rebellion or recognition:

> A girl, desperately fortified in my castle,
> The starched pure linen,
> Scalded plates, the sanitary air,
> The facile word killed soul-ferment.
> Six courses starved the spirit.
>   *And I said of laughter, mad,*
>   *And of mirth, what is it doing?*
> I dreamed of all things at man's mercy.

Nightingale was, of course, no Victorian angel in the house but a brilliant administrator and researcher, a fighter, with terrifying endurance and a keen sense of politics. She was also a driven woman; the split-second urgencies of her will come through in the jagged lines and verse paragraphs of the poem.

What I find compelling in the poems of Eleanor Taylor, besides the authority and originality of her language, is the underlying sense of how the conflicts of imaginative and intelligent women have driven them on, lashed them into genius or madness, how the home-nursing, the household administration, the patience and skill in relationships acquired at such expense in a family-centered life, became an essential part of the strength of a woman like Nightingale, but at tremendous price. *Welcome Eumenides* is a writing-large, in terms of a celebrated and powerful woman, of unanswered questions that hover throughout Eleanor Taylor's poems, and throughout the history and psychology of women.

Jane Eyre: The Temptations of a Motherless Woman (1973)

Like Thackeray's daughters, I read *Jane Eyre* in childhood, carried away "as by a whirlwind." Returning to Charlotte Brontë's most famous novel, as I did over and over in adolescence, in my twenties, thirties, now in my forties, I have never lost the sense that it contains, through and beyond the force of its creator's imagination, some nourishment I needed then and still need today. Other novels often ranked greater, such as *Persuasion, Middlemarch, Jude the Obscure, Madame Bovary, Anna Karenina, The Portrait of a Lady*—all offered their contradictory and compelling versions of what it meant to be born a woman. But *Jane Eyre* has for us now a special force and survival value.

Comparing *Jane Eyre* to *Wuthering Heights*, as people tend to do, Virginia Woolf had this to say:

> The drawbacks of being Jane Eyre are not far to seek. Always to be a governess and always to be in love is a serious limitation in a world which is full, after all, of people who are neither one nor the other. . . . [Charlotte Brontë] does not attempt to solve the problems of human life; she is even unaware that such problems exist; all her force, which is the more tremendous for being constricted, goes into the assertion, "I love," "I hate," "I suffer" . . .[1]

An earlier version of this essay was given as a lecture at Brandeis University, 1972; the essay was first published in *Ms.*, October 1973.

[1] Virginia Woolf, *The Common Reader* (New York: Harcourt Brace, 1948), pp. 221–22. A. R., 1978: Her *Common Reader* essays, so many of which were on women

She goes on to state that Emily Brontë is a greater poet than Charlotte because "there is no 'I' in *Wuthering Heights*. There are no governesses. There are no employers. There is love, but not the love of men and women." In short, and here I would agree with her, *Wuthering Heights* is mythic. The bond between Catherine and Heathcliff is the archetypal bond between the split fragments of the psyche, the masculine and feminine elements ripped apart and longing for reunion. But *Jane Eyre* is different from *Wuthering Heights*, and not because Charlotte Brontë lodged her people in a world of governesses and employers, of the love between men and women. *Jane Eyre* is not a novel in the Tolstoyan, the Flaubertian, even the Hardyesque sense. *Jane Eyre* is a tale.

The concern of the tale is not with social mores, though social mores may occur among the risks and challenges encountered by the protagonist. Neither is it an anatomy of the psyche, the fated chemistry of cosmic forces. It takes its place between the two: between the realm of the given, that which is changeable by human activity, and the realm of the fated, that which lies outside human control: between realism and poetry. The world of the tale is above all a "vale of soul-making," and when a novelist finds herself writing a tale, it is likely to be because she is moved by that vibration of experience which underlies the social and political, though it constantly feeds into both of these.

In her essay on *Jane Eyre*, critic Q. D. Leavis perceives the novel's theme as ". . . an exploration of how a woman comes to maturity in the world of the writer's youth."[2] I would suggest that a novel about how a man "comes to maturity in the world of the writer's youth"— *Portrait of the Artist*, for example—would not be dismissed as lack-

---

writers, bear nonetheless the marks of her struggle with masculine ideas of what is important, appropriate, or valid (a struggle eloquently described in her speech before the London/National Society for Women's Service, 1931, reprinted with Woolf's own manuscript revisions in *The Pargiters*, Mitchell Leaska, ed. [New York: NYPL/Readex Books, 1977]). So, in 1925, writing of *Jane Eyre*, the future author of *To the Lighthouse* (1927), *A Room of One's Own* (1929), and *Three Guineas* (1938) was able to declare that "Charlotte Brontë does not attempt to solve the problems of human life. She is even unaware that such problems exist." Woolf herself still meets with similar incomprehension today.

[2] Q. D. Leavis, Introduction to *Jane Eyre* (Baltimore: Penguin, 1966), p. 11.

ing in range, or, in Woolf's words, a sense of "human problems." I would suggest further, that Charlotte Brontë is writing—not a *Bildungsroman*—but the life story of a woman who is *incapable* of saying *I am Heathcliff* (as the heroine of Emily's novel does) because she feels so unalterably herself. Jane Eyre, motherless and economically powerless, undergoes certain traditional female temptations, and finds that each temptation presents itself along with an alternative—the image of a nurturing or principled or spirited woman on whom she can model herself, or to whom she can look for support.

II

In *Women and Madness* Phyllis Chesler notes that "women are motherless children in patriarchal society." By this she means that women have had neither power nor wealth to hand on to their daughters; they have been dependent on men as children are on women; and the most they can do is teach their daughters the tricks of surviving in the patriarchy by pleasing, and attaching themselves to, powerful or economically viable men:[3] Even the heiress in nineteenth-century fiction is incomplete without a man; her wealth, like Dorothea Brooke's or Isabel Archer's, must be devoted to the support of some masculine talent or dilettantism; economically the heiress is, simply, a "good match" and marriage her only real profession. In nineteenth-century England the poor and genteel woman had one possible source of independence if she did not marry: the profession of governess. But, as I have suggested, Jane Eyre is *not* "always a governess." She addresses us first as a literally motherless, and also fatherless child, under the guardianship of her aunt, Mrs. Reed, who despises and oppresses her. The tale opens with images of coldness, bleakness, banishment. Jane is seated behind the curtains in a

---

[3] A. R., 1978: Ground-breaking as *Women and Madness* (1972) was in its documentation of the antiwoman bias of the psychoanalytic and psychotherapeutic professions, Chesler oversimplified, I believe, the mother-daughter relationship, perceiving it as almost entirely, if tragically, negative. To a large extent she resorts to "blaming the mother" for the daughter's disadvantaged position in patriarchy. The more we learn of actual female history (to take but one example, of the history of black women) the less we can generalize about the failure of mothers to cherish and inspirit daughters in a strong, female tradition.

window-embrasure, trying to conceal herself from her aunt, her two girl cousins, and her boorish boy cousin John. With the icy coldness of the winter landscape outside on one hand, this chilly family circle on the other, she looks at a book of engravings of Arctic wastes and legendary regions of winter.

III

Moments after the novel begins, John Reed provokes Jane's childish rage by striking her in the face and taunting her with her poverty and dependency. Thus, immediately, the political/social circumstances of Jane's life are established: as a female she is exposed to male physical brutality and whim; as an economically helpless person she is vulnerable in a highly class-conscious society. Her response to John's gratuitous cruelty is to "fly at him" and thereat to be dragged off and locked into the "Red Room," where her uncle had died and which is rumored to be a haunted chamber.

Here begins the ordeal which represents Jane's first temptation. For a powerless little girl in a hostile household, where both psychic and physical violence are used against her, used indeed to punish her very spiritedness and individuality, the temptation of victimization is never far away. To see herself as the sacrificial lamb or scapegoat of this household, and act out that role, or conversely to explode into violent and self-destructive hysterics which can only bring on more punishment and victimization, are alternatives all too ready at hand.

In the Red Room, Jane experiences the bitter isolation of the outsider, the powerlessness of the scapegoat to please, the abjectness of the victim. But above all, she experiences her situation as unnatural:

> Unjust—unjust! said my reason, forced by the agonizing stimulus into precocious though transitory power; and Resolve, equally wrought up, instigated some strange expedient to achieve escape from insupportable oppression—as running away, or if that could not be effected, never eating or drinking more, and letting myself die.

I want to recall to you that the person who is going through this illumination—for "dark" and "turbid" as her feelings are, they are illuminating—is a girl of ten, without material means or any known recourse in the outer world, dependent on the household she lives in for physical support and whatever strands of human warmth she can cling to. She is, even so, conscious that it could be otherwise; she imagines alternatives, though desperate ones. It is at this moment that the germ of the person we are finally to know as Jane Eyre is born: a person determined to live, and to choose her life with dignity, integrity, and pride.

Jane's passion in the Red Room comes to its climax; she hallucinates, screams, is thrust back into the dreaded death-chamber, and blacks out. Her ensuing illness, like much female illness, is an acting-out of her powerlessness and need for affection, and a psychic crisis induced by these conditions. During her convalescence from this "fit," she experiences for the first time the decency of the family apothecary and the gentle and caring side of the sharp-tongued young servant Bessie. Bessie is the first woman to show Jane affection; and it is partly the alliance with her that makes it possible for the child Jane to maintain her hope for the future, her will to survive; which prevents her from running away—a self-destructive act under the circumstances—or from relapsing into mere hysteria or depression. It is this, too, which helps her retain the self-respect and the spirit of rebellion in which she finally confronts her aunt:

> Shaking from head to foot, thrilled with ungovernable excitement, I continued—

> "I am glad you are no relation of mine. I will never call you aunt again as long as I live. I will never come to see you when I am grown up; and if anyone asks me how I liked you, and how you treated me, I will say the very thought of you makes me sick, and that you treated me with miserable cruelty."

> . . . Ere I had finished this reply, my soul began to expand, to exult, with the strangest sense of freedom, of triumph, I ever felt. It seemed as if an invisible bond had burst and that I had struggled out into unhoped-for liberty.

This outburst, like much anger of the powerless, leaves Jane only briefly elated. The depressive, self-punishing reaction sets in; she is only pulled out of it by Bessie's appearance and a confirmed sense of Bessie's affection and respect for her. Bessie tells her that she must not act afraid of people, because it will make them dislike her—an odd aslant bit of counsel, yet Jane's precocious courage is able to respond. The next chapter finds Jane on her way to Lowood Insitution.

IV

Lowood is a charity school for the poor or orphaned genteel female destined to become a governess. It is a school for the poor controlled by the rich, an all-female world presided over by the hollow, Pharisaical male figure of Mr. Brocklehurst. He is the embodiment of class and sexual double-standards and of the hypocrisy of the powerful, using religion, charity, and morality to keep the poor in their place and to repress and humiliate the young women over whom he is set in charge. He is absolute ruler of this little world. However, within it, and in spite of his sadistic public humiliation of her, Jane finds two women unlike any she has ever met: the superintendent Miss Temple, and the older student Helen Burns.

Miss Temple has no power in the world at large, or against Mr. Brocklehurst's edicts; but she has great personal attractiveness, mental and spiritual charm and strength. Unlike the Reeds, she is of gentle birth yet not a snob; unlike Bessie she is not merely sympathetic but admirable. She cannot change the institution she is hired to administer but she does quietly try to make life more bearable for its inmates. She is maternal in a special sense: not simply sheltering and protective, but encouraging of intellectual growth. Of her Jane says later in the novel:

> . . . to her instruction, I owed the best part of my acquirements; her friendship and society had been my continual solace; she had stood me in the stead of mother, governess, and latterly, companion.

Helen Burns is strong of will, awkward and blundering in the practical world yet intellectually and spiritually mature beyond her years. Severe, mystical, convinced of the transitory and insignificant nature of earthly life, she still responds to Jane's hunger for contact with a humane and sisterly concern. She is consumptive, soon to die, burning with an other-worldly intensity. Jane experiences

Helen's religious asceticism as something impossible for herself, tinged with "an inexpressible sadness"; yet Helen gives her a glimpse of female character without pettiness, hysteria, or self-repudiation; it is Helen who tells her,

> "If all the world hated you, and believed you wicked, while your own conscience approved you, and absolved you from guilt, you would not be without friends."

Both Miss Temple's self-respect and sympathy, and Helen's transcendent philosophical detachment, are needed by Jane after her early humiliation by Mr. Brocklehurst. For if at Gateshead Hall Jane's temptations were victimization and hysteria, at Lowood, after her public ordeal, they are self-hatred and self-immolation.

Jane is acutely conscious of her need for love: she expresses it passionately to Helen Burns.

> ". . . to gain some real affection from you, or Miss Temple, or any other whom I truly love, I would willingly submit to have the bone of my arm broken, or to let a bull toss me, or to stand behind a kicking horse, and let it dash its hoof at my chest—"

Her need for love is compounded with a female sense that love must be purchased through suffering and self-sacrifice; the images that come to her are images of willing submission to violence, of masochism. Helen calms her, tells her she thinks "too much of the love of human beings," calls on her to think beyond this life to the reward God has prepared for the innocent beyond the grave. Like Simone Weil, like St. Teresa, like Héloïse, Helen Burns substitutes a masculine God for the love of earthly men (or women)—a pattern followed by certain gifted imaginative women in the Christian era.

The discipline of Lowood and the moral and intellectual force of Helen and Miss Temple combine to give the young Jane a sense of her own worth and of ethical choice. Helen dies of consumption with Jane in her arms held like "a little child"; Miss Temple later marries an "excellent clergyman" and leaves Lowood. Thus Jane loses her first real mothers. Yet her separation from these two women enables Jane to move forward into a wider realm of experience.

My world had for some years been in Lowood: my experience had been of its rules and systems; now I remembered that the real world was wide . . .

I desired liberty; for liberty I gasped; for liberty I uttered a prayer; it seemed scattered on the wind then faintly blowing. I abandoned it and framed a humbler supplication. For change, stimulus. That petition, too, seemed swept off into vague space. "Then," I cried, half desperate, "grant me at least a new servitude!"

One of the impressive qualities of Charlotte Brontë's heroines, the quality which makes them more valuable to the woman reader than Anna Karenina, Emma Bovary, and Catherine Earnshaw combined, is their determined refusal of the romantic. They are not immune to it; in fact, they are far more tempted by it than are the cooler-headed heroines of Jane Austen; there is far more in their circumstances of orphaned wandering and intellectual eroticism to heat their imaginations—they *have*, in fact, more imagination. Jane Eyre is a passionate girl and woman; but she displays early an inner clarity which helps her to distinguish between intense feelings which can lead to greater fulfillment, and those which can only lead to self-destructiveness. The thrill of masochism is not for her, though it is one of her temptations as we have seen; having tasted a drop of it, she rejects it. In the central episode of the novel, her meeting with Mr. Rochester at Thornfield, Jane, young, inexperienced, and hungry for experience, has to confront the central temptation of the female condition—the temptation of romantic love and surrender.

V

It is interesting that the Thornfield episode is often recalled or referred to as if it *were* the novel *Jane Eyre*. So truncated and abridged, that novel would become the following: A young woman arrives as governess at a large country house inhabited by a small French girl and an older housekeeper. She is told that the child is the ward of the master of the house, who is traveling abroad. Presently the master comes home and the governess falls in love with him, and he with her. Several mysterious and violent incidents occur in the house which seem to center around one of the servants, and which the master tells the governess will all be explained once they are married. On the wedding day, it is revealed that he has a wife still alive, a madwoman who is kept under guard in the upper part of the house and who is the source of the sinister incidents. The governess decides that her only course of action is to leave her lover forever. She steals away from the house and settles in another part of the country. After some time she returns to the manor house to find it has burned to the ground, the madwoman is dead, and her lover, though blinded and maimed by the fire, is free to marry her.

Thus described, the novel becomes a blend of Gothic horror and Victorian morality. That novel might have been written by many a contributor to ladies' magazines, but it is not the novel written by Charlotte Brontë. If the Thornfield episode is central, it is because in it Jane comes to womanhood and to certain definitive choices about what it means to her to be a woman. There are three aspects of this episode: the house, Thornfield itself; Mr. Rochester, the Man; and the madwoman, Jane's alter ego.

Charlotte Brontë gives us an extremely detailed and poetically convincing vision of Thornfield. Jane reaches its door by darkness, after a long journey; she scarcely knows what the house is like till the next day when Mrs. Fairfax, the housekeeper, takes her through it on a tour which ends in the upper regions, on the rooftop. The reader's sense of its luxury, its isolation, and its mysteries is precisely Jane's, seen with the eyes of a young woman just come from the dormitory of a charity school—a young woman of strong sensuality. But it is the upper regions of the house which are of crucial importance—the part of the house Jane lives in least, yet which most affects her life. Here she first hears that laugh—"distinct, formal, mirthless"—which is ascribed to the servant Grace Poole and which she will later hear outside her own bedroom door. Here, too, standing on the roof, or walking up and down in the corridor, close to the very door behind which the madwoman is kept hidden, she gives silent vent to those feelings which are introduced by the telling phrase: "Anybody may blame me who likes . . ."

The phrase introduces a passage which is Charlotte Brontë's feminist manifesto. Written one hundred and twenty-six years ago, it is still having to be written over and over today, in different language but with essentially the same sense that sentiments of this kind are still unacceptable to many, and that in uttering them one lays one-self open to blame and to entrenched resistance:

> It is in vain to say human beings ought to be satisfied with tranquility: they must have action; and they will make it if they cannot find it. Millions are condemned to a stiller doom than mine, and millions are in silent revolt against their lot. Nobody knows how many rebellions besides political rebellions ferment in the masses of life which people earth. Women are supposed to be very calm generally; but women feel just as men feel; they need exercise for their faculties, and a field for their efforts as much as their brothers do; they suffer from too rigid a re-straint, too absolute a stagnation, precisely as men would suffer; and it is narrow-minded in their more privileged fellow-creatures to say that they ought to confine themselves to making puddings and knitting stockings, to playing on the piano and embroidering bags. It is thought-less to condemn them, or laugh at them, if they seek to do more or learn more than custom has pronounced necessary for their sex.

Immediately thereafter we are made to hear again the laugh of the madwoman. I want to remind you of another mad wife who appears in a novel of our own time—the woman Lynda in Doris Lessing's *The Four-Gated City*, who inhabits not the upper story but the cellar, and with whom the heroine Martha (like Jane Eyre an em-ployee and in love with her employer) finally goes to live, experienc-ing her madness with her.

For Jane Eyre, the upper regions are not what Gaston Bachelard calls in *The Poetics of Space* "the rationality of the roof" as opposed to the unconscious and haunted world of the cellar.[4] Or, the roof is where Jane is visited by an expanding vision, but this vision, this illu-mination, brings her close to the madwoman captive behind the door. In Lessing's novel the madwoman is herself a source of illumi-nation. Jane has no such contact with Bertha Rochester. Yet Jane's sense of herself as a woman—as equal to and with the same needs as a man—is next-door to insanity in England in the 1840s. Jane never feels herself to be going mad, but there is a madwoman in the house who exists as her opposite, her image horribly distorted in a warped mirror, a threat to her happiness. Just as her instinct for self-preserva-

[4] Gaston Bachelard, *The Poetics of Space* (Boston: Beacon, 1967), pp. 17–18.

tion saves her from earlier temptations, so it must save her from becoming this woman by curbing her imagination at the limits of what is bearable for a powerless woman in the England of the 1840s.

VI

We see little of Bertha Rochester; she is heard and sensed rather than seen. Her presence is revealed by three acts when she escapes into the inhabited part of the house. Two of these are acts of violence against men—the attempted burning of Mr. Rochester in his bed-chamber, and the stabbing of her brother when he visits Thornfield. The third act is the visit to Jane's bedroom on the night before her wedding and the tearing of the wedding veil, the symbol of matri-mony. (She does not, interestingly enough, attack Jane.) Only after Bertha's existence is publicly revealed is Jane taken into the madwoman's chamber and sees again, waking, "that purple face—those bloated features." Bertha is described as big, corpulent, virile, with a "grizzled mane" of hair like an animal's; earlier Jane had seen her as resembling "the foul German spectre—the Vampyr." In all this she is the antithesis of Jane, as Mr. Rochester points out:

> "That is *my wife*," said he. "Such is the sole conjugal embrace I am ever to know—such are the endearments which are to solace my leisure hours! And *this* is what I wished to have" (laying his hand on my shoul-der) "this young girl, who stands so grave and quiet at the mouth of hell, looking collectedly at the gambols of a demon . . ."

In his long account of the circumstances of his marriage to Bertha—a marriage arranged for financial reasons by his father, but which he undertook for Bertha's dark sensual beauty—Rochester makes no pretense that he was not acting out of lust. Yet he repeat-edly asserts *her* coarseness, "at once intemperate and unchaste," as the central fact of his loathing for her. Once she is pronounced mad, he has her locked up, and goes forth on a life of sexual adventures, one result of which has been the child Adèle, daughter of his French mistress. Rochester's story is part Byronic romance, but it is based on a social and psychological reality: the nineteenth-century loose woman might have sexual feelings, but the nineteenth-century *wife* did not and must not; Rochester's loathing of Bertha is described repeatedly in terms of her physical strength and her violent will—both unacceptable qualities in the nineteenth-century female, raised to the nth degree and embodied in a monster.

VII

Mr. Rochester is often seen as the romantic Man of Fate, Byronic, brooding, sexual. But his role in the book is more interesting: he is certainly that which culture sees as Jane's fate, but he is not the fate she has been seeking. When she leaves Lowood for Thornfield, when she stands on the roof of Thornfield or walks across its fields longing for a wider, more expansive life, she is not longing for a man. We do not know what she longs for, she herself does not know; she uses terms like liberty, a new servitude, action. Yet the man appears, romantically and mysteriously, in the dusk, riding his horse— and slips and falls on the ice, so that Jane's first contact with him is with someone in need of help; he has to lean on her to regain his seat on horseback. Again at the novel's end it is she who must lead him, blinded by fire. There is something more working here than the introduction of a stock romantic hero.

Mr. Rochester offers Jane wider horizons than any she has known; travel, riches, brilliant society. Throughout the courtship there is a tension between her growing passion for him and her dislike of and uneasiness with the *style* of his love-making. It is not Rochester's sensuality that brings her up short, but his tendency to make her his object, his creature, to want to dress her up, lavish jewels on her, remake her in another image. She strenuously resists being romanticized as a beauty or a houri; she will, she tells him, be no part of his harem.

In his determination to possess Jane, Rochester is arrogant enough to lie to her three times. During the house party at which Jane, as governess, has to suffer the condescension and contempt of the ladies of the neighborhood, Rochester, disguised as an old Gypsy woman, comes to the door to read fortunes, and he attempts to trick Jane into revealing her feelings for him. It is clear, in this scene, that Rochester is well aware of the strength of Jane's character and is uneasy as

to the outcome of his courtship and the kind of marriage he is going
to propose to her. In making as if to read Jane's fate in her features,
he tells her:

> ". . . that brow professes to say—'I can live alone, if self-respect and
> circumstances require me to do so. I need not sell my soul to buy bliss.
> I have an inward treasure born with me, which can keep me alive if all
> the extraneous delights should be withheld, or offered only at a price I
> cannot afford to give.' "

Abruptly, at the end of this scene, he reveals himself. But he continues to carry on a flirtation with the heiress Miss Ingram, in order
to arouse Jane's jealousy; he pretends to the last possible moment
that he intends to marry Miss Ingram, till Jane, in turmoil at the
prospect, confesses her grief at having to leave him. Her grief—but
also, her anger at the position in which she has been placed:

> "I tell you I must go!" I retorted, roused to something like passion. "Do
> you think I can stay to become nothing to you? Do you think I am au-
> tomaton?—a machine without feelings? . . . Do you think because I
> am poor, obscure, plain, and little, I am soulless and heartless? You
> think wrong!—I have as much soul as you—and full as much heart!
> . . . I am not talking to you now through the medium of custom, con-
> ventionalities, nor even of mortal flesh: it is my spirit that addresses
> your spirit; just as if both had passed through the grave and we stood at
> God's feet, equal—as we are!"

(Always a governess and always in love? Had Virginia Woolf really
read this novel?)

VIII

Jane's parting interview with Mr. Rochester is agonizing; he plays
on every chord of her love, her pity and sympathy, her vulnerability.
On going to bed, she has a dream. Carried back to the Red Room,
the scene of her first temptation, her first ordeal, in the dream, Jane
is reminded of the "syncope," or swoon, she underwent there, which
became a turning point for her; she is then visited by the moon, sym-

bol of the matriarchal spirit and the "Great Mother of the night sky."[5]

> I watched her come—watched with the strangest anticipation; as though some word of doom were to be written on her disc. She broke forth as moon never yet burst from cloud: a hand first penetrated the sable folds and waved them away; then, not a moon, but a white human form shone in the azure, inclining a glorious brow earthward. It gazed and gazed on me. It spoke to my spirit: immeasurably distant was the tone, yet so near, it whispered in my heart—
>
> "My daughter, flee temptation."
>
> "Mother, I will."

Her dream is profoundly, imperiously, archetypal. She is in danger, as she was in the Red Room; but her own spiritual consciousness is stronger in womanhood than it was in childhood; she is in touch with the matriarchal aspect of her psyche which now warns and protects her against that which threatens her integrity. Bessie, Miss Temple, Helen Burns, even at moments the gentle housekeeper Mrs. Fairfax, have acted as mediators for her along the way she has come thus far; even, it may be said, the terrible figure of Bertha has come between Jane and a marriage which was not yet ripe, which would have made her simply the dependent adjunct of Mr. Rochester instead of his equal. Individual women have helped Jane Eyre to the point of her severest trial; at that point she is in relation to the Great Mother herself. On waking from this dream, she leaves Thornfield, with a few pieces of clothing and twenty shillings in her purse, to set forth on foot to an unknown destination.

Jane's rebellion against Rochester's arrogance—for in pleading with her to stay with him against the laws of her own integrity, he is still arrogant—forces her to act on her own behalf even if it causes him intense suffering, even though she still loves him. Like many women in similar circumstances, she feels that such an act of self-preservation requires her to pay dearly. She goes out into the world without a future, without money, without plans—a "poor, obscure,

[5] Erich Neumann, *The Great Mother* (Princeton, N. J.: Princeton University, 1972), pp. 55–59.

plain, and little" figure of a woman, risking exposure to the elements, ostracism, starvation. By an act which one can read as a final unconscious sacrificial gesture, she forgets her purse with its few shillings in the stagecoach, and thus is absolutely destitute, forced to beg for the leftovers a farmer's wife is about to feed to her pig. In this whole portion of the novel, in which Jane moves through the landscape utterly alone, there is a strong counterpull between female self-immolation—the temptation of passive suicide—and the will and courage which are her survival tools.

She is literally saved from death by two sisters, Diana and Mary, living in a parsonage with their brother, the clergyman St. John Rivers. Diana and Mary bear the names of the pagan and Christian aspects of the Great Goddess—Diana or Artemis, the Virgin huntress, and Mary the Virgin Mother. These women are unmarried bluestockings; they delight in learning; in their remote parsonage they study German and read poetry aloud. They live as intellectual equals with their brother; yet with Jane, in her illness and convalescence, they are maternally tender and sensitive. As time passes and Jane recovers and begins to teach in the village school, Diana and Mary become her friends; for the first time since the death of Helen Burns she has an intellectually sympathetic companionship with young women of her own age.

Once again, a man offers her marriage. St. John has been observing her for his own purposes, and finding her "docile, diligent, disinterested, faithful, constant, and courageous; very gentle, and very heroic" he invites her to accompany him as his fellow-missionary to India, where he intends to live and die in the service of his God. He needs a helpmate to work among Indian women; he offers her marriage without love, a marriage of duty and service to a cause. The cause is of course defined by him; it is the cause of patriarchal religion: self-denying, stern, prideful, and ascetic. In a sense he offers her the destiny of Milton's Eve: "He for God only, she for God in him." What St. John offers Jane is perhaps the deepest lure for a spiritual woman, that of adopting a man's cause or career and making it her own. For more than one woman, still today, the felt energy of her own existence is still diffuse, the possibilities of her life vague; the man who pressures to define it for her may be her most confusing temptation. *He* will give shape to her search for meaning, her desire for service, her feminine urge toward self-abnegation: in short—as Jane becomes soon aware—he will *use* her.

But St. John is offering Jane this "meaning" under the rubric of marriage—and from this "use" of herself she draws back in healthy repulsion.

> Can I receive from him the bridal ring, endure all the forms of love (which I doubt not he would scrupulously observe) and know that the spirit was quite absent? Can I bear the consciousness that every endearment he bestows is a sacrifice made on principle? No: such martyrdom would be monstrous. . . .

> As his curate, his comrade, all would be right: I would cross oceans with him in that capacity; toil under Eastern suns, in Asian deserts with him . . . admire and emulate his courage and devotion . . . smile undisturbed at his ineradicable ambition; discriminate the Christian from the man; profoundly esteem the one, and freely forgive the other. . . . But as his wife—at his side always, and always restrained, and always checked—forced to keep the fire of my nature continually low . . . *this* would be unendurable. . . .

> "If I were to marry you, you would kill me. You are killing me now" [she tells him].

> His lips and cheeks turned white—quite white.

> "*I should kill you—I am killing you?* Your words are such as ought not to be used—they are violent, unfeminine [*sic!*] and untrue . . ."

So she refuses his cause; and so he meets her refusal. In the meantime she has inherited an income; she has become independent; and at this point an extrasensory experience calls her back to Thornfield.

IX

"Reader, I married him." These words open the final chapter of *Jane Eyre*. The question is, how and why is this a happy ending? Jane returns to Thornfield to find it "a blackened ruin"; she discovers Rochester, his left hand amputated and his eyes blinded by the fire in which he vainly attempted to save the life of his mad wife. Rochester has paid his dues; a Freudian critic would say he has been symboli-

cally castrated. Discarding this phallic-patriarchal notion of his ordeal, we can then ask, what kind of marriage is possible for a woman
like Jane Eyre?

Certainly not marriage with a castrate, psychic or physical. (St.
John repels Jane in part because he is *emotionally* castrated.) The
wind that blows through this novel is the wind of sexual equality—
spiritual and practical. The passion that Jane feels as a girl of twenty
or as a wife of thirty is the same passion—that of a strong spirit
demanding its counterpart in another. Mr. Rochester needs Jane
now—

> ". . . to bear with my infirmities . . . to overlook my deficiencies."
>
> "Which are none, sir, to me."

She feels, after ten years of marriage, that "I am my husband's life
as fully as he is mine." This feeling is not that of romantic love or
romantic marriage.

> To be together is for us to be at once as free as in solitude, as gay as in
> company. We talk—I believe, all day long; to talk to each other is but a
> more animated and an audible thinking.

Coming to her husband in economic independence and by her
free choice, Jane can become a wife without sacrificing a grain of her
Jane Eyre-ity. Charlotte Brontë sets up the possibility of this relationship in the early passages of the Thornfield episode, the verbal
sparring of this couple who so robustly refuse to act out the para-
digms of romantic, Gothic fiction. We believe in the erotic and intellectual sympathy of this marriage because it has been prepared by
the woman's refusal to accept it under circumstances which were
mythic, romantic, or sexually oppressive. The last paragraphs of the
novel concern St. John Rivers: whose ambition is that of "the high
master-spirit, which aims to a place in the first rank of those who are
redeemed from the earth—who stand without fault before the throne
of God, who share the last victories of the Lamb, who are called, and
chosen, and faithful." We can translate St. John's purism into any of
a number of kinds of patriarchal arrogance of our own day, whether
political, intellectual, aesthetic, or religious. It is clear that Charlotte

Brontë believes that human relations require something quite different: a transaction between people which is "without painful shame or damping humiliation" and in which nobody is made into an object for the use of anybody else.

In telling the tale of Jane Eyre, Charlotte Brontë was quite conscious, as she informed her publisher, that she was not telling a moral tale. Jane is not bound by orthodoxy, though superficially she is a creature of her time and place. As a child, she rejects the sacredness of adult authority; as a woman, she insists on regulating her conduct by the pulse of her own integrity. She will not live with Rochester as his dependent mistress because she knows that relationship would become destructive to her; she would live unmarried with St. John as an independent co-worker; it is he who insists this would be immoral. The beauty and depth of the novel lie in part in its depiction of alternatives—to convention and traditional piety, yes, but also to social and cultural reflexes internalized within the female psyche. In *Jane Eyre*, moreover, we find an alternative to the stereotypical rivalry of women; we see women in real and supportive relationship to each other, not simply as points on a triangle or as temporary substitutes for men. Marriage is the completion of the life of Jane Eyre, as it is for Miss Temple and Diana and Mary Rivers; but for Jane at least it is marriage radically understood for its period, in no sense merely a solution or a goal. It is not patriarchal marriage in the sense of a marriage that stunts and diminishes the woman; but a continuation of this woman's creation of herself.

Caryatid: Two Columns (1973)

The short pieces under the title "Caryatid" were written as regular columns for the *American Poetry Review* in January and June of 1973. The bombing of Southeast Asia continued as an insistent fact of American life, punctuated by actual or promised ceasefires. The repression of dissent in the United States had already been initiated with the killing of black student demonstrators at Jackson State University in Mississippi and white students at Kent State in Ohio, in 1970.

When the *American Poetry Review*, then a new periodical, invited me to contribute a regular column on any topics I wished, I agreed to do so, thinking that it would give me a chance to say in print things which were taking root in my mind, to work through ideas about art and politics which concerned me, and to reach a new audience with those ideas. I contributed four such columns, but early came to mistrust the "liberal" policy which could accomodate my feminism, or occasional utterances by black writers, to a predominantly white and sexist content, and a pervasive lack of purpose— poetic or political. Over the next few years my differences with APR deepened. They were to be sure no greater than my growing differences with the masculine literary arena as a whole: its male solipsism, its frequent trivialization of literature, its pornographic celebrations of and rewards for phallic violence. But I learned something of value in writing for APR: that women's words, even where they are not edited, can get flattened and detonated in a context which is predominantly masculine and misogynist, and that the attempt to "reach" readers through such a context can be a form of self-delusion. The words I wrote for APR have more meaning and cogency here in this book than they could have possessed in the lukewarm flux of that periodical.

The emergence of a range of feminist journals, in which art, politics, and criticism resonate off each other, has been the best hope for women of seeing our words in relationship to the thought of others who believe in the integrity and preciousness of women's lives. Not uncritical or sheeplike others, but others concerned for our spiritual as well as physical survival. Moreover, when we write for women we imagine an audience which *wants* our words—which desires our courage, our anger, our verve, our active powers, instead of fearing or loathing them. We write for ourselves and each other— an ever-expanding sense of whom is part of our imagining—passionately listening and reading as we write because other women's words are vital to our own. This is precisely the kind of cultural ferment out of which transforming art has always grown; not from the effort to "belong" to some mainstream, some congregation of false inclusion. As long as I wrote in the hope of "reaching" men, I was setting bounds on my own mind, holding back; trying to make the subversive sound unthreatening, the unthinkable reassuring. And so I used terms like "androgynous," "bisexual," or "human liberation" which, almost as soon as I wrote them, rang flat and ineffectual to me, and which *were* effective only as checks on my own thought.

〜〜〜〜〜〜〜

I Vietnam and Sexual Violence

When you read this, the bombs may be falling still, or falling again; or a temporary lull may have been ordered, or a cease-fire may be in effect. This peace-around-the-corner, while children, invalids, and old people are blown into mass graves, has been the latest, most visible testimony to the power now handled by a few men—which begins to seem like the power of nature, to bring on famine, plague, or cyclone and take it away again at will. It has reduced the Left to reactive responses: when technology, the product of human reason, can be made to seem like a destructive force of nature, how do intelligence and compassion respond except ritually, through the old gatherings and marches, the old desperate gestures of sabotage, the old litanies?

A while back a slogan of the antiwar movement was: *Bring the war home*. Which was taken to mean: disrupt "business as usual" here, stop traffic, obstruct the passage of military supplies, bring guerilla theater into the streets, implant Vietnam in the foreground of public attention. But the war was never brought home, nor has it yet come home, even for most of those whose long, honorable, often dangerous efforts to end it have lasted over a decade. In focusing on the war as a specific, undeniable atrocity, in struggling to raise the consciousness of others, in projecting their angry and compassionate imaginations across half the world and identifying with the people of North Vietnam, the New Left and the antiwar movement did begin to make connections which needed to be made before further connections were possible. The collusion of the universities with military-industrial power, with ghetto repression and the development of counterinsurgency methods, was for students and some intellectuals in the sixties one of the most significant of such connections; it located force and coercion squarely in the midst of the "humanistic" enclaves—where they still are.

But the danger was that in viewing the sickness of institutions, or of the class system, or the war itself as the central and corrosive factor, in projecting our efforts for understanding and change out there somewhere beyond ourselves, we would fail really to understand and therefore really to change anything. The bombings, for example, if they have anything to teach us, must be understood in the light of something closer to home, both more private and painful, and more general and endemic, than institutions, class, racial oppression, the hubris of the Pentagon, or the ruthlessness of a right-wing administration: the bombings are so wholly sadistic, gratuitous and demonic that they can finally be seen, if we care to see them, for what they are: acts of concrete sexual violence, an expression of the congruence of violence and sex in the masculine psyche.

Consider this: A man, or two men together, or a gang of men, rape a woman, then strangle her, then repeatedly stab her dead body. Such acts occur all the time. The incidence of rape is growing; recently in the *New York Times* various local sheriffs were quoted as blaming it on the prevalence of young women hitch-hikers. The assumption is that men *are* rapists, that this is simply a fact of nature, that women had better plan accordingly. Until recently, rape was considered to be a crime committed by black men against white women; and black men have been lynched, castrated, tortured, and imprisoned for the suspicion of such a crime. The long history of legitimized rape of black women by white men, of white women by white men, of women—black and white—by their husbands and lovers, daughters by their fathers, sisters by their brothers, has only recently, with the emergence of a militant women's consciousness, begun to be documented. Moreover, women are coming to understand better the meaning of the verbalized fantasies of the men they have slept with.

The equation of manhood—potency—with the objectification of another's person and the domination of another's body, is the venereal disease that lives alike in the crimes of Vietnam and the lies of sexual liberation (another creation of the sixties)—as it lives in the imaginations of pornographers, in the fantasies of poets and presidents, professors and policemen, surgeons and salesmen. In the demonic sadism of the bombings, this lesion has simply been more visible, because there it seemed to be something outside of us, we could pretend it was something separate from our inner lives.

Rape is the ultimate outward and physical act of coercion and depersonalization practiced on women by men. Most male readers of this paper would perhaps deny having gone so far: the honest would admit to fantasies, urges of lust and hatred, or lust and fear, or to a "harmless" fascination with pornography and sadistic art. Men, and women too, have accepted the fact-of-nature attitude, the fatalistic stance: "that's what we are"; "men are like that." Women, too, have been coerced into accepting our own rape—psychic, social, political, physical—we have been led to feel that the guilt and responsibility were ours, or to pity our rapists. Of course women too have reported rape fantasies; taught to view our bodies as our totality, our genitals as our chief source of fascination and value, many women have become dissociated from their own bodies, obsessed with the mirror-image, viewing themselves as objects to be possessed by men rather than as the subjects of an existence. And in fact rape has been seen, as I will note later, as an archetypal experience for woman.

The acts of coercion and domination in Southeast Asia, and the tacit assent of a majority of citizens—not merely in the U.S. but in the West at large—have been variously ascribed to a numbing of the public moral sense, an exhaustion of outrage, the violent repression of dissent on the campuses of the seventies, and to an atomization among people which enables them to see only that which touches their private interest in a very short-run vision. But patriarchal man is in dangerous confusion about his "private" interest. For centuries, patriarchy has maintained itself by asking what was good for males, has assumed male norms and values as universal ones, has allowed the differences of "otherness," the division of male and female consciousness, to become a terrifying dissociation of sensibility. The idea of woman exists at a strangely primitive level in the male psyche. She remains, for all his psychological self-consciousness, the object-figure on which can be projected all that man does not understand, all that he needs, all that he dreads, in his own experience. (Erich Neumann, in an essay on matriarchal consciousness which appeared in the Jungian journal *Spring*, went so far as to say that man's consequent fear and hatred of woman has been so deep that were it not for his sexual need of women they could have been extirpated as a group.) Denying his own feminine aspects, always associating his manhood with his ability to possess and dominate women, man the patriarch has slowly, imperceptibly, over time, achieved a degree of self-estrangement, self-hatred, and self-mutilation which is coming to have almost irreversible effects on human relationships and on the natural world.

It was assumed by the disciples of Marx and Freud alike that man exists in one of two modes: the political or the psychological. This division is a classic "two horn'd reasoning cloven Fiction" of patriarchal thought. The women's movement of our generation is the first mass political and social movement to have seen the utter fallaciousness of this division, to look for new forms of social organization and human relationship which might begin to close it: to demand that we transform, not merely our institutions, but ourselves.

Many contemporary male poets suffer from this divided consciousness, know they are suffering, yet seem unaware what it is about. On the first page of the first issue of *APR* appeared a poem by Pablo Neruda succinctly entitled "Love." It begins:

> What's wrong with you, with us,
> what's happening to us? . . .

> What's wrong with you? I look at you
> and I find nothing in you but two eyes
> like all eyes, a mouth
> lost among a thousand mouths that I have kissed, more beautiful,
> a body just like those that have slipped
> beneath my body without leaving any memory.

And how empty you went through the world!
like a wheatcolored jar
without air, without sound, without substance!
I vainly sought in you
depth for my arms
that dig, without cease, beneath the earth;
beneath your skin, beneath your eyes
nothing . . .

and it ends:

Why, why, why,
my love, why?

Possibly the answer is implicit in "Not Only the Fire," where he tells
the woman how he recalls their moments of ecstasy, but also how

I see you
washing my handkerchiefs
hanging at the window
my worn-out socks . . .
little wife
of every day,
again a human being,
humbly human,
proudly poor,
as you have to be in order to be
not the swift rose
that love's ash dissolves
but all of life,
all of life with soap and needles . . .

Ah my life,
it is not only fire that burns between us
but all of life,
the simple story,
the simple love
of a woman and a man
like everyone.

One method of dealing with a dishonest sexuality is to sentimentalize it; to create of it a kind of warm limpid nostalgia; this is perhaps

the most regressive and diseased poetry that can be written, and it is written frequently by poets who are considered politically and aesthetically radical.

Richard Hugo, writing in the second issue of *APR,* is more honest, and I think of more concern to us, not only for his delineations of a man's fear and hatred of women but because he gives us, in the poem "Announcement" a striking metaphor of the masculine fatalism which underlies much masculine self-pity:

> Tomorrow morning at four, the women will be herded
> into the public square to hear their rights read aloud.
> I'm pleased to sign this new law. No longer
> will women be obliged to kneel and be flayed
> by our southern farmers. This law says, farmers
> must curb their mean instincts. From now on
> women as well as men may use county water.
>
> I'm sorry the farmers grumble. A way of life
> is passing. But good things remain . . .
>   And women's tears
> at the wonderment of tide will always be legal
> reminding us over and over of their depth of feeling.
> Our laws have always respected women . . .
>
> In our wisdom we change what can be changed
> and leave the other alone. We don't play around
> with those inviolable structures of wind
> that pile the souls of our ancestors high
> on the evening horizon in luminous banks of gold
> and the basic right we all have to die.
> We grant stars what is theirs and fight misery.

The irony of this poem, which I take (hope) to be conscious, lies in its assumption that men—the men in power, those who sign the "new laws"—are *sure* what can and can't be changed. The sexual fatalism deep in contemporary male poetry is one with the political fatalism for which radicals blame the uncommitted or even, in times of despair, themselves.

Daniel Hoffman, in the same issue, has a taut little poem connecting the assassin's fear of women and his "need for love" (perceived by a woman) with his need to murder. But the "need for love" which Joplin's voice still rivets in our ears, and the "need for a woman" are really phrases disguising a profound inner emptiness, the neurotic emptiness which no quantity of love, no quantity of fucking, can fill. A woman can pour herself, for a lifetime, into such emptiness, believing herself the redemptive female whose mission it is to "save" the man, humanize him, forgive him when he cannot forgive himself.

The "need for love" is not the same thing as a desire for relation; the desire for relation implies a degree of wholeness, which needs a fellow-being not for completion of the self but for extension and challenge of the self. The "need for a woman" can be the man's need for a receptacle for his own fear, vulnerability, tears, uncertainty for which he has made no psychic room; or, for an object-creation to be painted with the mask of Medea, Circe, Medusa, Helen, or Salomé; then used, raped, idolized, or punished accordingly.

Rape has always been a part of war; and rape in war may be an act of vengeance on the male enemy "whose" women are thus used. The apparently well-organized rape of at least 400,000 women of Bangladesh (the latest estimate of the International Planned Parenthood Federation) on the part of Pakistani soldiers seems to have been carried out with military thoroughness; women were rounded up and interned for the purpose.[1] In Godard's film, *Les Carabiniers*, rape is used as a bribe to the peasants being impressed for service, as one of the perquisites of the military: as part of an invading army one has carte blanche to loot property and rape women. Again, the assumption is that men always want to rape and are only prevented by the restrictions of society. I know of no statistics as yet on the rape of Vietnamese women by American or Vietnamese troops; but with the mechanization of the war and its further depersonalization of the people involved, its lifting of the invaders out of body-range, it signifies something that the bombing of civilian populations was intensified, that schools and hospitals became normal targets: coercion heaped on the vulnerable, carried to the most ruthless degree of sadism.

Rape is a part of war; but it may be more accurate to say that the capacity for dehumanizing another which so corrodes male sexuality

[1] A. R., 1978: See note 13, in "The Antifeminist Woman," p. 81.

is carried over from sex into war. The chant of the basic training drill: ("This is my rifle, this is my gun [cock]; This is for killing, this is for fun") is not a piece of bizarre brainwashing invented by some infantry sergeant's fertile imagination; it is a recognition of the fact that when you strike the chord of sexuality in the patriarchal psyche, the chord of violence is likely to vibrate in response; and vice versa.

In *The Great Mother*, Erich Neumann says that "abduction, rape, marriage of death, and separation are the great motifs underlying the Eleusinian mysteries" (matriarchal rites which survived into the patriarchal period in Greece). The myth of Demeter, who let earth grow waste and sterile in her anger at Hades's rape and abduction of her daughter Perserphone, has a suggestive ring today: earth herself is being raped, more ruthlessly than ever before in history; but the ecologically concerned, like the Marxist and the pacifist, are concerned with too narrow a vision. The propagandists of patriarchal technology tell us that science can forestall mass famine, as if the natural world were a source of food and nothing more, as if insect, bole, schist, meadow, canyon, forest had no meaning for us psychologically and we could actually exist, scientifically nourished, "homeless between the earth and sky." This is patriarchal thinking, rational, head-centered, efficient on its own terms.

But as Neumann tells it; "The one essential element in the Eleusinian matriarchal mysteries is the *heuresis* of the daughter by the mother, the 'finding again' of Korê [Persephone] by Demeter, the reunion of mother and daughter. Psychologically, this 'finding again' signifies the annulment of the male rape and incursion, the restoration after marriage of the matriarchal unity of mother and daughter . . ." This process of transformation enacted in the mysteries is the transformation of Korê or virgin into Demeter or powerful, mature goddess of life—but also her union "on a higher plane with the spiritual aspect of the Feminine, the Sophia aspect of the Great Mother."

The mysteries seem to have recognized rape, victimization, and separation from the mother as central experiences in the development of the female; but the re-finding of mother and daughter by each other—the ritual return to female primacy—was essential to the survival of life and the fertility of earth. Men as well as women were initiates of these mysteries; according to Neumann, "the male initiate . . . sought to identify himself with Demeter, i.e., with his own feminine aspect." The Eleusinian worshiper knew that the Feminine was not merely fertility, relation to the earth and to natural cycles, but Sophia, who "does not vanish in the nirvana-like abstraction of a masculine spirit" but "always remains attached to the earthly foundation of reality."

By a curious process of differentiation, the New Left and the "counterculture" of the early sixties appeared to define themselves in opposition to the patriarchal culture. For awhile it seemed that a more "feminine" consciousness was spreading among the young men of that generation: distrust for arbitrary authority, for hierarchical structures, care for persons, for nature, for the pain of others. But the Left was, and is, dominated intellectually be men, and leftist women were, and are, no more in a position to demasculinize the nature of society than women of any other political persuasion. At present a stronger unconscious, psychic alliance exists between the men of the worldwide Left and the men ruling the most powerful patriarchy in history, than between the men of the Left and the feminist movement. That psychic alliance must change; that way no human liberation lies. The poet has a destiny in all this. We need a poetry which will dare to explore, and to begin exploding, the phallic delusions which are now endangering consciousness itself.

II Natalya Gorbanevskaya

Natalya Gorbanevskaya is a Russian poet and activist, thirty-six years old, the mother of two children. Her poetry, praised by Akhmatova, has appeared largely in *samizdat*—underground collections. She was one of the signers of a letter demanding an open hearing for Alexander Ginzburg and others who opposed the Daniel-Sinyavsky trial, and she participated in demonstrations against that trial.

Pregnant and threatened with a miscarriage, Gorbanevskaya entered a hospital in early 1968. She soon found herself a political prisoner there. She was transferred to a mental hospital, but after a time was released because she was still pregnant.

Her political activity continued. In August 1968, she took part in a demonstration in Red Square protesting the invasion of Czechoslovakia. With her was her three-month-old son. She was arrested, but released as the mother of an infant. She then addressed a letter to the world press (published in the *New York Times*) describing the demonstration and its consequences. Shortly after this, she was ordered to appear before a commission of "psychiatric experts" (the Serbsky Institute of Forensic Psychiatry) which diagnosed her as having "a possibility of low-profile schizophrenia," recommending a diagnosis of insanity and incarceration in a "penal category" psychiatric hospital. She was, temporarily, released to the guardianship of her mother as "mentally unstable."

Despite these intimidations, Gorbanevskaya continued her political activity. She became a founder of the Action Group for the Defense of Civil Rights in the USSR, and signed a protest letter on the anniversary of the Soviet invasion of Czechoslovakia. She was arrested four months later, again examined by the Institute for Forensic Psychiatry and sent for compulsory treatment to a "special" psychiatric hospital in Kazan. "Emotional coldness and indifference" were cited as evidence of her insanity. The woman lawyer who defended her was not permitted to attach to her record any letters or other documents expressing her affection and consideration for her mother and family. After three years, she was released. She intends to continue her political activity.

I obtained the above facts from a copy of an article by Daniel Weissbort, accompanying translations of Gorbanevskaya's poetry, and from a recent volume of translations of her poetry along with an account of her political harassment and a number of documents relating to her case.[1] Weissbort's translations and his description of her ordeal are sensitive and intelligent; what he perhaps could not be expected to grasp are the ways in which Gorbanevskaya's detention reflects the special vulnerability of women in noncapitalist as in capitalist societies. Both men and women suffer in Soviet mental prisons, as do both men and women in the prisons of the U.S. But the use of Gorbanevskaya's threatened miscarriage as a means of de-

---

[1] Daniel Weissbort, ed., *Natalya Gorbanevskaya: Poems: The Trial: Prison* (Oxford: Carcanet Press, 1972).

taining her, the attacks on her sanity under conditions in which a
woman is peculiarly vulnerable emotionally, the use of her children
(motherhood) as grounds for release and the corresponding use of her
emotional temperature ("coldness and indifference," as measured by
the State) as grounds for incarcerating her again, reflect not simply
the methods of totalitarianism but the methods specifically available
against women in male-dominated society. In all societies women
are in double jeopardy; on the one hand we are expected to con-
form to certain emotional standards in our relationships with others,
at the penalty of being declared insane; on the other, our political
perceptions can be labeled "irrational" and "hysterical." There is torture for both men and women but there is a peculiar torture in fearing not merely for oneself but for a second life in one's body. Gorbanevskaya's notes written in the maternity hospital bear witness to
this:

> Here they took away even the multi-vitamins and gluconate. I am
> afraid they will use force to inject something into me, and then things
> will look really bad for my child. I must be got away from here as
> quickly as possible, as any barbarity is possible . . .
>
> I've realized how important is tomorrow's conversation with the doctor.
> Even my intention to keep the baby might be regarded almost as a
> symptom of schizophrenia by the doctors . . .

and also to the courage and lucidity she brought to bear on her situation:

> I was quite calm those days (in the psychiatric hospital). I gathered all
> my inner strength so as not to harm the child, and not to lose my grip
> by tormenting myself and getting all worked up. When I considered the
> possibility of their not discharging me, of their holding on to me for
> weeks, maybe months, I told myself with unexpected firmness: "People
> give birth in hospitals, don't they? What does it matter? And without
> visits, without parcels, without apples and oranges." So if they had not
> released me, in other words had openly declared war on me, I would
> have come out of it with honour, and victoriously . . .
>
> The final thing which I ought to say is that if they did want to frighten
> me, knock me off the rails, traumatise me, they did not succeed. I am
> awaiting the birth of my child quite calmly, and neither my pregnancy

nor his birth will prevent me from doing what I wish—which includes
participating in every protest against any act of tyranny.

The woman who has spent time in a hospital fearing to lose the
child in her body, the woman who has suffered the judgment of her
sanity by a jury of male experts, knows something of Gorbanevskaya's ordeal. Her poems, as rendered by Weissbort, are
strong and sensuous, only obliquely political; but like Akhmatova's,
they bear the thumb-print of an era which still goes on. Like Akhmatova, Gorbanevskaya, a woman living in the jeopardy shared by all
women, in a society as ruthless in its way as our own, continues to
throw her weight on the side of those who have no voice in that society.[2]

(A. R., 1978: After much difficulty, Natalya Gorbanevskaya was
able to leave the Soviet Union in 1975. She is now living in France.)

[2]A.R., 1978: The use of psychiatric controls for political pacification has been, of
course, by no means limited to the Soviet Union. On February 24 and March 30,
1972, the *Congressional Record* published Peter Breggin's papers on "The Return of
Lobotomy and Psychosurgery" and "New Information in the Debate over Psychosurgery," documenting the use of psychosurgery on "hyperactive" children in Japan,
Thailand, and India, and in the U.S., notably at the University of Mississippi, on
children as young as five years. (The Soviet Union had, in fact, outlawed lobotomy
and psychosurgery in 1951.) In the U.S., persons evincing "inappropriate anxiety,"
"depression," "neurosis," "schizophrenia," "anxiety-tension states," and other "strong
emotions" are considered candidates for surgery, anger being diagnosed as biological
in origin. The majority of persons operated on are "age: older; sex: female; race: black;
and occupational role: the 'simpler' ones." Black women have been considered the
"most successful" candidates.

As of summer 1978, the State of Massachusetts had appropriated over $500,000 for
the construction of a maximum security unit for so-called violent women at Worcester
State Hospital. Due to pressures from the feminist community and the Coalition to
Stop Institutional Violence, an appeals process for women being transferred to the
unit is under consideration, and construction of the ward has been temporarily halted.
See "The Worcester Ward: Violence Against Women" in *Science for the People*,
November/December 1978. As Blanche Wiesen Cook observes in a note to her article, "Surveillance and Mind Control," in Howard Frazier, ed., *Uncloaking the CIA*
(New York: Free Press, 1978), p. 175, "psychosurgery has now been given the government's stamp of approval. Experimental psychosurgery has been designated a psychological 'therapy.' " Cook emphasizes the necessity for public vigilance and protest
against these medical and technological "solutions" to family and societal disorders.

Anne Sexton: 1928–1974
(1974)

I met Anne Sexton only once or twice. I was teaching at City College in New York when she died, and the still-tenuous women's community there decided to hold a memorial for her. Recalling the effect on so many young women poets of Sylvia Plath's suicide (an imaginative obsession with victimization and death, unfair to Plath herself and her own struggle for survival), I wanted to try to speak to the question of identification which a suicide always arouses. This was my attempt to do so.

～～～～～～

Anne Sexton was a poet and a suicide. She was not in any conscious or self-defined sense a feminist, but she did some things ahead of the rebirth of the feminist movement. She wrote poems alluding to abortion, masturbation, menopause, and the painful love of a powerless mother for her daughters, long before such themes became validated by a collective consciousness of women, and while writing and publishing under the scrutiny of the male literary establishment. In 1966 I helped organize a read-in against the Vietnam War, at Harvard, and asked her to participate. Famous male poets and novelists were there, reading their diatribes against McNamara, their napalm poems, their ego-poetry. Anne read—in a very quiet, vulnerable voice—"Little Girl, My Stringbean, My Lovely Woman"—setting the first-hand image of a mother's affirmation of her daughter against the second-hand images of death and violence hurled that evening by men who had never seen a bombed village. That poem is dated 1964, and it is a feminist poem. Her head was often patriarchal, but in her blood and her bones, Anne Sexton knew.

Many women writers, learning of her death, have been trying to reconcile our feelings about her, her poetry, her suicide at forty-five, with the lives we are trying to stay alive in. We have had enough suicidal women poets, enough suicidal women, enough of self-destructiveness as the sole form of violence permitted to women.

I would like to list, in Anne's honor and memory, some of the ways in which we destroy ourselves. Self-trivialization is one. Believing the lie that women are not capable of major creations. Not taking ourselves or our work seriously enough; always finding the needs of others more demanding than our own. Being content to produce intellectual or artistic work in which we imitate men, in which we lie to ourselves and each other, in which we do not press to our fullest possibilities, to which we fail to give the attention and hard work we would give to a child or a lover. Horizontal hostility—contempt for women—is another: the fear and mistrust of other women, because other women *are* ourselves. The conviction that "women are never really going to do anything," that women's self-determination and survival are secondary to the "real" revolution made by men, that "our worst enemies are women." We become our own worst enemies when we allow our inculcated self-hatred to turn such shallow projections on each other. Another kind of destructiveness is misplaced compassion. A woman I know was recently raped; her first—and typical—instinct was to feel sorry for the rapist, who had held her at knife-point. When we begin to feel compassion for ourselves and each other instead of for our rapists, we will begin to be immune to suicide. A fourth way is addiction. Addiction to "Love"—to the idea of selfless, sacrificial love as somehow redemptive, a female career; to sex as a junkie-trip, a way of self-blurring or self-immolation. Addiction to depression—the most acceptable way of living out a female existence, since the depressed cannot be held responsible, doctors will prescribe us pills, alcohol offer its blanket of blankness. Addiction to male approval: as long as you can find a man to vouch for you, sexually or intellectually, you must be somehow all right, your existence vindicated, whatever the price you pay.

Self-trivialization, contempt for women, misplaced compassion, addiction; if we could purge ourselves of this quadruple poison, we would have minds and bodies more poised for the act of survival and rebuilding.

I think of Anne Sexton as a sister whose work tells us what we have to fight, in ourselves and in the images patriarchy has held up to us. Her poetry is a guide to the ruins, from which we learn what women have lived and what we must refuse to live any longer. Her death is an arrest: in its moment we have all been held, momentarily, in the grip of a policeman who tells us we are guilty of being female, and powerless. But because of her work she is still a presence; and as Tillie Olsen has said: "Every woman who writes is a survivor."

Toward a Woman-Centered University (1973–74)

Early in my thinking about this essay, it had two titles. The first stands at the head of this page. The second grew out of a passge in Mary Beard's *Woman as Force in History*, where she describes the conditions of thought and education at the time of the Renaissance, prior to discussing the role played by women in intellectual life.

> In the promotion of the new learning, two tasks had to be carried out. The first included the recovery of additional classical works, the preparation of critical editions, the re-issue of the best . . . and critical study of the new texts. The second was the dissemination of the knowledge obtained from this critical study.
>
> In the dissemination of the new learning . . . five methods were widely and intensively employed: tutoring and self-directed study in families, education in schools, humanist lecturing, conversations in small private groups and larger coteries, and correspondence. [1]

I had just been reading the syllabi of women's studies programs and courses all over the country, and it was natural to translate Beard's description into terms of this new curriculum, as well as of the feminist study groups, conferences, periodicals, and "conversa-

---

Written for a volume sponsored by the Carnegie Commission on Higher Education: *Women and the Power to Change*, edited by Florence Howe, and published by Mc-Graw-Hill, 1975. Some excerpts from this essay were reprinted in the *Chronicle of Higher Education*, vol. 10, no. 19.

[1] Mary Beard, *Woman as Force in History* (New York: Collier/Macmillan, 1971), p. 260; first published 1945.

tions in small private groups and larger coteries" that have become legion over the past few years. And so for a while the working title of this essay was "Notes toward a Feminist Renaissance." It is by now clear that a feminist renaissance is under way, that in the struggle to discover women and our buried or misread history, feminists are doing two things: questioning and reexploring the past, and demanding a humanization of intellectual interests and public measures in the present. In the course of this work, we are recovering lost sources of knowledge and of spiritual vitality, while familiar texts are receiving a fresh critical appraisal, and the whole process is powered by a shift in perspective far more extraordinary and influential than the shift from theology to humanism of the European Renaissance. Much of this research, discussion, and analysis is already being carried on in the university, but even more is taking place outside it, in precisely the kind of unofficial, self-created groups described by Mary Beard. It could be said that a women's university-without-walls exists already in America, in the shape of women reading and writing with a new purposefulness, and the growth of feminist bookstores, presses, bibliographic services, women's centers, medical clinics, libraries, art galleries, and workshops, all with a truly educational mission; and that the members of this university are working and studying out of intense concern for the quality of human life as distinct from the ego-bound achievement of individual success. With the help of the duplicating machine, documents, essays, poems, statistical tables are moving from hand to hand, passing through the mails; the "dissemination of the knowledge obtained from this study" is not accountable in terms of the sales of a single edition or even dependent solely on commercial publication.

I returned to my original title—less elegant, more blunt, some might say more provocative—because immense forces in the university, as in the whole patriarchal society, are intrinsically opposed to anything resembling an actual feminist renaissance, wherever that process appears to be a serious undertaking and not merely a piece of decorative reformism. If the phrase "woman-centered university" sounds outrageous, biased, or improbable, we need only try the sound of its opposite, the "man-centered university"—not forgetting that grammar reveals the truth and that "man," the central figure of that earlier renaissance, was indeed the male, as he still is. Or, as the catalog of one "coeducational" institution has it:

> Brandeis University has set itself to develop the whole man, the sensitive, cultured, open-minded citizen who grounds his thinking in facts, who is intellectually and spiritually aware, who believes that life is significant, and who is concerned with society and the role he will play in it. [2]

This is no semantic game or trivial accident of language. What we have at present *is* a man-centered university, a breeding ground not of humanism, but of masculine privilege. As women have gradually and reluctantly been admitted into the mainstream of higher education, they have been made participants in a system that prepares men to take up roles of power in a man-centered society, that asks questions and teaches "facts" generated by a male intellectual tradition, and that both subtly and openly confirms men as the leaders and shapers of human destiny both within and outside academia. The exceptional women who have emerged from this system and who hold distinguished positions in it are just that: the required exceptions used by every system to justify and maintain itself. That all this is somehow "natural" and reasonable is still an unconscious assumption even of many who grant that women's role in society is changing, and that it needs to change.

Since this condition reflects the unspoken—and outspoken—assumptions of man-centered society, it would be naive to imagine that the university can of itself be a vanguard for change. It is probable that the unrecognized, unofficial university-without-walls I have described will prove a far more important agent in reshaping the foundations on which human life is now organized. The orthodox university is still a vital spot, however, if only because it is a place where people can find each other and begin to hear each other. (It is also a source of certain kinds of power. [3])

[2] Brandeis University Bulletin, 1972–1973, p. 11.

[3] See A. Leffler, D. Gillespie, E. Ratner, "Academic Feminists and the Women's Movement," *Ain't I a Woman?*, vol. 4, no. 1, 1973, p. 7.

Women in the university therefore need to address themselves—against the opprobrium and obstruction they do and will encounter—to changing the center of gravity of the institution as far as
possible; to work toward a woman-centered university because only if
that center of gravity can be shifted will women really be free to
learn, to teach, to share strength, to explore, to criticize, and to convert knowledge to power. It will be objected that this is merely "reverse chauvinism." But given the intensive training all women go
through in every society to place our own long-term and collective
interests second or last and to value altruism at the expense of independence and wholeness—and given the degree to which the university reinforces that training in its every aspect—the most urgent
need at present is for women to recognize, and act on, the priority of
recreating ourselves and each other, after our centuries of intellectual and spiritual blockading. A by-product of such a shift in priorities will of course ultimately mean an opening-out of intellectual
challenges for men who are emotionally mature and intuitively daring
enough to recognize the extent to which man-centered culture has
also limited and blindered them.

A few male scholars have been examining the academic tradtion
from the point of view of its sexual bias. Walter J. Ong, S.J., suggests
that the very origins of academic style are peculiarly masculine.

> Rhetoric . . . developed in the past as a major expression of the ration-
> al level of the ceremonial combat which is found among males and
> typically only among males at the physical level throughout the entire
> animal kingdom. . . . Rhetoric became particularly attached to
> Learned Latin, which the male psyche appropriated to itself as in ex-
> trafamilial language when Latin ceased to be a "mother" tongue (that
> is, was no longer spoken in the home by one's mother). Latin, spoken
> and written for 1500 years with totally negligible exceptions only by
> males, became a ceremonial language institutionalizing with particular
> force the ceremonial polemic which set the style for all education until
> romanticism. For until the romantic age, academic education was all
> but exclusively focused on defending a position (thesis) or attacking the
> position of another person—even medicine was taught this way.[4]

[4] Walter Ong, "Review of Brian Vickers' *Classical Rhetoric in English Poetry,*
College English, February 1972.

Ong remarks that "the ancient art of rhetoric did not and could not survive coeducation"—a statement that unfortunately is true only in the most literal sense.

A contemporary view is provided by Leonard Kriegel:

> . . . my teachers at Columbia . . . knew the value of reputation, and they would bank it with all the fierce pride of Wall St. lawyers. . . . The process of attaining a reputation was part of a Columbia graduate education, and we were exposed to it as soon as classes began. A man needed reserve and style and distance here; intelligence was not enough. . . .

> The "name" professors, those faculty whose shoulders were burdened with the reputation of the department, possessed that distance and propriety. They possessed other qualities, too. Some of them possessed contempt for their students. . . . Two professors of modern drama dueled each other for students, insisted on declarations of allegiance, of commitment not to a critical perspective but to themselves. . . .

> I soon found out that importance was measured not in terms of scholarship but of power within the department. The majority of graduate students . . . were so caught up in the game, so victimized by their desire for careers, so willing to preserve a place at any cost at the side of some academic eminence, that their lives became mere extensions of the dehumanization of the university. . . . We emulated our models, working for the day when we, too, might claim professorial status for ourselves . . . worshippers at the shrine of making it.

> . . . For most of us, the academic world had promised a way in which we could ignore the lure of materialism. Unfortunately, we turned into the consenting victims of what we claimed to ignore. If a student wished to buy the academic world, then it followed that he had to buy the rest of America also.[5]

Certain terms in the above quotations have a familiar ring: *defending, attacking, combat, status, banking, dueled, power, making it*. They suggest the connections—actual and metaphoric—between the style of the university and the style of a society invested in military and economic aggression. In each of these accounts what stands

[5] Leonard Kriegel, *Working Through: A Teacher's Journey in the Urban University* (New York: Saturday Review Press, 1972), pp. 43–44, 49–51.

out is not the passion for "learning for its own sake" or the sense of an intellectual community, but the dominance of the masculine ideal, the race of men against one another, the conversion of an end to a means. If the university can thus become an alienating environment even for the men who have primary rights within it, it is an insidiously exploitative environment for women.

A number of other male writers have begun to acknowledge the sexual roots of the failure of masculine culture, and of the masculine order characterized by depersonalization, fragmentation, waste, artificial scarcity, and emotional shallowness, not to mention its suicidal obsession with power and technology as ends rather than as means. Some predict the reemergence of the "feminine principle" as the salvation of the species. For recent statements of this kind, one by a sociologist and one by a poet, see Philip Slater's *The Pursuit of Loneliness*: "Women are in a better position to liberate our society emotionally"[6] or Robert Bly's essay, "I Came Out of the Mother Naked": ". . . the Great Mother is moving again in the psyche. Every day her face becomes clearer"[7] However, even when these writers acknowledge the problem as rooted in sexual disbalance, they seem to hope for some miraculous transformation of values brought about, not by actual women working to change actual conditions and exercising actual power, but by an intangible "feminine principle" or "mother consciousness." Neither Bly nor Slater acknowledges the existence of a women's movement or talks about how it might affect men; Slater in fact ignorantly and complacently predicted, as late as 1970, that "such is extremely unlikely to occur." Herbert Marcuse sees the women's liberation movement as a "radical force" and a "free society" as a "*female* society"; he hastens to add that this "has nothing to do with matriarchy of any sort," but with the "*femalization* of the male" (to be achieved through what specifics he does not tell us). He never deals with the fact that it is, after all, men who have created and profited from patriarchy, except insofar as he suggests that "the patriarchal society has created a female image, a female counter-force, which may still become one of the gravedig-

[6] Philip Slater, *The Pursuit of Loneliness* (Boston: Beacon, 1970), p. 89.

[7] Robert Bly, in *Sleepers Joining Hands* (New York: Harper & Row, 1973), pp. 29–51.

gers of patriarchal society." (Somehow, the women's movement would seem to have been created by men.) "In this sense too, the woman holds the promise of liberation."[8]

Evidently, it is not to men that we shall be looking for more concrete and less wishful thinking about centers of change, or new constructs by which change may become diffused through the society. This essay is an attempt to suggest some ways in which one particular institution—the university—might become a focus and magnet for a "female counter-force." My description will be tentative and partial; it would be premature and absurd to assume that we know precisely what forms will best accommodate the changes we want, or that the forms themselves will not change and develop. And, of course, my description presupposes simultaneous changes in every other cell of the social body.

II

The early feminists, the women intellectuals of the past, along with educated men, assumed that the intellectual structure as well as the contents of the education available to men was viable: that is, enduring, universal, a discipline civilizing to the mind and sensitizing to the spirit. It claims for both humanism and objectivity went unquestioned. One of the few voices to question this was that of Virginia Woolf, in her still little-read and extraordinary *Three Guineas*, an essay connecting war and fascism directly with the patriarchal system, and with the exclusion of women from learning and power. Far more radical in its vision than the more famous *A Room of One's Own*, it does not simply protest this exclusion but questions the very nature of the professions as practiced by men, the very quality of the intellectual heritage protected by the university.

> The questions that we have to ask and to answer about that [academic] procession during this moment of transition are so important that they may well change the lives of all men and women forever. For we have to ask ourselves, here and now, do we wish to join that procession, or don't we? On what terms shall we join that procession? Above all,

[8] Herbert Marcuse, *Counterrevolution and Revolt* (Boston: Beacon, 1972), pp. 75–78.

where is it leading us, the procession of educated men? . . . Let us
never cease from thinking,—what is this "civilization" in which we find
ourselves? What are these ceremonies and why should we take part in
them? What are these professions and why should we make money out
of them? Where in short is it leading us, the procession of the sons of
educated men?[9]

The major educational question for the nineteenth and earlier
twentieth centuries was whether the given educational structure and
contents should be made available to women. In the nineteenth century the issue to be resolved was whether a woman's mind and body
were intended by "nature" to grapple with intellectual training. In
the first sixty years of our own century the "problem" seemed to be
that education was "wasted" on women who married, had families,
and effectively retired from intellectual life. These issues, of course,
though they had to be argued, really veiled (as the question of "standards" veils the issue of nonwhite participation in higher education)
the core of politics and social power. Why women gave up their careers after marriage, why even among the unmarried or childless so
few were found in the front ranks of intellectual life were questions
that opened up only when women began to ask them and to explore
the answers.

Until the 1960s, the university continued to be seen as a privileged
enclave, somehow more defensible than other privileged enclaves,
criticized if at all for being too idealistic, too little in touch with the
uses and abuses of power; and romanticized as a place where knowledge is loved for its own sake, every opinion has an open-minded
hearing, "the dwelling place of permanent values . . . of beauty, of
righteousness, of freedom," as the Brandeis University bulletin in-
tones. The radical student critique—black and white—of the sixties
readily put its finger on the facts underlying this fiction: the racism of
the academy and its curriculum, its responsiveness to pressures of
vested interest, political, economic, and military; the use of the
academy as a base for research into weapons and social control and
as a machinery for perpetuating the power of white, middle-class

[9] Virginia Woolf, *Three Guineas* (New York: Harcourt Brace, 1966) pp. 62–63;
first published 1938.

men. Today the question is no longer whether women (or non-whites) are intellectually and "by nature" equipped for higher education, but whether this male-created, male-dominated structure is really capable of serving the humanism and freedom it professes.

Woolf suggested that women entering the professions must bring with them the education—unofficial, unpaid for, unvalued by society—of their female experience, if they are not to become part of the dehumanizing forces of competition, money lust, the lure of personal fame and individual aggrandizement, and of "unreal loyalties." In other words, we must choose what we will accept and what we will reject of institutions already structured and defined by patriarchal values. Today, more crucial even than the number of teaching jobs open to women—crucial as that continues to be—is the process of deciding "on what terms we shall join that procession." Woolf, for all the charges of lack of class consciousness thrown at her, was in fact extremely conscious of the evils of exclusivity and elitism. She had to a marked degree the female knowledge of what it means to be kept outside, alienated from power and knowledge, and of how subtly a place "inside" corrupts even liberal spirits.

> . . . the professions have a certain undeniable effect upon the professors. They make the people who practise them possessive, jealous of any infringement of their rights, and highly combative if anyone dares dispute them. . . . Therefore this guinea, which is to help you help women to enter the professions, has this condition as a first condition attached to it. You shall swear that you will do all in your power to insist that any woman who enters any profession shall in no way hinder any other human being, whether man or woman, white or black, provided that he or she is qualified to enter that profession, from entering it; but shall do all in her power to help them.[10]

What present-day radical feminists have come to recognize, is that in order to become a force against elitism and exclusivity we must learn to place each other and ourselves first, not to hinder other human beings, but to tap the kinds of power and knowledge that exist—buried, diffused, misnamed, sometimes misdirected—within

[10] Ibid., p. 66.

women.[11] At this point we need the university, with its libraries, laboratories, archives, collections, and some—but not all—of the kinds of trained thinking and expertise it has to offer. We need to consciously and critically select what is genuinely viable and what we can use from the masculine intellectual tradition, as we possess ourselves of the knowledge, skills, and perspectives that can refine our goal of self-determination with discipline and wisdom. (Certainly we do *not* need the university to continue replicating the tradition that has excluded us, or to become "amateur males.") The university is by no means the only place where this work will be carried on; nor, obviously, can the university become more woman-centered and less elitist while the society remains androcentric.

III

There are two ways in which a woman's integrity is likely to be undermined by the process of university education. This education is, of course, yet another stage in the process of her entire education, from her earliest glimpses of television at home to the tracking and acculturating toward "femininity" that become emphatic in high school. But when a woman is admitted to higher education—particularly graduate school—it is often made to sound as if she enters a sexually neutral world of "disinterested" and "universal" perspectives. It is assumed that coeducation means the equal education, side by side, of women and men. Nothing could be further from the truth; and nothing could more effectively seal a woman's sense of her secondary value in a man-centered world than her experience as a "privileged" woman in the university—if she knows how to interpret what she lives daily.

In terms of the *content* of her education, there is no discipline that does not obscure or devalue the history and experience of women as

[11] The urge to leap across feminism to "human liberation" is a tragic and dangerous mistake. It deflects us from our real sources of vision, recycles us back into old definitions and structures, and continues to serve the purposes of patriarchy, which will use "women's lib," as it contemptuously phrases it, only to buy more time for itself—as both capitalism and socialism are now doing. Feminism is a criticism and subversion of *all* patriarchal thought and institutions—not merely those currently seen as reactionary and tyrannical.

a group. What Otto Rank said of psychology has to be said of every other discipline, including the "neutral" sciences: it is "not only mand-made . . . but masculine in its mentality."[12] Will it seem, in forty years, astonishing that a book should have been written in 1946 with the title *Woman as Force in History?* The title does not seem bizarre to us now. Outside of women's studies, though liberal male professors may introduce material about women into their courses, we live with textbooks, research studies, scholarly sources, and lectures that treat women as a subspecies, mentioned only as peripheral to the history of men. In every discipline where we *are* considered, women are perceived as the objects rather than the originators of inquiry, thus primarily through male eyes, thus as a special category. That the true business of civilization has been in the hands of men is the lesson absorbed by every student of the traditional sources. How this came to be, and the process that kept it so, may well be the most important question for the self-understanding and survival of the human species; but the extent to which civilization has been built on the bodies and services of women—unacknowledged, unpaid, and unprotested in the main—is a subject apparently unfit for scholarly decency. The witch persecutions of the fourteenth through seventeenth centuries, for example, involved one of the great historic struggles—a class struggle and a struggle for knowledge—between the illiterate but practiced female healer and the beginnings of an aristocratic nouveau science, between the powerful patriarchal Church and enormous numbers of peasant women, between the pragmatic experience of the wisewoman and the superstitious practices of the early male medical profession.[13] The phenomena of woman-fear and woman-hatred illuminated by those centuries of gynocide are with us still; certainly a history of psychology or history of science that was not hopelessly one-sided would have to confront and examine this period and its consequences. Like the history of slave revolts, the history of women's resistance to domination awaits discovery by the offspring of the dominated. The chronicles, systems, and investigations of the humanities and the sciences are in

[12] Otto Rank, *Beyond Psychology* (New York: Dover, 1958), p. 37.

[13] B. Ehrenreich and D. English, *Witches, Midwives and Nurses: A History of Women Healers* (Old Westbury, N. Y.: Feminist Press, 1973).

fact a collection of half-truths and lacunae that have worked enormous damage to the ability of the sexes to understand themselves and
one another.

If this is changing within the rubric of women's studies, it is doing
so in the face of prejudice, contempt, and outright obstruction. If it
is true that the culture recognized and transmitted by the university
has been predominantly white Western culture, it is also true that
within black and Third World studies the emphasis is still predominantly masculine, and the female perspective needs to be fought for
and defended there as in the academy at large.

I have been talking about the content of the university curriculum, that is, the mainstream of the curriculum. Women in colleges
where a women's studies program already exists, or where feminist
courses are beginning to be taught, still are often made to feel that
the "real" curriculum is the male-centered one; that women's studies
are (like Third World studies) a "fad"; that feminist teachers are
"unscholarly," "unprofessional," or "dykes." But the content of
courses and programs is only the more concrete form of undermining experienced by the woman student. More invisible, less amena-
ble to change by committee proposal or fiat, is the hierarchal image,
the structure of relationships, even the style of discourse, including
assumptions about theory and practice, ends and means, process and
goal.

The university is above all a hierarchy. At the top is a small cluster
of highly paid and prestigious persons, chiefly men, whose careers
entail the services of a very large base of ill-paid or unpaid persons,
chiefly women: wives, research assistants, secretaries, teaching assistants, cleaning women, waitresses in the faculty club, lower-echelon
administrators, and women students who are used in various ways to
gratify the ego. Each of these groups of women sees itself as distinct
from the others, as having different interests and a different destiny.
The student may become a research assistant, mistress, or even wife;
the wife may act as secretary or personal typist for her husband, or
take a job as lecturer or minor administrator; the graduate student
may, if she demonstrates unusual brilliance and carefully follows the
rules, rise higher into the pyramid, where she loses her identification
with teaching fellows, as the wife forgets her identification with the
student or secretary she may once have been. The waitress or clean-

ing woman has no such mobility, and it is rare for other women in the university, beyond a few socially aware or feminist students, to support her if she is on strike or unjustly fired. Each woman in the university is defined by her relationship to the men in power instead of her relationship to other women up and down the scale.

Now, this fragmentation among women is merely a replication of the fragmentation from each other that we undergo in the society outside; in accepting the premise that advancement and security—even the chance to do one's best work—lie in propitiating and identifying with men who have some power, we have always found ourselves in competition with each other and blinded to our common struggles. This fragmentation and the invisible demoralization it generates work constantly against the intellectual and emotional energies of the woman student.

The hidden assumptions on which the university is built comprise more than simply a class system. In a curious and insidious way the "work" of a few men—especially in the more scholarly and prestigious institutions—becomes a sacred value in whose name emotional and economic exploitation of women is taken for granted. The distinguished professor may understandably like comfort and even luxury and his ego requires not merely a wife and secretary but an au pair girl, teaching assistant, programmer, and student mistress; but the justification for all this service is the almost religious concept of "his work." (Those few women who rise to the top of their professions seem in general to get along with less, to get their work done along with the cooking, personal laundry, and mending without the support of a retinue.) In other words, the structure of the man-centered university constantly reaffirms *the use of women as means* to the end of male "work"—meaning male careers and professional success. Professors of Kantian ethics or Marxist criticism are no more exempt from this exploitation of women than are professors of military science or behavioral psychology. In its very structure, then, the university encourages women to continue perceiving themselves as means and not as ends—as indeed their whole socialization has done.

It is sometimes pointed out that because the majority of women working in the university are in lower-status positions, the women student has few if any "role models" she can identify with in the form

of women professors or even high-ranking administrators. She therefore can conceive of her own future only in terms of limited ambi-
tions. But it should be one of the goals of a woman-centered university to do away with the pyramid itself, insofar as it is based on sex,
age, color, class, and other irrelevant distinctions. I will take this up
again further on.

IV

For reasons both complex and painful, the "exceptional" woman
who receives status and tenure in the university has often been less
than supportive to young women beginning their own careers. She
has for her own survival learned to vote against other women, absorb
the masculine adversary style of discourse, and carefully avoid any
style or method that could be condemned as "irrational" or "emotionally charged." She chooses for investigation subjects as remote as
possible from her self-interest as a woman,[14] or if women are the objects of her investigation, she manages to write about them as if they
belonged to a distant tribe. The kinds of personal knowledge and
reflection that might illuminate the study of, say, death fantasies
during pregnancy, or the recurrent figure of the Beautiful Dead
Woman in male art, or that might lead to research on a method of
birth control comparable with other developments in medicine and
technology—such are ruled out lest she appear "unscholarly" or
"subjective." (It is a grotesque fact that the professional literature
available on the female orgasm and on lesbianism is almost entirely
by male researchers.) Of course, the advent of feminist studies has
been rapidly changing this scene, and will continue to change it. But
again, the usually younger feminist scholar-teacher is in most places

[14] "Until recently, most academic women have avoided women's subjects like the
plague; to do otherwise was to diminish their chances of being considered serious contenders in traditionally male fields" (Barbara Sicherman, "The Invisible Woman," in
Women in Higher Education [Washington, D.C.: American Council on Education,
1972], p. 76). Leffler, et al. op. cit., pp. 12–13) suggest that although more recently a
reverse trend is seen among "academic feminists," they "rarely research new topics or
develop new ideas on the gender problem. Rather, they tend to trail in the movement's wake . . . (without acknowledging movement inspiration, naturally)."

untenured and struggling, and the style and concerns of masculine scholarship still represent the mainstream.

The mental hospital and the psychotherapeutic situation have been described as replicating the situation of women in the patriarchal family.[15] The university is likewise a replica of the patriarchal family. The male teacher may have a genuinely "fatherly" relation to his gifted student-daughter, and many intellectual women have been encouraged and trained by their gifted fathers, or gifted male teachers. But it is the *absence* of the brilliant and creative mother, or woman teacher, that is finally of more significance than the presence of the brilliant and creative male. Like the father's favorite daughter in the patriarchal family, the promising woman student comes to identify with her male scholar-teacher more strongly than with her sisters. He may well be in a position to give her more, in terms of influence, training, and emotional gratification, than any academic woman on the scene. In a double sense, he confirms her suspicion that she is "exceptional." If she succeeds, it is partly that she has succeeded in pleasing *him*, winning his masculine interest and attention. The eroticism of the father-daughter relationship resonates here, and romance and flirtation are invisibly present even where there is no actual seduction. Alice Rossi has pointed out the potential undermining of a woman's self-confidence when she is engaged in an actual sexual alliance with her mentor: how can she be sure that his praise is not a form of seduction, that her recommendations were not won in bed?[16] And not infrequently the professor marries his gifted woman student and secures her for life as a brain as well as a body, the critic and editor of his books, "without whom . . . ," as the dedications all say. A woman-centered university would be a place in which the much-distorted mother-daughter relationship could find a new model: where women of maturer attainments in every field would provide intellectual guidance along with concern for the wholeness of their young women students, an older woman's

[15] Phyllis Chesler, *Women and Madness* (New York: Doubleday, 1972), p. 35.

[16] Alice S. Rossi, "Looking Ahead: Summary and Prospects," in Rossi and Ann Calderwood, eds., *Academic Women on the Move* (New York: Russell Sage, 1973), ch. 21.

sympathy and unique knowledge of the processes younger women were going through, along with the power to give concrete assistance and support. Under such circumstances it is likely that far less eroticism would glamorize the male teacher, and the woman student could use whatever he had to offer her without needing to identify with him or adopt his perspective for her own.[17]

V

I have tried to show that the androcentric university not only undermines and exploits women but forces men who wish to succeed in it further into the cul-de-sac of one-sided masculinity. In this it is simply a microcosm of society. Virginia Woolf was a forerunner of contemporary feminist analysts in criticizing the drive for goals without consideration of means and process, the glorification of competition, the confusion between human beings and objects as products of this one-sided masculinity of culture; and in this century we have seen culture brought low and discredited because of them. Without pretending that we can in our present stage of understanding and of mystification through language define crisply and forever what is "masculine" and what is "feminine," we *can* at least say that the above corruptions and confusions are products of a male-dominated history.

The world as a whole is rapidly becoming Westernized. In no culture more than in Western culture is the failure of ideas like "industrialization" and "development" more evident; for without famine, without authentic scarcity, without the naked struggle to stay alive, and with the apparent "freedom" of unveiled and literate women, the condition of woman has remained that of a nonadult, a person whose exploitation—physical, economic, or psychic—is accepted *no matter to what class she belongs*. A society that treats any group of adults as nonadult—that is, unfit to assume utmost responsbility in society and unfit for doing the work of their choice—will end by

[17] For the other side of the coin—exclusion of women from the protégé system on a sexual basis—see American Sociological Association, *The Status of Women in Sociology* (Washington, D.C.: 1973), pp. 26–28). On both sides of the coin, dependency on the male teacher is the rule.

treating most of its citizens as patriarchal society has treated children—that is, lying to them and using force, overt or manipulative, to control them.

I want to suggest two categories of women's needs that would, if genuinely met, change the nature of the university and to some extent the community outside the university, and I am suggesting further that these needs of women are congruent with the humanizing of the community-at-large. The first category includes both the content of education and the style in which it is treated. The second includes institutionalized obstacles that effectively screen out large numbers of able women from full or partial engagement in higher education.

First, as to curriculum: As the hitherto "invisible" and marginal agent in culture, whose native culture has been effectively denied, women need a reorganization of knowledge, of perspectives and analytical tools that can help us know our foremothers, evaluate our present historical, political, and personal situation, and take ourselves seriously as agents in the creation of a more balanced culture. Some feminists foresee this culture as based on female primacy, others as "androgynous"; whatever it is to become, women will have the primary hand in its shaping. This does not and need not mean that the entire apparatus of masculine intellectual achievement should be scrapped, or that women should simply turn the whole apparatus inside out and substitute "she" for "he." Some of the structures will be seen as unhealthy for human occupation even while their grandeur in its own day can be appreciated; like old and condemned buildings, we may want to photograph these for posterity and tear them down; some may be reconstructed along different lines; some we may continue to live and use. But a radical reinvention of subject, lines of inquiry, and method will be required. As Mary Daly has written:

> The tyranny of methodolatry hinders new discoveries. It prevents us from raising questions never asked before and from being illumined by ideas that do not fit into pre-established boxes and forms. . . . Under patriarchy, Method has wiped out women's questions so totally that even women have not been able to hear and formulate our own questions to meet our own experiences.

Daly also calls for "breaking down the barriers between technical knowledge and that deep realm of intuitive knowledge which some theologians call ontological reason".[18] In fact, it is in the realm of the apparently unimpeachable sciences that the greatest modifications and revaluations will undoubtedly occur. It may well be in this domain that has proved least hospitable or attractive to women—theoretical science—that the impact of feminism and of woman-centered culture will have the most revolutionary impact. It was a woman, Simone Weil, who wrote, in the early thirties:

> . . . the technicians are ignorant of the theoretical basis of the knowledge which they employ. The scientists in their turn not only remain out of touch with technical problems but in addition are cut off from that over-all vision which is the very essence of theoretical culture. One could count on one's fingers the number of scientists in the entire world who have a general idea of the history and development of their own particular science; there is not one who is really competent as regards sciences other than his own . . .[19]

A more recent writer points out the historical origins for the scientist's claim to neutrality, his [sic] assertion of normative freedom, and his "conscious rejection and ignorance of the subjective and the a-rational in human activity."[20] He suggests that every attempt to bring public and social sanctions to bear on the scientist's designs has hitherto met with defeat and that every attempt to extend the boundaries of accepted epistemology, including psychoanalysis, has been labeled "pseudoscience." (He fails, however, to mention the healing and midwifery of wisewomen that were even more violently driven underground. Mendelsohn's article, in fact, though it is concerned with the return of science to the service of human needs, and though it was delivered as a lecture to a Radcliffe Institute symposium on women, never touches on the connection between the masculiniza-

[18] Mary Daly, *Beyond God the Father* (Boston: Beacon, 1973), pp. 11–12; 39.

[19] Richard Rees, *Simone Weil: A Sketch for a Portrait* (London: Oxford, 1966), pp. 20–21.

[20] Everett Mendelsohn, "A Human Reconstruction of Science," prepared for "Women: Recourse for a Changing World," Radcliffe Institute Symposium, 1972; *Boston University Journal*, vol. 21, no. 2, spring 1973, p. 48.

tion of the sciences and their elitism, indifference to values, and rigidity of method.) He ends, however, by calling for certain kinds of change in the procedures and priorities of the science that can be applied by extension to the entire body of knowledge and method that the university has adopted for its province:

> A reconstructed science would value truth, but also compassion. It would have an inbuilt ethic that would defend both being and living; that is, knowledge that would be non-violent, non-coercive, non-exploitative, non-manipulative . . . that would renounce finally the Faustian quest to achieve the limits of the universe or total knowledge, that would work to construct models that would be more explanatory and more inclusive—science practiced among and derived from the public. What if we were to say that we would not undertake to develop what could not be understood and publicly absorbed, that we were intent on building a science not confined to academies and institutions.[21]

Certainly a major change will be along the lines already seen in women's studies: a breakdown of traditional departments and "disciplines," of that fragmentation of knowledge that weakens thought and permits the secure ignorance of the specialist to protect him from responsibility for the applications of his theories. It is difficult to imagine a woman-centered curriculum where quantitative method and technical reason would continue to be allowed to become means for the reduction of human lives, and where specialization would continue to be used as an escape from wholeness.[22]

It has been almost a given of women's courses that style and content are inseparable. A style has evolved in the classroom, more dialogic, more exploratory, less given to pseudo-objectivity, than the traditional mode. A couple of examples of the feminist approach are quoted below. The first comes from a description of an applied psy-

---

[21] Ibid., p. 52.

[22] Mina P. Shaughnessy has written of the failures of measurement to account for actual events in the teaching process: "In how many countless and unconscious ways do we capitulate to the demand for numbers? . . . In how many ways has the need for numbers forced us to violate the language itself, ripping it from the web of discouse in order to count those things that can be caught in the net of numbers?" ("Open Admissions and the Disadvantaged Teacher," keynote speech at the Conference on College Composition and Communication, New Orleans, April 1973 [unpublished]).

chology course on discrimination against women, taught at the University of Wales in Cardiff:

> A "personal style" was adopted. By this I mean a style of communication which avoided such constructions as "it is said," "it is thought," "it is considered." In short, I acknowledged the subjective element by not avoiding the use of the personal pronoun. This style is more appropriate to a non-exploitative, non-patriarchal interaction between students and teacher. It is conducive to a greater degree of academic rigour. . . . It seems to me that the form of many communications in academia, both written and verbal, is such as to not only obscure the influence of the personal or subjective but also to give the impression of divine origin—a mystification composed of sybilline statements—from beings supposedly emptied of the "dross" of self. Additionally I believe that a "personal style" probably encourages greater creativeness. Further, it seems to me, that, when teaching, such a style encourages the active involvement of all concerned. It is opposed to any form of alienation. It seems particularly appropriate that women's studies should counteract the misleading tendency in academe to camouflage the influence of the subject.

The second example comes from the actual syllabus handed to students in a course, "The Education of Women in Historical Perspective."

> I am teaching this course because I believe that education is the key to social change. Despite the generally conservative role that formal institutions play in society, philosophers, statesmen and parents have looked to schools for improving the *status quo*. Access to schools has been used as a method of social control, as have curriculum and teaching methods. The schools can become vehicles for indoctrination, for oppression, as well as for healthy stimulation of individual and societal freedom; the line between "education" and indoctrination is difficult to define, but essential to look for.

> . . . I look at issues historically; that has been my training, and my primary interest. I have trouble with the twentieth century, far preferring the puzzle of the nineteenth. In women's education, this was when the biggest changes took place, when education for women was a revolutionary question. However, we may be in the midst of another revolutionary time, and an understanding of the past is essential for appreci-

ation of the contemporary scene. History can be a delightful escape into a world where there is a finite number of questions. . . . This course is my attempt to escape from my ostrich tendencies, to understand my own role in the present movement.

I want to stress this problem of bias because scholarship is supposed to be as bias-free as possible. We will look at all questions and issues from as many sides as we can think of; but I am inescapably a feminist. . . . You must question my assumptions, my sources, my information; that is part of learning to learn. You should also question your own assumptions. Skepticism about oneself is essential to continued growth and a balanced perspective.[23]

The underlying mode of the feminist teaching style is thus by nature antihierarchical.

VI

I have described the university as a hierarchy built on exploitation. To become truly educated and self-aware, against the current of patriarchal education, a woman must be able to discover and explore her root connection with *all women*. Her previous education has taught her only of her prescribed relationships with men, or "Women beware women." Any genuine attempt to fill this need would become a force for the dehierarchizing of the university. For it would have to involve all women in the institution, simultaneously, as students and as teachers, besides drawing on the special experience of nonacademic women, both within and outside the university—the grandmothers, the high-school dropouts, the professionals, the artists, the political women, the housewives. And it would involve them at an organic level, not as interesting exhibits or specimens.

There is one crucial hub around which all the above revolves— one need that is primary if women are to assume any real equality in the academic world, one challenge that the university today, like the society around it, evades with every trick in its possession. This is the issue of childcare. The welfare mother badgered to get out and work,

[23] Deborah Rosenfelt, ed., *Female Studies*, vol. 7 (Old Westbury, N.Y.: Feminist Press, 1973), pp. 10; 187.

the cafeteria worker whose child wears a latchkey, the student or assistant professor constantly uncertain about the source and quality of the next baby-sitter, all have this at stake; all are constantly forced to improvise or to give up in the struggle to fill this social vacuum. Full-time mothering is a peculiar and late-arrived social phenomenon and is assumed to be the "normal" mode of childrearing in the United States; but full-time mothering, even by choice, is not an option for the majority of women. There is no improvisation of childcare—even if it be the child's own father who "generously" agrees to share the chores—that can begin to substitute for an excellent, dependable, nonsexist, imaginative system of care, cheap enough for all, and extending identical opportunities to the children of the poorest and the highest-paid women on the campus.

Alice Rossi has described some of the possibilities and practical solutions to this question in her "Equality between the Sexes: An Immodest Proposal,"[24] and much of what I am going to say here will merely develop what she earlier sketched out. Perhaps I shall say it with a greater sense of urgency, because even in the years since her essay was written, the struggle over childcare and the need for it have become more clear-cut. Attention to how children are to be cared for and socialized can be seen as a kind of test of the "humanism" of the university, which has hitherto been so responsive to the masters of war. In the past the university has *used* children, in its special kindergartens and laboratory schools, as guinea pigs for tests and new methods, just as it has used the community around it for such purposes.

The degree to which patriarchal society has neglected the problem of childcare is in some ways reflective of its need to restrict the lives of women. Even in "revolutionary" socialist societies, where women are a needed sector of the labor force, and where state-supported collective childcare exists, the centers are staffed by women and women bear the ultimate responsibility for children. This may not in itself be undesirable; but the relegation of this responsibility to women reflects a reactionary thinking about sexual roles rather than a conscious decision made in the light of a feminist analysis. In both

[24] In Robert J. Lifton, ed., *The Woman in America* (Boston: Beacon, 1968), pp. 121–24.

China and the Soviet Union the grandmother is an important adjunct to collective day care; the grandfather goes unmentioned in this role.[25] In the United States, the rapid increase in single-parent families and female heads of households does not alter the fact that, as of today, the fantasy of the family as consisting of a breadwinning father, a homemaking mother, and children is the model on which most social constructs are based. School holidays and lunch and coming-home hours, for example, often reflect the assumption that there is a nonworking mother whose major responsibility is to be there when the children come home. Even within the women's movement, childcare for women who wish to be politically or culturally active is sometimes a neglected priority in the arranging of conferences and workshops.

It is difficult to imagine, unless one has lived it, the personal division, endless improvising, and creative and intellectual holding back that for most women accompany the attempt to combine the emotional and physical demands of parenthood and the challenges of work. To assume one can naturally combine these has been a male privilege everywhere in the world. For women, the energy expended in both the conflict and the improvisation has held many back from starting a professional career and has been a heavy liability to careers once begun. The few exceptions in this country have been personal solutions; for the majority of mothers no such options exist.

Since this essay is concerned, not with an ideal future but with some paths toward it, I am assuming that within the foreseeable future few if any adequate community children's centers will be available, certainly on the scale and of the excellence we need. Until such exist in every community, it will be necessary for any university concerned with shifting its androcentric imbalance to provide them. But again, they cannot be merely token custodial units, or testing

[25] Ruth Sidel (*Women and Child-Care in China* [New York: Hill & Wang, 1972], p. 25) reports of China: "All nursery and kindergarten teachers are women. There seems to be no effort to recruit men into fields in which they would be working with small children. And there seems to be no concern for breaking down the traditional sex roles in professions such as teaching and nursing, both of which are virtually all female." See also Toni Blanken, "Preschool Collectives in the Soviet Union," in Pamela Roby, ed., *Child Care: Who Cares?* (New York: Basic Books, 1973), pp. 386–97.

grounds run by the university for its own experimental ends. The kind of childcare I am going to describe would be designed first of all in the interests of the children and mothers it serves.

(1)   Childcare would be available for children of all students, staff, and faculty, with additional places for community children, at a subsidized rate that would make it effectively open to all. This is an absolutely necessary, though not sufficient, condition for the kinds of change we envision.

(2)   Childcare would be of the highest quality; no merely custodial center would be tolerated. The early nuture and education of the children would be as flexible and imaginative as possible. There would be a conscious counterthrust against the sex-role programming of patriarchal society.

(3)   The centers would be staffed, under experienced and qualified directorship, by women and men who have chosen and been trained for this kind of work. They would be assisted by several kinds of people:

   (a)   College students, female and male, who want experience in early education or just want to spend time with children. (Several experienced baby-sitters could work with several times the number of children they ordinarily "sit" with in private homes, and with more expert supervision.)

   (b)   High-school students similar to the college students in (a).

   (c)   Older women and men from the community—"grandparents" with special qualifications, informal or formal.

   (d)   Parents who want to share their children's lives on a parttime basis during the working day.

   (e)   Apprentices from graduate programs in education, pediatrics, psychology, the arts, etc.

   The children would thus be in contact with a wide range of women and men, of different ages, as "nurturant" figures from an early age. The core staff of the centers should be as sexually balanced and as permanent as possible.

I am aware that some feminists, including some lesbian mothers, might prefer to see the nurture and acculturation of young children entirely in the hands of women—not as an acting out of traditional roles, but as a cultural and political choice. I tend, however, to agree with Michelle Rosaldo when she writes:

> . . . American society is . . . organized in a way that creates and exploits a radical distance between private and public, domestic and social, female and male . . . this conflict is at the core of the contemporary rethinking of sex roles. . . . If the public world is to open its doors to more than an elite among women, the nature of work itself will have to be altered, and the asymmetry between work and the home reduced. For this we must . . . bring men into the sphere of domestic concerns and responsibilities.[26]

(4) There should be flexibility enough to allow parents to, say, take their children to the university museum or for lunch in the cafeteria if they so desire. Nursing mothers should be able to come and feed their babies.

(5) A well-baby clinic, with both medical and dental care, should be regularly provided for all the children as a service of the centers. A referral service for mothers with physical or psychic problems should be available.

(6) There should be opportunities for staff and parents of the centers to discuss, in small groups, ideas of childrearing, criticisms of the running of the center, and ways in which it can better serve its clients.

While excellent universal early childhood care should be a major priority in any reasonably humane society, the primary and moving impulse behind the children's center would be to help equalize the position of women.[27]

[26] In M. Rosaldo and L. Lamphere, eds., *Woman, Culture and Society* (Stanford, Calif.: Stanford University, 1974), p. 42.

[27] See Simmons and Chayes, "University Day Care," and Hagen, "Child Care and Women's Liberation," in Roby, op. cit. Obviously, day care is both an educational and a political issue and can evoke different ideas of goal and quality from different groups. For example, the heterosexual mother and the lesbian mother may each see

VII

The notion of the "full-time" student has penalized both women and the poor. The student with a full-time job and a full-time academic program is obviously more handicapped than the student who can afford to go to college without working. Many women—married, divorced, or single mothers—have the equivalent of an unpaid full-time job at home and are discouraged from considering advanced study. Until universal and excellent childcare is developed these women are handicapped in undertaking a full-time program. Sometimes only a year or so of part-time study would make the difference between continuing their education and dropping out, or between real achievement and a frantic attempt to muddle through.[28]

But in a university not dedicated primarily to reduplicating the old pyramid, two other groups will need the availability of part-time study. Women faculty should make it one of their special concerns that staff and community women be brought into the educational process. All staff—women and men—should have paid time off for auditing or taking courses for credit, as well as access to libraries and to academic counseling. Community women must be taken seriously as potential users of the university. Many of these women have suffered from the burdens of both race and sex; tracked into the nonacademic stream in high school, carrying the responsibilities of early marriages and large families, they have worked hard both within and outside the home and yet have often been dismissed in the most offhand stereotyping both by the radical male left and by male "liberals."

---

quite different objectives for the kind of center in which she would want to place her child. (See *Ain't I a Woman*, double issue on childcare, spring 1973.) These differences will undoubtedly emerge and have to be worked through, sometimes painfully; but I agree with Gross and MacEwen (in Roby, p. 295) that it must be the parents (I would say particularly the mothers) who establish goals for the center and that the university should be seen purely as a provider of space and funding.

[28] K. Patricia Cross ("The Woman Student," in *Women in Higher Education*, op. cit., p. 49 ff) observes furthermore that "mature women constitute a significant segment of the [new student] population" and asserts the need for a recognition of American mobility (in which the wife is uprooted by the husband's career) through systems of transferable credits and credit-by-examination.

Whether invisible as scrubwomen or cafeteria workers, or vaguely perceived as shoppers in the local supermarket or mothers pushing prams in the community, these women are also becoming increasingly awake to expectations they have been denied.[29] The working women employed by the university and the women of its local community both have claims upon the resources it so jealously guards. They should be able to look to a nonelitist university for several kinds of resources: a women's health center, with birth-control and abortion counseling, Pap tests, pamphlets and talks on women's health problems; a rape crisis center; an adult education program in which women at first too shy or uncertain to enroll for college classes might test their interests and abilities (this might include remedial reading and writing, math, women's history, basic economics, current events, community organizing workshops, poetry and art workshops, etc.); a woman-staffed women's psychological counseling center with both group and individual counseling; a law clinic. A large university should be prepared to integrate services contributed to such centers with the other academic commitments of any faculty member willing and qualified to work in them. And, undoubtedly, a great deal of reciprocal education would be going on as women of very different backgrounds and shades of opinion began to meet, hold discussions, and discover their common ground.

I can anticipate one response to these recommendations, partly because it has been leveled at me in conversation, partly because I have leveled it at myself. The university cannot, it may be argued, become all to each; it cannot serve the education of young adults, train future specialists, provide a conduit for research and scholarship, and do all these other things you are suggesting. I have, I confess, thought long and hard on that side of the question. Part of my

[29] A *New York Times Magazine* article carried a series of transcribed conversations with middle-aged, mostly blue-collar, second-generation Italian and Jewish women in East Flatbush, all in their forties and members of a consciousness-raising group, all concerned with changing and expanding their lives now that their children are grown up. One recalls "how hard I fought for my girls to go to college." The author comments that "two main concerns spurred their interest in feminism: the feeling that society in general, and their husbands in particular, no longer viewed them as sexually interesting . . . and the realization that they were 'out of a job' in the same sense as a middle-aged man who is fired by his employer of 20 years" (Susan Jacoby, "What Do I Do for the Next Twenty Years?" *New York Times Magazine*, June 17, 1973).

final resolution comes from the fact that we are talking about a process involving simultaneous changes both in society "out there" and in the university, and that when the local or national community becomes able to develop strong and responsive centers such as I have been describing for all its citizens, the burden would not have to fall on the university. Ideally, I imagine a very indistinct line between "university" and "community" instead of the familiar city-on-a-hill frowning down on its neighbors, or the wrought-iron gates by which town and gown have traditionally defined their relationship. For centuries women were by definition people of the town, not of the gown; and still, there are many more of us "down there."

Moreover, the university in contemporary America has not been at such pains to refrain from providing services to *certain* communities: consulting for industry and government, conducting classified military research, acting as a recruitment center for the military-industrial and intelligence communities. What I am really suggesting is that it change its focus but still continue its involvement outside the ivy—or graffiti—covered walls. Instead of serving such distant and faceless masters as the "challenge of Sputnik," Cold War "channeling," or the Air Force, a university responsive to women's needs would serve the needs of the human, visible community in which it sits—the neighborhood, the city, the rural county, its true environment. In a sense the solution I am proposing is anarchistic: that the university should address itself to the microcosms of national problems and issues that exist locally, and that it should do so with the greatest possible sense that it will not simply be giving, but be receiving, because academe has a great deal to learn from women and from other unprivileged people.

I have described the kinds of ad hoc teaching that might take place under university auspices. As a research institution, it should organize its resources around problems specific to its community; for example, adult literacy; public health; safer, cheaper, and simpler birth control; drug addiction; community action; geriatrics and the sociology and psychology of aging and death; the history and problems of women and those of people in nonwhite, non–middle-class cultures; urban (or rural) adolescence; public architecture; child development and pediatrics; urban engineering with the advice and consent of the engineered; folk medicine; the psychology, architecture, economics, and diet of prisons; union history; the economics of the small farmer—the possibilities would vary from place to place. The "community" is probably a misleading term. In fact, most large urban universities have many communities. The "community" around Columbia University, for example, is not simply black and Puerto Rican, but white middle-class, poor and aged, Jewish, Japanese, Cuban, etc. A sympathetic and concerned relationship with all these groups would involve members of the university in an extremely rich cluster of problems. And the nature of much research (and its usefulness) might be improved if it were conceived as research *for*, rather than *on*, human beings.

VIII

I have been trying to think of a celebrated literary utopia written by a woman. The few contenders would be contemporary: Monique Wittig's *Les Guerillères*, but that is really a vision of epic struggle, or Elizabeth Gould Davis's early chapters in *The First Sex*, but those are largely based on Bachofen. Shulamith Firestone noted the absence of a female utopia in *The Dialectic of Sex* and proceeded, in the last chapter, to invent her own. These thoughts occur because any vision of things-other-than-as-they-are tends to meet with the charge of "utopianism," so much power has the way-things-are to denude and impoverish the imagination. Even minds practiced in criticism of the status quo resist a vision so apparently unnerving as that which foresees an end to male privilege and a changed relationship between the sexes. The university I have been trying to imagine does not seem to me utopian, though the problems and contradictions to be faced in its actual transformation are of course real and severe. For a long time, academic feminists, like all feminists, are going to have to take personal risks—of confronting their own realities, of speaking their minds, of being fired or ignored when they do so, of becoming sterotyped as "man-haters" when they evince a primary loyalty to women. They will also encounter opposition from successful women who have been the token "exceptions." This opposition—this female misogyny—is a leftover of a very ancient competitiveness and self-hatred forced on women by patriarchal culture. What is now required of the fortunate exceptional

women are the modesty and courage to see why and how they have
been fortunate at the expense of other women, and to begin to acknowledge their community with them. As one of them has written:

> The first responsibility of a "liberated" woman is to lead the fullest,
> freest and most imaginative life she can. The second responsibility is
> her solidarity with other women. She may live and work and make love
> with men. But she has no right to represent her situation as simpler, or
> less suspect, or less full of compromises than it really is. Her good rela-
> tions with men must not be bought at the price of betraying her sis-
> ters.[30]

To this I would add that from a truly feminist point of view these two
responsibilities are inseparable.

I am curious to see what corresponding risks and self-confronta-
tions men of intelligence and goodwill will be ready to undergo on
behalf of women. It is one thing to have a single "exceptional"
woman as your wife, daughter, friend, or protégée, or to long for a
humanization of society by women; another to face each feminist
issue—academic, social, personal—as it appears and to evade none.
Many women have felt publicly betrayed time and again by men on
whose good faith and comradeship they had been relying on account
of private conversations. I know that academic men are now hard-
pressed for jobs and must fear the competition of women entering
the university in greater numbers and with greater self-confidence.
But masculine resistance to women's claims for full humanity is far
more ancient, deeply rooted, and irrational than this year's job market. Misogyny should itself become a central subject of inquiry
rather than continue as a desperate clinging to old, destructive fears
and privileges. It will be interesting to see how many men are prepared to give more than rhetorical support today to the sex from
which they have, for centuries, demanded and accepted so much.

If a truly universal and excellent network of childcare can begin to
develop, if women in sufficient numbers pervade the university at all
levels—from community programs through college and professional
schools to all ranks of teaching and administration—if older,

[30] Susan Sontag, "The Third World of Women," *Partisan Review*, vol. 40, no. 2,
1973, p. 206.

more established faculty women begin to get in touch with their (always, I am convinced) latent feminism, if even a few men come forward willing to think thròugh and support feminist issues beyond their own immediate self-interest, there is a strong chance that in our own time we would begin to see some true "universality" of values emerging from the inadequate and distorted corpus of patriarchal knowledge. This will mean not a renaissance but a *nascence*, partaking of some inheritances from the past but working imaginatively far beyond them.

It is likely that in the immediate future various alternatives will be explored. Women's studies programs, where they are staffed by feminists, will serve as a focus for feminist values even in a patriarchal context. Even where staffed largely by tokenists, their very existence will make possible some rising consciousness in students. Already, alternate feminist institutes are arising to challenge the curriculum of established institutions.[31] Feminists may use the man-centered university as a base and resource while doing research and writing books and articles whose influence will be felt far beyond the academy. Consciously woman-centered universities—in which women shape the philosophy and the decision making though men may choose to study and teach there—may evolve from existing institutions. Whatever the forms it may take, the process of women's repossession of ourselves is irreversible. Within and without academe, the rise in women's expectations has gone far beyond the middle class and has released an incalculable new energy—not merely for changing institutions but for human redefinition; not merely for equal rights but for a new kind of being.

[31]A. R., 1978: For example, the Feminist Studio Workshop in Los Angeles, the Sagaris Institute, Maiden Rock Institute in Minnesota, the projected Feminist Art Institute in New York.

Vesuvius at Home: The Power of Emily Dickinson (1975)

This essay was read in its earliest form as a lecture at Brandeis University, and in its present version as one of the Lucy Martin Donnelley lectures at Bryn Mawr College. It was first printed in *Parnassus: Poetry in Review*. The problem of taking Emily Dickinson seriously is still with us today. "The Belle of Amherst," a specious and reductive "one-woman show" based on Dickinson's most familiar poems and on the legendary version of her life and character, was a Broadway and television hit in 1976–77, and is now being made into a film. There is still almost no adequate criticism of Dickinson's poetry. The best scholarly efforts have centered on her life (e.g., Jay Leyda's *The Days and Hours of Emily Dickinson*; Richard Sewall's respectful and useful two-volume biography) but most biographers have been condescending, clinical, or sentimental. Virtually all criticism of this poet's work suffers from the literary and historical silence and secrecy surrounding intense woman-to-woman relationships—a central element in Dickinson's life and art; and by the assumption that she was asexual or heterosexually "sublimated."* As Toni McNaron has written: "I am not waiting to turn Dickinson into a practicing lesbian. . . . What I do want is a lesbian-feminist reading of her poetry and her life as the most accurate way to handle that otherwise confusing constellation of myth and fact surrounding her."** The

* This includes Albert Gelpi's sensitive, imaginative, and exceptionally sympathetic essay on Dickinson in his *The Tenth Muse: The Psyche of the American Poet* (Cambridge, Mass.: Harvard University, 1975).

** Toni McNaron, "The Necessary Struggle to Name Ourselves," to be included in an anthology tentatively entitled *The Lesbian Perspective in Research and Teaching*, edited by Sarah Hoagland and Julia P. Stanley.

distinction made here is a vital one: to "prove" that a woman of the nineteenth century did or did not sleep with another woman, or women, is beside the point. But lesbian/feminist criticism has the power to illuminate the work of *any* woman artist, beyond proving her a "practicing lesbian" or not. Such a criticism will ask questions hitherto passed over; will not search obsessively for heterosexual romance as the key to a woman artist's life and work; will ask how she came to be for-herself and how she identified with and was able to use women's culture, a women's tradition; and what the presence of other women meant in her life. It will thus identify images, codes, metaphors, strategies, points of stress, unrevealed by conventional criticism which works from a male/mainstream perspective. And this process will make women artists of the past—and present—available to us in ways we cannot yet predict or imagine.

~~~~~~~~

I am traveling at the speed of time, along the Massachusetts Turnpike. For months, for years, for most of my life, I have been hovering like an insect against the screens of an existence which inhabited Amherst, Massachusetts, between 1830 and 1886. The methods, the exclusions, of Emily Dickinson's existence could not have been my own; yet more and more, as a women poet finding my own methods, I have come to understand her necessities, could have been witness in her defense.

"Home is not where the heart is," she wrote in a letter, "but the house and the adjacent buildings." A statement of New England realism, a directive to be followed. Probably no poet ever lived so much and so purposefully in one house; even, in one room. Her niece Martha told of visiting her in her corner bedroom on the second floor at 280 Main Street, Amherst, and of how Emily Dickinson made as if to lock the door with an imaginary key, turned, and said: "Matty: here's freedom."

I am traveling at the speed of time, in the direction of the house and buildings.

Western Massachusetts: the Connecticut Valley: a countryside still full of reverberations: scene of Indian uprisings, religious revivals, spiritual confrontations, the blazing-up of the lunatic fringe of the Puritan coal. How peaceful and how threatened it looks from Route 91, hills gently curled above the plain, the tobacco barns standing in fields sheltered with white gauze from the sun, and the sudden urban sprawl: ARCO, MacDonald's, shopping plazas. The country that broke the heart of Jonathan Edwards, that enclosed the genius of Emily Dickinson. It lies calmly in the light of May, cloudy skies breaking into warm sunshine, light-green spring softening the hills, dogwood and wild fruit-trees blossoming in the hollows.

From Northampton bypass there's a four-mile stretch of road to Amherst—Route 9—between fruit farms, steakhouses, super-markets. The new University of Massachusetts rears its skyscrapers up from the plain against the Pelham Hills. There is new money here, real estate, motels. Amherst succeeds on Hadley almost with-out notice. Amherst is green, rich-looking, secure; we're suddenly in the center of town, the crossroads of the campus, old New England college buildings spread around two village greens, a scene I re-member as almost exactly the same in the dim past of my undergrad-uate years when I used to come there for college weekends.

Left on Seelye Street, right on Main; driveway at the end of a yellow picket fence. I recognize the high hedge of cedars screening the house, because twenty-five years ago I walked there, even then drawn toward the spot, trying to peer over. I pull into the driveway behind a generous nineteenth-century brick mansion with wings and porches, old trees and green lawns. I ring at the back door—the door through which Dickinson's coffin was carried to the cemetery a block away.

For years I have been not so much envisioning Emily Dickinson as trying to visit, to enter her mind, through her poems and letters, and through my own intimations of what it could have meant to be one of the two mid–nineteenth-century American geniuses, and a woman, living in Amherst, Massachusetts. Of the other genius, Walt Whitman, Dickinson wrote that she had heard his poems were "disgraceful." She knew her own were unacceptable by her world's standards of poetic convention, and of what was appropriate, in par-ticular, for a woman poet. Seven were published in her lifetime, all edited by other hands; more than a thousand were laid away in her bedroom chest, to be discovered after her death. When her sister dis-covered them, there were decades of struggle over the manuscripts, the manner of their presentation to the world, their suitability for publication, the poet's own final intentions. Narrowed-down by her early editors and anthologists, reduced to quaintness or spinsterish oddity by many of her commentators, sentimentalized, fallen-in-love with like some gnomic Garbo, still unread in the breadth and depth of her full range of work, she was, and is, a wonder to me when I try to imagine myself into that mind.

I have a notion that genius knows itself; that Dickinson chose her seclusion, knowing she was exceptional and knowing what she needed. It was, moreover, no hermetic retreat, but a seclusion which included a wide range of people, of reading and correspondence. Her sister Vinnie said, "Emily is always looking for the rewarding person." And she found, at various periods, both women and men: her sister-in-law Susan Gilbert, Amherst visitors and family friends such as Benjamin Newton, Charles Wadsworth, Samuel Bowles, editor of the Springfield *Republican*, and his wife; her friends Kate Anthon and Helen Hunt Jackson, the distant but significant figures of Elizabeth Barrett, the Brontës, George Eliot. But she carefully selected her society and controlled the disposal of her time. Not only the "gentlewomen in plush" of Amherst were excluded; Emerson visited next door but she did not go to meet him; she did not travel or receive routine visits; she avoided strangers. Given her vocation, she was neither eccentric nor quaint; she was determined to survive, to use her powers, to practice necessary economies.

Suppose Jonathan Edwards had been born a woman; suppose William James, for that matter, had been born a woman? (The invalid seclusion of his sister Alice is suggestive.) Even from men, New England took its psychic toll; many of its geniuses seemed peculiar in one way or another, particularly along the lines of social intercourse. Hawthorne, until he married, took his meals in his bedroom, apart from the family. Thoreau insisted on the values both of solitude and of geographical restriction, boasting that "I have traveled much in Concord." Emily Dickinson—viewed by her bemused contemporary Thomas Higginson as "partially cracked," by the twentieth century as fey or pathological—has increasingly struck me as a practical woman, exercising her gift as she had to, making choices. I have come to imagine her as somehow too strong for her environment, a figure of powerful will, not at all frail or breathless, someone whose personal dimensions would be felt in a household. She was her father's favorite daughter though she professed being afraid of him. Her sister dedicated herself to the everyday domestic labors which would free Dickinson to write. (Dickinson herself baked the bread, made jellies and gingerbread, nursed her mother through a long illness, was a skilled horticulturalist who grew pomegranates, calla lilies, and other exotica in her New England greenhouse.)

Upstairs at last: I stand in the room which for Emily Dickinson was "freedom." The best bedroom in the house, a corner room, sunny, overlooking the main street of Amherst in front, the way to her brother Austin's house on the side. Here, at a small table with one drawer, she wrote most of her poems. Here she read Elizabeth Barrett's *Aurora Leigh*, a woman poet's narrative poem of a woman poet's life; also George Eliot; Emerson; Carlyle; Shakespeare; Charlotte and Emily Brontë. Here I become, again, an insect, vibrating at the frames of windows, clinging to panes of glass, trying to connect. The scent here is very powerful. Here in this white-curtained, high-ceilinged room, a red-haired woman with hazel eyes and a contralto voice wrote poems about volcanoes, deserts, eternity, suicide, physical passion, wild beasts, rape, power, madness, separation, the daemon, the grave. Here, with a darning needle, she bound these poems—heavily emended and often in variant versions—into booklets, secured with darning thread, to be found and read after her death. Here she knew "freedom," listening from above-stairs to a visitor's piano-playing, escaping from the pantry where she was mistress of the household bread and puddings, watching, you feel, watching ceaselessly, the life of sober Main Street below. From this room she glided downstairs, her hand on the polished bannister, to meet the complacent magazine editor, Thomas Higginson, unnerve him while claiming she herself was unnerved. "Your scholar," she signed herself in letters to him. But she was an independent scholar, used his criticism selectively, saw him rarely and always on *her* premises. It was a life deliberately organized on her terms. The terms she had been handed by society—Calvinist Protestantism, Romanticism, the nineteenth-century corseting of women's bodies, choices, and sexuality—could spell insanity to a woman genius. What this one had to do was retranslate her own unorthodox, subversive, sometimes volcanic propensities into a dialect called metaphor: her native lan-

guage. "Tell all the Truth—but tell it Slant—." It is always what is
under pressure in us, especially under pressure of concealment—
that explodes in poetry.

The women and men in her life she equally converted into metaphor. The masculine pronoun in her poems can refer simultaneously
to many aspects of the "masculine" in the patriarchal world—the
god she engages in dialogue, again on *her* terms; her own creative
powers, unsexing for a woman, the male power-figures in her immediate environment—the lawyer Edward Dickinson, her brother Austin, the preacher Wadsworth, the editor Bowles—it is far too limiting
to trace that "He" to some specific lover, although that was the chief
obsession of the legend-mongers for more than half a century. Obviously, Dickinson was attracted by and interested in men whose
minds had something to offer her; she was, it is by now clear, equally
attracted by and interested in women whose minds had something to
offer. There are many poems to and about women, and some which
exist in two versions with alternate sets of pronouns. Her latest biographer, Richard Sewall, rejecting an earlier Freudian biographer's
theory that Dickinson was essentially a psychopathological case, the
by-product of which happened to be poetry, creates a context in
which the importance, and validity, of Dickinson's attachments to
women may now, at last, be seen in full. She was always stirred by
the existences of women like George Eliot or Elizabeth Barrett, who
possessed strength of mind, articulateness, and energy. (She once
characterized Elizabeth Fry and Florence Nightingale as "holy"—
one suspects she merely meant, "great.")

But of course Dickinson's relationships with women were more
than intellectual. They were deeply charged, and the sources both of
passionate joy and pain. We are only beginning to be able to consider then in a social and historical context. The historian Carroll
Smith-Rosenberg has shown that there was far less taboo on intense,
even passionate and sensual, relationships between women in the
American nineteenth-century "female world of love and ritual," as
she terms it, than there was later in the twentieth century. Women
expressed their attachments to other women both physically and verbally; a marriage did not dilute the strength of a female friendship, in
which two women often shared the same bed during long visits, and
wrote letters articulate with both physical and emotional longing.

The nineteenth-century close woman friend, according to the many diaries and letters Smith-Rosenberg has studied, might be a far more important figure in a woman's life than the nineteenth-century husband. None of this was perceived or condemned as "lesbianism." [1] We will understand Emily Dickinson better, read her poetry more perceptively, when the Freudian imputation of scandal and aberrance in women's love for women has been supplanted by a more informed, less misogynistic attitude toward women's experiences with each other.

But who, if you read through the seventeen hundred and seventy-five poems—who—woman or man—could have passed through that imagination and not come out transmuted? Given the space created by her in that corner room, with its window-light, its potted plants and work-table, given that personality, capable of imposing its terms on a household, on a whole community, what single theory could hope to contain her, when she'd put it all together in that space?

"Matty: here's freedom," I hear her saying as I speed back to Boston along the turnpike, as I slip the ticket into the toll-collector's hand. I am thinking of a confined space in which the genius of the nineteenth-century female mind in America moved, inventing a language more varied, more compressed, more dense with implications, more complex of syntax, than any American poetic language to date; in the trail of that genius my mind has been moving, and with its language and images my mind still has to reckon, as the mind of a woman poet in America today.

In 1971, a postage stamp was issued in honor of Dickinson; the portrait derives from the one existing daguerrotype of her, with straight, center-parted hair, eyes staring somewhere beyond the camera, hands poised around a nosegay of flowers, in correct nineteenth-century style. On the first-day-of-issue envelope sent me by a friend there is, besides the postage stamp, an engraving of the poet as popular fancy has preferred her, in a white lace ruff and with hair as bouffant as if she had just stepped from a Boston beauty-parlor. The poem chosen to represent her work to the American public is engraved, alongside a dew-gemmed rose, below the portrait:

[1] "The Female World of Love and Ritual: Relations between Women in Nineteenth-Century America," *Signs*, vol. 1, no. 1.

If I can stop one heart from breaking
I shall not live in vain
If I can ease one life the aching
Or cool one pain
Or help one fainting robin
Unto his nest again
I shall not live in vain.

Now, this is extremely strange. It is a fact that, in 1864, Emily
Dickinson wrote this verse; and it is a verse which a hundred or more
nineteenth-century versifiers could have written. In its undistinguished language, as in its conventional sentiment, it is remarkably untypical of the poet. Had she chosen to write many poems like
this one we would have no "problem" of nonpublication, of editing,
of estimating the poet at her true worth. Certainly the sentiment—a
contented and unambiguous altruism—is one which even today
might in some quarters be accepted as fitting from a female ver-
sifier—a kind of Girl Scout prayer. But we are talking about the
woman who wrote:

He fumbles at your Soul
As Players at the Keys
Before they drop full Music on—
He stuns you by degrees—
Prepares your brittle Nature
For the Ethereal Blow
By fainter Hammers—further heard—
Then nearer—Then so slow
Your breath has time to straighten—
Your brain—to bubble Cool—
Deals—One—imperial—Thunderbolt—
That scalps your naked Soul—

When Winds take Forests in their Paws—
The Universe—is still—

(#315)

Much energy has been invested in trying to identify a concrete,
flesh-and-blood male lover whom Dickinson is supposed to have
renounced, and to the loss of whom can be traced the secret of her

seclusion and the vein of much of her poetry. But the real question, given that the art of poetry is an art of transformation, is how this woman's mind and imagination may have used the masculine element in the world at large, or those elements personified as masculine—including the men she knew; how her relationship to this reveals itself in her images and language. In a patriarchal culture, specifically the Judeo-Christian, quasi-Puritan culture of nineteenth-century New England in which Dickinson grew up, still inflamed with religious revivals, and where the sermon was still an active, if perishing, literary form, the equation of divinity with maleness was so fundamental that it is hardly surprising to find Dickinson, like many an early mystic, blurring erotic with religious experience and imagery. The poem I just read has intimations both of seduction and rape merged with the intense force of a religious experience. But are these metaphors for each other, or for something more intrinsic to Dickinson? Here is another:

> He put the Belt around my life—
> I heard the Buckle snap—
> And turned away, imperial,
> My Lifetime folding up—
> Deliberate, as a Duke would do
> A Kingdom's Title Deed—
> Henceforth, a Dedicated sort—
> A member of the Cloud.
>
> Yet not too far to come at call—
> And do the little Toils
> That make the Circuit of the Rest—
> And deal occasional smiles
> To lives that stoop to notice mine—
> And kindly ask it in—
> Whose invitation, know you not
> For Whom I must decline?
>
> (#273)

These two poems are about possession, and they seem to me a poet's poems—that is, they are about the poet's relationship to her own power, which is exteriorized in masculine form, much as masculine poets have invoked the female Muse. In writing at all—particularly an unorthodox and original poetry like Dickinson's—women have often felt in danger of losing their status as women. And this status has always been defined in terms of relationship to men—as daughter, sister, bride, wife, mother, mistress, Muse. Since the most powerful figures in patriarchal culture have been men, it seems natural that Dickinson would assign a masculine gender to that in herself which did not fit in with the conventional ideology of womanliness. To recognize and acknowledge our own interior power has always been a path mined with risks for women; to acknowledge that power and commit oneself to it as Emily Dickinson did was an immense decision.

Most of us, unfortunately, have been exposed in the schoolroom to Dickinson's "little-girl" poems, her kittenish tones, as in "I'm Nobody! Who Are You?" (a poem whose underlying anger translates itself into archness) or

> I hope the Father in the skies
> Will lift his little girl—
> Old fashioned—naughty—everything—
> Over the stile of "Pearl."

                                                                    (#70)

or the poems about bees and robins. One critic—Richard Chase—has noted that in the nineteenth century "one of the careers open to women was perpetual childhood." A strain in Dickinson's letters and some—though by far a minority—of her poems was a self-diminutivization, almost as if to offset and deny—or even disguise—her actual dimensions as she must have experienced them. And this emphasis on her own "littleness," along with the deliberate strangeness of her tactics of seclusion, have been, until recently, accepted as the prevailing character of the poet: the fragile poetess in white, sending flowers and poems by messenger to unseen friends, letting down baskets of gingerbread to the neighborhood children from her bedroom window; writing, but somehow naively. John Crowe Ransom, arguing for the editing and standardization of Dickinson's punctuation and typography, calls her "a little home-keeping person" who, "while she had a proper notion of the final destiny of her poems . . .

was not one of those poets who had advanced to that later stage of operations where manuscripts are prepared for the printer, and the poet's diction has to make concessions to the publisher's style-book." (In short, Emily Dickinson did not wholly know her trade, and Ransom believes a "publisher's style-book" to have the last word on poetic diction.) He goes on to print several of her poems, altered by him "with all possible forbearance." What might, in a male writer— a Thoreau, let us say, or a Christopher Smart or William Blake— seem a legitimate strangeness, a unique intention, has been in one of our two major poets devalued into a kind of naiveté, girlish ignorance, feminine lack of professionalism, just as the poet herself has been made into a sentimental object. ("Most of us are half in love with this dead girl," confesses Archibald MacLeish. Dickinson was fifty-five when she died.)

It is true that more recent critics, including her most recent biographer, have gradually begun to approach the poet in terms of her greatness rather than her littleness, the decisiveness of her choices instead of the surface oddities of her life or the romantic crises of her legend. But unfortunately anthologists continue to plagiarize other anthologies, to reprint her in edited, even bowdlerized versions; the popular image of her and of her work lags behind the changing consciousness of scholars and specialists. There still does not exist a selection from her poems which depicts her in her fullest range. Dickinson's greatness cannot be measured in terms of twenty-five or fifty or even five hundred "perfect" lyrics; it has to be seen as the accumulation it is. Poets, even, are not always acquainted with the full dimensions of her work, or the sense one gets, reading in the one-volume complete edition (let alone the three-volume variorum edition) of a mind engaged in a lifetime's musing on essential problems of language, identity, separation, relationship, the integrity of the self; a mind capable of describing psychological states more accurately than any poet except Shakespeare. I have been surprised at how narrowly her work, still, is known by women who are writing poetry, how much her legend has gotten in the way of her being repossessed, as a source and a foremother.

I know that for me, reading her poems as a child and then as a young girl already seriously writing poetry, she was a problematic figure. I first read her in the selection heavily edited by her niece which

appeared in 1937; a later and fuller edition appeared in 1945 when I
was sixteen, and the complete, unbowdlerized edition by Johnson
did not appear until fifteen years later. The publication of each of
these editions was crucial to me in successive decades of my life.
More than any other poet, Emily Dickinson seemed to tell me that
the intense inner event, the personal and psychological, was inseparable from the universal; that there was a range for psychological poetry beyond mere self-expression. Yet the legend of the life was
troubling, because it seemed to whisper that a woman who undertook such explorations must pay with renunciation, isolation, and
incorporeality. With the publication of the *Complete Poems*, the
legend seemed to recede into unimportance beside the unquestionable power and importance of the mind revealed there. But taking possession of Emily Dickinson is still no simple matter.

The 1945 edition, entitled *Bolts of Melody*, took its title from a
poem which struck me at the age of sixteen and which still, thirty
years later, arrests my imagination:

> I would not paint—a picture—
> I'd rather be the One
> Its bright impossibility
> To dwell—delicious—on—
> And wonder how the fingers feel
> Whose rare—celestial—stir
> Evokes so sweet a Torment—
> Such sumptuous—Despair—
>
> I would not talk, like Cornets—
> I'd rather be the One
> Raised softly to the Ceilings—
> And out, and easy on—
> Through Villages of Ether
> Myself endured Balloon
> By but a lip of Metal
> The pier to my Pontoon—
>
> Nor would I be a Poet—
> It's finer—own the Ear—
> Enamored—impotent—content—
> The License to revere,
> A privilege so awful

> What would the Dower be,
> Had I the Art to stun myself
> With Bolts of Melody!

(#505)

This poem is about choosing an orthodox "feminine" role: the receptive rather than the creative; viewer rather than painter, listener rather than musician; acted-upon rather than active. Yet even while ostensibly choosing this role she wonders "how the fingers feel/ whose rare-celestial—stir—/ Evokes so sweet a Torment—" and the "feminine" role is praised in a curious sequence of adjectives: "Enamored—*impotent*—content—." The strange paradox of this poem— its exquisite irony—is that it is about choosing not to be a poet, a poem which is gainsaid by no fewer than one thousand seven hundred and seventy-five poems made during the writer's life, including itself. Moreover, the images of the poem rise to a climax (like the Balloon she evokes) but the climax happens as she describes, not what it is to be the receiver, but the maker and receiver at once: "A Privilege so awful/ What would the Dower be/ Had I the Art to stun myself/ With Bolts of Melody!"—a climax which recalls the poem: "He fumbles at your Soul/ As Players at the Keys/ Before they drop full Music on—" And of course, in writing those lines she possesses herself of that privilege and that Dower. I have said that this is a poem of exquisite ironies. It is, indeed, though in a very different mode, related to Dickinson's "little-girl" strategy. The woman who feels herself to be Vesuvius at home has need of a mask, at least, of innocuousness and of containment.

> On my volcano grows the Grass
> A meditative spot—
> An acre for a Bird to choose
> Would be the General thought—
>
> How red the Fire rocks below—
> How insecure the sod
> Did I disclose
> Would populate with awe my solitude.

(#1677)

Power, even masked, can still be perceived as destructive.

> A still—Volcano—Life—
> That flickered in the night—
> When it was dark enough to do
> Without erasing sight—
>
> A quiet—Earthquake style—
> Too subtle to suspect
> By natures this side Naples—
> The North cannot detect
>
> The Solemn—Torrid—Symbol—
> The lips that never lie—
> Whose hissing Corals part—and shut—
> And Cities—ooze away—

(#601)

Dickinson's biographer and editor Thomas Johnson has said that she often felt herself possessed by a daemonic force, particularly in the years 1861 and 1862 when she was writing at the height of her drive. There are many poems besides "He put the Belt around my Life" which could be read as poems of possession by the daemon—poems which can also be, and have been, read, as poems of possession by the deity, or by a human lover. I suggest that a woman's poetry about her relationship to her daemon—her own active, creative power—has in patriarchal culture used the language of heterosexual love or patriarchal theology. Ted Hughes tells us that

> the eruption of [Dickinson's] imagination and poetry followed when she shifted her passion, with the energy of desperation, from [the] lost man onto his only possible substitute,—the Universe in its Divine aspect. . . . Thereafter, the marriage that had been denied in the real world, went forward in the spiritual . . . just as the Universe in its Divine aspect became the mirror-image of her "husband," so the whole religious dilemma of New England, at that most critical moment in history, became the mirror-image of her relationship to him, of her "marriage" in fact. [2]

[2] Hughes, ed., A Choice of Emily Dickinson's Verse (London: Faber & Faber, 1968), p. 11.

This seems to me to miss the point on a grand scale. There are facts we need to look at. First, Emily Dickinson did not marry. And her nonmarrying was neither a pathological retreat as John Cody sees it, nor probably even a conscious decision; it was a fact in her life as in her contemporary Christina Rossetti's; both women had more primary needs. Second: unlike Rossetti, Dickinson did not become a religiously dedicated woman; she was heretical, heterodox, in her religious opinions, and stayed away from church and dogma. What, in fact, *did* she allow to "put the Belt around her Life"—what *did* wholly occupy her mature years and possess her? For "Whom" did she decline the invitations of other lives? The writing of poetry. Nearly two thousand poems. Three hundred and sixty-six poems in the year of her fullest power. What was it like to be writing poetry you knew (and I am sure she did know) was of a class by itself—to be fueled by the energy it took first to confront, then to condense that range of psychic experience into that language; then to copy out the poems and lay them in a trunk, or send a few here and there to friends or relatives as occasional verse or as gestures of confidence? I am sure she knew who she was, as she indicates in this poem:

> Myself was formed—a Carpenter—
> An unpretending time
> My Plane—and I, together wrought
> Before a Builder came—
>
> To measure our attainments
> Had we the Art of Boards
> Sufficiently developed—He'd hire us
> At Halves—
>
> My Tools took Human—Faces—
> The Bench, where we had toiled—
> Against the Man—persuaded—
> We—Temples Build—I said—

(#488)

This a poem of the great year 1862, the year in which she first sent a few poems to Thomas Higginson for criticism. Whether it antedates or postdates that occasion is unimportant; it is a poem of knowing one's measure, regardless of the judgments of others.

There are many poems which carry the weight of this knowledge.
Here is another one:

> I'm ceded—I've stopped being Theirs—
> The name They dropped upon my face
> With water, in the country church
> Is finished using, now,
> And They can put it with my Dolls,
> My childhood, and the string of spools,
> I've finished threading—too—
>
> Baptized before, without the choice,
> But this time, consciously, of Grace—
> Unto supremest name—
> Called to my Full—The Crescent dropped—
> Existence's whole Arc, filled up,
> With one small Diadem.
>
> My second Rank—too small the first—
> Crowned—Crowing—on my Father's breast—
> A half unconscious Queen—
> But this time—Adequate—Erect—
> With Will to choose, or to reject—
> And I choose, just a Crown—

                                                    (#508)

Now, this poem partakes of the imagery of being "twice-born" or, in
Christian liturgy, "confirmed"—and if this poem had been written
by Christina Rossetti I would be inclined to give more weight to a
theological reading. But it was written by Emily Dickinson, who
used the Christian metaphor far more than she let it use her. This is
a poem of great pride—not pridefulness, but *self*-confirmation—and
it is curious how little Dickinson's critics, perhaps misled by her
diminutives, have recognized the will and pride in her poetry. It is a
poem of movement from childhood to womanhood, of transcending
the patriarchal condition of bearing her father's name and "crow-
ing—on my Father's breast—." She is now a conscious Queen
"Adequate—Erect/ With Will to choose, or to reject—."

There is one poem which is the real "onlie begetter" of my
thoughts here about Dickinson; a poem I have mused over, repeated
to myself, taken into myself over many years. I think it is a poem

about possession by the daemon, about the dangers and risks of such possession if you are a woman, about the knowledge that power in a woman can seem destructive, and that you cannot live without the daemon once it has possessed you. The archetype of the daemon as masculine is beginning to change, but it has been real for women up until now. But this woman poet also perceives herself as a lethal weapon:

> My life had stood—a Loaded Gun—
> In Corners—till a Day
> The Owner passed—identified—
> And carried Me away—
>
> And now We roam in Sovereign Woods—
> And now We hunt the Doe—
> And every time I speak for Him—
> The Mountains straight reply—
>
> And do I smile, such cordial light
> Upon the Valley glow—
> It is as a Vesuvian face
> Had let its pleasure through—
>
> And when at Night—Our good Day done—
> I guard My Master's Head—
> 'Tis better than the Eider-Duck's
> Deep Pillow—to have shared—
>
> To foe of His—I'm deadly foe—
> None stir the second time—
> On whom I lay a Yellow Eye—
> Or an emphatic Thumb—
>
> Though I than He—may longer live
> He longer must—than I—
> For I have but the power to kill,
> Without—the power to die—

(#754)

Here the poet sees herself as split, not between anything so simple as "masculine" and "feminine" identity but between the hunter, admittedly masculine, but also a human person, an active, willing being, and the gun—an object, condemned to remain inactive until the hunter—the *owner*—takes possession of it. The gun contains an energy capable of rousing echoes in the mountains and lighting up the valleys; it is also deadly, "Vesuvian"; it is also its owner's defender against the "foe." It is the gun, furthermore, who *speaks for him*. If there is a female consciousness in this poem it is buried deeper than the images: it exists in the ambivalence toward power, which is extreme. Active willing and creation in women are forms of aggression, and aggression is both "the power to kill" and punishable by death. The union of gun with hunter embodies the danger of identifying and taking hold of her forces, not least that in so doing she risks defining herself—and being defined—as aggressive, as unwomanly ("and now we hunt the Doe"), and as potentially lethal. That which she experiences in herself as energy and potency can also be experienced as pure destruction. The final stanza, with its precarious balance of phrasing, seems a desperate attempt to resolve the ambivalence; but, I think, it is no resolution, only a further extension of ambivalence.

> Though I than He—may longer live
> He longer must—than I—
> For I have but the power to kill,
> Without—the power to die—

The poet experiences herself as loaded gun, imperious energy; yet without the Owner, the possessor, she is merely lethal. Should that possession abandon her—but the thought is unthinkable: "He longer *must* than I." The pronoun is masculine; the antecedent is what Keats called "The Genius of Poetry."

I do not pretend to have—I don't even wish to have—explained this poem, accounted for its every image; it will reverberate with new tones long after my words about it have ceased to matter. But I think that for us, at this time, it is a central poem in understanding Emily Dickinson, and ourselves, and the condition of the woman artist, particularly in the nineteenth century. It seems likely that the nineteenth-century woman poet, especially, felt the medium of poetry as dangerous, in ways that the woman novelist did not feel the medium of fiction to be. In writing even such a novel of elemental sexuality

and anger as *Wuthering Heights*, Emily Brontë could at least theo-
retically separate herself from her characters; they were, after all, fic-
titious beings. Moreover, the novel is or can be a construct, planned
and organized to deal with human experiences on one level at a
time. Poetry is too much rooted in the unconscious; it presses too
close against the barriers of repression; and the nineteenth-century
woman had much to repress. It is interesting that Elizabeth Barrett
tried to fuse poetry and fiction in writing *Aurora Leigh*—perhaps
apprehending the need for fictional characters to carry the charge of
her experience as a woman artist. But with the exception of *Aurora
Leigh* and Christina Rossetti's "Goblin Market"—that extraordinary
and little-known poem drenched in oral eroticism—Emily Dickinson's is the only poetry in English by a woman of that century which
pierces so far beyond the ideology of the "feminine" and the conventions of womanly feeling. To write it at all, she had to be willing to
enter chambers of the self in which

> Ourself behind ourself, concealed—
> Should startle most—

and to relinquish control there, to take those risks, she had to create a
relationship to the outer world where she could feel in control.

It is an extremely painful and dangerous way to live—split between a publicly acceptable persona, and a part of yourself that you
perceive as the essential, the creative and powerful self, yet also as
possibly unacceptable, perhaps even monstrous.

> Much Madness is divinest Sense—
> To a discerning Eye—
> Much Sense—the starkest Madness—
> 'Tis the Majority
> In this, as All, prevail—
> Assent—and you are sane—
> Demur—you're straightway dangerous—
> And handled with a Chain—

> (#435)

For many women the stresses of this splitting have led, in a world so
ready to assert our innate passivity and to deny our independence

and creativity, to extreme consequences: the mental asylum, self-imposed silence, recurrent depression, suicide, and often severe loneliness.

Dickinson is *the* American poet whose work consisted in exploring states of psychic extremity. For a long time, as we have seen, this fact was obscured by the kinds of selections made from her work by timid if well-meaning editors. In fact, Dickinson was a great psychologist; and like every great psychologist, she began with the material she had at hand: herself. She had to possess the courage to enter, through language, states which most people deny or veil with silence.

> The first Day's Night had come—
> And grateful that a thing
> So terrible—had been endured—
> I told my Soul to sing—
>
> She said her Strings were snapt—
> Her Bow—to Atoms blown—
> And so to mend her—gave me work
> Until another Morn—
>
> And then—a Day as huge
> As Yesterdays in pairs,
> Unrolled its horror in my face—
> Until it blocked my eyes—
>
> My Brain—begun to laugh—
> I mumbled—like a fool—
> And tho' 'tis Years ago—that Day—
> My Brain keeps giggling—still.
>
> And Something's odd—within—
> That person that I was—
> And this One—do not feel the same—
> Could it be Madness—this?
>
> (#410)

Dickinson's letters acknowledge a period of peculiarly intense personal crisis; her biographers have variously ascribed it to the pangs of renunciation of an impossible love, or to psychic damage deriving from her mother's presumed depression and withdrawal after her birth. What concerns us here is the fact that she chose to probe the nature of this experience in language:

> The Soul has Bandaged moments—
> When too appalled to stir—
> She feels some ghastly Fright come up
> And stop to look at her—
>
> Salute her—with long fingers—
> Caress her freezing hair—
> Sip, Goblin, from the very lips
> The Lover—hovered—o'er—
> Unworthy, that a thought so mean
> Accost a Theme—so—fair—
>
> The soul has moments of Escape—
> When bursting all the doors—
> She dances like a Bomb, abroad,
> And swings upon the Hours. . . .
>
> The Soul's retaken moments—
> When, Felon led along,
> With shackles on the plumed feet,
> And staples, in the Song,
>
> The Horror welcomes her, again,
> These, are not brayed of Tongue—

> (#512)

In this poem, the word "Bomb" is dropped, almost carelessly, as a correlative for the soul's active, liberated states—it occurs in a context of apparent euphoria, but its implications are more than euphoric—they are explosive, destructive. The Horror from which in such moments the soul escapes has a masculine, "Goblin" form, and suggests the perverse and terrifying rape of a "Bandaged" and powerless self. In at least one poem, Dickinson depicts the actual process of suicide:

> He scanned it—staggered—
> Dropped the Loop
> To Past or Period—

Caught helpless at a sense as if
His mind were going blind—

Groped up, to see if God was there—
Groped backward at Himself—
Caressed a Trigger absently
And wandered out of Life.

(#1062)

The precision of knowledge in this brief poem is such that we must assume that Dickinson had, at least in fantasy, drifted close to that state in which the "Loop" that binds us to "Past or Period" is "Dropped" and we grope randomly at what remains of abstract notions of sense, God, or self, before—almost absent-mindedly—reaching for a solution. But it's worth noting that this is a poem in which the suicidal experience has been distanced, refined, transformed through a devastating accuracy of language. It is not suicide that is studied here, but the dissociation of self and mind and world which precedes.

Dickinson was convinced that a life worth living could be found within the mind and against the grain of external circumstance: "Reverse cannot befall/ That fine prosperity/ Whose Sources are interior—" (#395). The horror, for her, was that which set "Staples in the Song"—the numbing and freezing of the interior, a state she describes over and over:

There is a Languor of the Life
More imminent than Pain—
'Tis Pain's Successor—When the Soul
Has suffered all it can—

A Drowsiness—diffuses—
A Dimness like a Fog
Envelopes Consciousness—
As Mists—obliterate a Crag.

The Surgeon—does not blanch—at pain—
His Habit—is severe—
But tell him that it ceased to feel—
The creature lying there—

And he will tell you—skill is late—
A Mightier than He—
Has ministered before Him—
There's no Vitality.

(#396)

I think the equation surgeon-artist is a fair one here; the artist can
work with the materials of pain; she cuts to probe and heal; but she is
powerless at the point where

After great pain, a formal feeling comes—
The Nerves sit ceremonious, like Tombs—
The stiff Heart questions was it He, that bore,
And Yesterday, or Centuries before?

The Feet, mechanical, go round—
Of Ground, or Air, or Ought—
A Wooden way
Regardless grown,
A Quartz contentment, like a stone—

This is the Hour of Lead
Remembered, if outlived
As Freezing persons, recollect the Snow—
First—Chill—then Stupor—then the letting go—

(#341)

For the poet, the terror is precisely in those periods of psychic death,
when even the possibility of work is negated; her "occupation's
gone." Yet she also describes the unavailing effort to numb emotion:

Me from Myself—to banish—
Had I Art—
Impregnable my Fortress
Unto All Heart—

But since Myself—assault Me—
How have I peace
Except by subjugating
Consciousness?

> And since We're mutual Monarch
> How this be
> Except by Abdication—
> Me—of Me?

(#642)

The possibility of abdicating oneself—of ceasing to be—remains.

> Severer Service of myself
> I—hastened to demand
> To fill the awful Longitude
> Your life had left behind—
>
> I worried Nature with my Wheels
> When Hers had ceased to run—
> When she had put away Her Work
> My own had just begun.
>
> I strove to weary Brain and Bone—
> To harass to fatigue
> The glittering Retinue of nerves—
> Vitality to clog
>
> To some dull comfort Those obtain
> Who put a Head away
> They knew the Hair to—
> And forget the color of the Day—
>
> Affliction would not be appeased—
> The Darkness braced as firm
> As all my stratagem had been
> The Midnight to confirm—
>
> No Drug for Consciousness—can be—
> Alternative to die
> Is Nature's only Pharmacy
> For Being's Malady—

(#786)

Yet consciousness—not simply the capacity to suffer, but the capacity to experience intensely at every instant—creates of death not a blotting-out but a final illumination:

This Consciousness that is aware
Of Neighbors and the Sun
Will be the one aware of Death
And that itself alone

Is traversing the interval
Experience between
And most profound experiment
Appointed unto Men—

How adequate unto itself
Its properties shall be
Itself unto itself and none
Shall make discovery.

Adventure most unto itself
The Soul condemned to be—
Attended by a single Hound
Its own identity.

(#822)

The poet's relationship to her poetry has, it seems to me—and I am not speaking only of Emily Dickinson—a twofold nature. Poetic language—the poem on paper—is a concretization of the poetry of the world at large, the self, and the forces within the self; and those forces are rescued from formlessness, lucidified, and integrated in the act of writing poems. But there is a more ancient concept of the poet, which is that she is endowed to speak for those who do not have the gift of language, or to see for those who—for whatever reasons— are less conscious of what they are living through. It is as though the risks of the poet's existence can be put to some use beyond her own survival.

The Province of the Saved
Should be the Art—To save—
Through Skill obtained in Themselves—
The Science of the Grave

No Man can understand
But He that hath endured
The Dissolution—in Himself—
That Man—be qualified

To qualify Despair
To Those who failing new—
Mistake Defeat for Death—Each time—
Till acclimated—to—

(#539)

The poetry of extreme states, the poetry of danger, can allow its readers to go further in our own awareness, take risks we might not have dared; it says, at least: "Someone has been here before."

The Soul's distinct Connection
With immortality
Is best disclosed by Danger
Or quick Calamity—

As Lightning on a Landscape
Exhibits Sheets of Place—
Not yet suspected—but for Flash—
And Click—and Suddenness.

(#974)

Crumbling is not an instant's Act
A fundamental pause
Dilapidation's processes
Are organized Decays.

'Tis first a Cobweb on the Soul
A Cuticle of Dust
A Borer in the Axis
An Elemental Rust—

Ruin is formal—Devil's work
Consecutive and slow—
Fail in an instant—no man did
Slipping—is Crash's law.

(#997)

I felt a Cleaving in my Mind
As if my Brain had split—

I tried to match it—Seam by Seam—
But could not make them fit.

The thought behind, I strove to join
Unto the thought before—
But Sequence ravelled out of Sound
Like Balls—upon a Floor.

(#937)

There are many more Emily Dickinsons than I have tried to call up here. Wherever you take hold of her, she proliferates. I wish I had time here to explore her complex sense of Truth; to follow the thread we unravel when we look at the numerous and passionate poems she wrote to or about women; to probe her ambivalent feelings about fame, a subject pursued by many male poets before her; simply to examine the poems in which she is directly apprehending the natural world. No one since the seventeenth century had reflected more variously or more probingly upon death and dying. What I have tried to do here is follow through some of the origins and consequences of her choice to be, not only a poet but a woman who explored her own mind, without any of the guidelines of orthodoxy. To say "yes" to her powers was not simply a major act of nonconformity in the nineteenth century; even in our own time it has been assumed that Emily Dickinson, not patriarchal society, was "the problem." The more we come to recognize the unwritten and written laws and taboos underpinning patriarchy, the less problematical, surely, will seem the methods she chose.

Women and Honor: Some Notes on Lying (1975)

These notes were first read at the Hartwick Women Writers' Workshop, founded and directed by Beverly Tanenhaus, at Hartwick College, Oneonta, New York, in June 1975. They were published as a pamphlet by Motheroot Press in Pittsburgh, 1977; in *Heresies: A Feminist Magazine of Art and Politics*, vol. 1, no. 1; and in a French translation by the Québecois feminist press, Les Editions du Remue-Ménage, 1979.

It is clear that among women we need a new ethics; as women, a new morality. The problem of speech, of language, continues to be primary. For if in our speaking we are breaking silences long established, "liberating ourselves from our secrets" in the words of Beverly Tanenhaus, this is in itself a first kind of action. I wrote *Women and Honor* in an effort to make myself more honest, and to understand the terrible negative power of the lie in relationships between women. Since it was published, other women have spoken and written of things I did not include: Michelle Cliff's "Notes on Speechlessness" in *Sinister Wisdom* no. 5 led Catherine Nicolson (in the same issue) to write of the power of "deafness," the frustration of our speech by those who do not want to hear what we have to say. Nelle Morton has written of the act of "hearing each other into speech."* How do we listen? How do we make it possible for another to break her silence? These are some of the questions which follow on the ones I have raised here.

~~~~~~~~~

* Nelle Morton, "Beloved Image!", paper delivered at the National Conference of the American Academy of Religion, San Francisco, California, December 28, 1977.

(These notes are concerned with relationships between and among women. When "personal relationship" is referred to, I mean a relationship between two women. It will be clear in what follows when I am talking about women's relationships with men.)

The old, male idea of honor. A man's "word" sufficed—to other men—without guarantee.

"Our Land Free, Our Men Honest, Our Women Fruitful"—a popular colonial toast in America.

Male honor also having something to do with killing: *I could not love thee, Dear, so much/Lov'd I not Honour more,* ("To Lucasta, On Going to the Wars"). Male honor as something needing to be avenged: hence, the duel.

Women's honor, something altogether else: virginity, chastity, fidelity to a husband. Honesty in women has not been considered important. We have been depicted as generically whimsical, deceitful, subtle, vacillating. And we have been rewarded for lying.

Men have been expected to tell the truth about facts, not about feelings. They have not been expected to talk about feelings at all.

Yet even about facts they have continually lied.

We assume that politicians are without honor. We read their statements trying to crack the code. The scandals of their politics: not that men in high places lie, only that they do so with such indifference, so endlessly, still expecting to be believed. We are accustomed to the contempt inherent in the political lie.

• • •

To discover that one has been lied to in a personal relationship, however, leads one to feel a little crazy.

• • •

Lying is done with words, and also with silence.

The woman who tells lies in her personal relationships may or may not plan or invent her lying. She may not even think of what she is doing in a calculated way.

A subject is raised which the liar wishes buried. She has to go downstairs, her parking meter will have run out. Or, there is a telephone call she ought to have made an hour ago.

She is asked, point-blank, a question which may lead into painful talk: "How do you feel about what is happening between us?" Instead of trying to describe her feelings in their ambiguity and confusion, she asks, "How do *you* feel?" The other, because she is trying to establish a ground of openness and trust, begins describing her own feelings. Thus the liar learns more than she tells.

And she may also tell herself a lie: that she is concerned with the other's feelings, not with her own.

But the liar is concerned with her own feelings.

The liar lives in fear of losing control. She cannot even desire a relationship without manipulation, since to be vulnerable to another person means for her the loss of control.

The liar has many friends, and leads an existence of great loneliness.

• • •

The liar often suffers from amnesia. Amnesia is the silence of the unconscious.

To lie habitually, as a way of life, is to lose contact with the unconscious. It is like taking sleeping pills, which confer sleep but blot out dreaming. The unconscious wants truth. It ceases to speak to those who want something else more than truth.

In speaking of lies, we come inevitably to the subject of truth. There is nothing simple or easy about this idea. There is no "the truth," "a truth"—truth is not one thing, or even a system. It is an increasing complexity. The pattern of the carpet is a surface. When we look closely, or when we become weavers, we learn of the tiny multiple threads unseen in the overall pattern, the knots on the underside of the carpet.

This is why the effort to speak honestly is so important. Lies are usually attempts to make everything simpler—for the liar—than it really is, or ought to be.

In lying to others we end up lying to ourselves. We deny the importance of an event, or a person, and thus deprive ourselves of a part of our lives. Or we use one piece of the past or present to screen out another. Thus we lose faith even with our own lives.

The unconscious wants truth, as the body does. The complexity and fecundity of dreams come from the complexity and fecundity of the unconscious struggling to fulfill that desire. The complexity and fecundity of poetry come from the same struggle.

• • •

An honorable human relationship—that is, one in which two people have the right to use the word "love"—is a process, delicate, violent, often terrifying to both persons involved, a process of refining the truths they can tell each other.

It is important to do this because it breaks down human self-delusion and isolation.

It is important to do this because in so doing we do justice to our own complexity.

It is important to do this because we can count on so few people to go that hard way with us.

• • •

I come back to the questions of women's honor. Truthfulness has not been considered important for women, as long as we have remained physically faithful to a man, or chaste.

We have been expected to lie with our bodies: to bleach, redden, unkink or curl our hair, pluck eyebrows, shave armpits, wear padding in various places or lace ourselves, take little steps, glaze finger and toe nails, wear clothes that emphasized our helplessness.

We have been required to tell different lies at different times, depending on what the men of the time needed to hear. The Victorian wife or the white southern lady, who were expected to have no sensuality, to "lie still"; the twentieth-century "free" woman who is expected to fake orgasms.

We have had the truth of our bodies withheld from us or distorted; we have been kept in ignorance of our most intimate places. Our instincts have been punished: clitoridectomies for "lustful" nuns or for "difficult" wives. It has been difficult, too, to know the lies of our complicity from the lies we believed.

The lie of the "happy marriage," of domesticity—we have been complicit, have acted out the fiction of a well-lived life, until the day we testify in court of rapes, beatings, psychic cruelties, public and private humiliations.

Patriarchal lying has manipulated women both through falsehood and through silence. Facts we needed have been withheld from us. False witness has been borne against us.

And so we must take seriously the question of truthfulness between women, truthfulness among women. As we cease to lie with our bodies, as we cease to take on faith what men have said about us, is a truly womanly idea of honor in the making?

• • •

Women have been forced to lie, for survival, to men. How to unlearn this among other women?

"Women have always lied to each other."
"Women have always whispered the truth to each other."
Both of these axioms are true.

"Women have always been divided against each other."
"Women have always been in secret collusion."
Both of these axioms are true.

In the struggle for survival we tell lies. To bosses, to prison guards, the police, men who have power over us, who legally own us and our children, lovers who need us as proof of their manhood.

There is a danger run by all powerless people: that we forget we are lying, or that lying becomes a weapon we carry over into relationships with people who do not have power over us.

• • •

I want to reiterate that when we talk about women and honor, or women and lying, we speak within the context of male lying, the lies of the powerful, the lie as false source of power.

Women have to think whether we want, in our relationships with each other, the kind of power that can be obtained through lying.

Women have been driven mad, "gaslighted," for centuries by the refutation of our experience and our instincts in a culture which validates only male experience. The truth of our bodies and our minds has been mystified to us. We therefore have a primary obligation to each other: not to undermine each others' sense of reality for the sake of expediency; not to gaslight each other.

Women have often felt insane when cleaving to the truth of our experience. Our future depends on the sanity of each of us, and we have a profound stake, beyond the personal, in the project of describing our reality as candidly and fully as we can to each other.

• • •

There are phrases which help us not to admit we are lying: "my privacy," "nobody's business but my own." The choices that underlie these phrases may indeed be justified; but we ought to think about the full meaning and consequences of such language.

Women's love for women has been represented almost entirely through silence and lies. The institution of heterosexuality has forced the lesbian to dissemble, or be labeled a pervert, a criminal, a sick or dangerous woman, etc., etc. The lesbian, then, has often been forced to lie, like the prostitute or the married women.

Does a life "in the closet"—lying, perhaps of necessity, about ourselves to bosses, landlords, clients, colleagues, family, because the law and public opinion are founded on a lie—does this, can it, spread into private life, so that lying (described as *discretion*) becomes an easy way to avoid conflict or complication? can it become a strategy so ingrained that it is used even with close friends and lovers?

Heterosexuality as an institution has also drowned in silence the erotic feelings between women. I myself lived half a lifetime in the lie of that denial. That silence makes us all, to some degree, into liars.

When a woman tells the truth she is creating the possibility for more truth around her.

• • •

The liar leads an existence of unutterable loneliness.

The liar is afraid.

But we are all afraid: without fear we become manic, hubristic, self-destructive. What is this particular fear that possesses the liar?

She is afraid that her own truths are not good enough.

She is afraid, not so much of prison guards or bosses, but of something unnamed within her.

The liar fears the void.

The void is not something created by patriarchy, or racism, or capitalism. It will not fade away with any of them. It is part of every woman.

"The dark core," Virginia Woolf named it, writing of her mother. The dark core. It is beyond personality; beyond who loves us or hates us.

We begin out of the void, out of darkness and emptiness. It is part of the cycle understood by the old pagan religions, that materialism denies. Out of death, rebirth; out of nothing, something.

The void is the creatrix, the matrix. It is not mere hollowness and anarchy. But in women it has been identified with lovelessness, barrenness, sterility. We have been urged to fill our "emptiness" with children. We are not supposed to go down into the darkness of the core.

Yet, if we can risk it, the something born of that nothing is the beginning of our truth.

The liar in her terror wants to fill up the void, with anything. Her lies are a denial of her fear; a way of maintaining control.

· · ·

Why do we feel slightly crazy when we realize we have been lied to in a relationship?

We take so much of the universe on trust. You tell me: "In 1950 I lived on the north side of Beacon Street in Somerville." You tell me: "She and I were lovers, but for months now we have only been good friends." You tell me: "It is seventy degrees outside and the sun is shining." Because I love you, because there is not even a question of lying between us, I take these accounts of the universe on trust: your address twenty-five years ago, your relationship with someone I know only by sight, this morning's weather. I fling unconscious tendrils of belief, like slender green threads, across statements such as these, statements made so unequivocally, which have no tone or shadow of tentativeness. I build them into the mosaic of my world. I allow my universe to change in minute, significant ways, on the basis of things you have said to me, of my trust in you.

I also have faith that you are telling me things it is important I should know; that you do not conceal facts from me in an effort to spare me, or yourself, pain.

Or, at the very least, that you will say, "There are things I am not telling you."

When we discover that someone we trusted can be trusted no longer, it forces us to reexamine the universe, to question the whole instinct and concept of trust. For awhile, we are thrust back onto some bleak, jutting ledge, in a dark pierced by sheets of fire, swept by sheets of rain, in a world before kinship, or naming, or tenderness exist; we are brought close to formlessness.

• • •

The liar may resist confrontation, denying that she lied. Or she may use other language: forgetfulness, privacy, the protection of someone else. Or, she may bravely declare herself a coward. This allows her to go on lying, since that is what cowards do. She does not say, *I was afraid*, since this would open the question of other ways of handling her fear. It would open the question of what is actually feared.

She may say, *I didn't want to cause pain*. What she really did not want is to have to deal with the other's pain. The lie is a short-cut through another's personality.

• • •

Truthfulness, honor, is not something which springs ablaze of itself; it has to be created between people.

This is true in political situations. The quality and depth of the politics evolving from a group depends in very large part on their understanding of honor.

Much of what is narrowly termed "politics" seems to rest on a longing for certainty even at the cost of honesty, for an analysis which, once given, need not be reexamined. Such is the deadendedness—for women—of Marxism in our time.

Truthfulness anywhere means a heightened complexity. But it is a movement into evolution. Women are only beginning to uncover our own truths; many of us would be grateful for some rest in that struggle, would be glad just to lie down with the sherds we have painfully unearthed, and be satisfied with those. Often I feel this like an exhaustion in my own body.

The politics worth having, the relationships worth having, demand that we delve still deeper.

• • •

The possibilities that exist between two people, or among a group of people, are a kind of alchemy. They are the most interesting thing in life. The liar is someone who keeps losing sight of these possibilities.

When relationships are determined by manipulation, by the need for control, they may possess a dreary, bickering kind of drama, but they cease to be interesting. They are repetitious; the shock of human possibilities has ceased to reverberate through them.

When someone tells me a piece of the truth which has been withheld from me, and which I needed in order to see my life more clearly, it may bring acute pain, but it can also flood me with a cold, sea-sharp wash of relief. Often such truths come by accident, or from strangers.

It isn't that to have an honorable relationship with you, I have to understand everything, or tell you everything at once, or that I can know, beforehand, everything I need to tell you.

It means that most of the time I am eager, longing for the possibility of telling you. That these possibilities may seem frightening, but not destructive, to me. That I feel strong enough to hear your tentative and groping words. That we both know we are trying, all the time, to extend the possibilities of truth between us.

The possibility of life between us.

Motherhood in Bondage
(1976)

E very great new movement in human consciousness arouses both
hope and terror. The understanding that male-female relationships have been founded on the status of the female as the property of the male, or of male-dominated institutions, continues to be
difficult for both women and men. It is painful to acknowledge that
our identity has been dictated and diminished by others, or that we
have let our identity depend on the diminishment and exploitation
of other humans. This idea still meets with the resistance that has
always risen when unsanctioned, long-stifled realities begin to stir
and assert themselves.

Resistance may take many forms. Protective deafness—the inabil-
ity to hear what is actually being said—is one. Trivialization is another: the reduction of a troubling new complexity to a caricature, or
a clinical phenomenon. A literary critic, reviewing two recent anthologies of women's poetry, declares that "the notion that the world
has been put together exclusively by men, and solely for their own
benefit, and that they have conspired together for generations to dis-
criminate against their mothers and sisters, wives and daughters,
lovers and friends, is a neurosis for which we do not yet have a
name." It is striking that, even in his denial, this writer can describe
women only as appendages to men.

In her history of birth control in America, the Marxist historian

Published on the "Op-Ed" page of the *New York Times*, November 20, 1976.

Linda Gordon writes, "For women . . . heterosexual relations are always intense, frightening, high-risk situations which ought, if a woman has any sense of self-preservation, to be carefully calculated."[1] The power politics of the relations between the sexes, long unexplored, is still a charged issue. To raise it is to cut to the core of power relations throughout society, to break down irreparably the screens of mystification between "private life" and "public affairs."

But even more central a nerve is exposed when motherhood is analyzed as a political institution. This institution—which affects each woman's personal experience—is visible in the male dispensation of birth control and abortion; the guardianship of men over children in the courts and the educational system; the subservience, through most of history, of women and children to the patriarchal father; the economic dominance of the father over the family; the usurpation of the birth process by a male medical establishment. The subjectivity of the fathers (who are also sons) has prescribed how, when, and even where women should conceive, bear, nourish, and indoctrinate their children. The experience of motherhood by women—both mothers and daughters—is only beginning to be described by women themselves.

Until very recently, the choice to be or not to be a mother was virtually unavailable to most women; even today, the possibility of choice remains everywhere in jeopardy. This elemental loss of control over her body affects every woman's right to shape the imagery and insights of her own being. We speak of women as "nonmothers" or "childless"; we do not speak of "nonfathers" or "childless men." Motherhood is admirable, however, only so long as mother and child are attached to a legal father: Motherhood out of wedlock, or under the welfare system, or lesbian motherhood, are harassed, humiliated, or neglected. In the 1970s in the United States, with 26 million children of wage-earning mothers, 8 million in female-headed households, the late nineteenth-century stereotype of the "mother at home" is still assumed as the norm—a "norm" that has, outside of a small middle-class minority, never existed.

In trying to distinguish the two strands: motherhood as *experience*,

[1] Linda Gordon, *Woman's Body, Woman's Right: A Social History of Birth Control in America* (New York: Viking Grossman, 1976).

one possible and profound experience for women, and motherhood as enforced identity and as political *institution*, I myself only slowly began to grasp the centrality of the institution, and how it connects with the dread of difference that infects all societies. Under that institution, all women are seen primarily as mothers; all mothers are expected to experience motherhood unambivalently and in accordance with patriarchal values; and the "nonmothering" woman is seen as deviant.

Since the "deviant" is outside the law, and "abnormal," the pressure on all women to assent to the "mothering" role is intense. To speak of maternal ambivalence; to examine the passionate conflicts and ambiguities of the mother-daughter relationship, and the role of the mother in indoctrinating her daughters to subservience and her sons to dominance; to identify the guilt mothers are made to feel for societal failures beyond their control; to acknowledge that a lesbian can be a mother and a mother a lesbian, contrary to popular stereotypes; to question the dictating by powerful men as to how women, especially the poor and nonwhite, shall use their bodies, or the indoctrination of women toward a one-sided emotional nurturing of men, is to challenge deeply embedded phobias and prejudices.

Such themes anger and terrify, precisely because they touch us at the quick of human existence. But to flee them, or trivialize them, to leave the emotions they arouse in us unexamined, is to flee both ourselves and the dawning hope that women *and* men may one day experience forms of love and parenthood, identity and community that will not be drenched in lies, secrets, and silence.

"It Is the Lesbian in Us . . ."
(1976)

I was born in 1929. In that year, Virginia Woolf was writing of the necessity for a literature that would reveal "that vast chamber where nobody has been"—the realm of relationships between women.

Whatever is unnamed, undepicted in images, whatever is omitted from biography, censored in collections of letters, whatever is misnamed as something else, made difficult-to-come-by, whatever is buried in the memory by the collapse of meaning under an inadequate or lying language—this will become, not merely unspoken, but *unspeakable*.

Two women, one white, one black, were the first persons I loved and who I knew loved me. Both of them sang me my first songs, told me my first stories, became my first knowledge of tenderness, passion, and, finally, rejection. Each of them, over time, surrendered me to the judgment and disposition of my father and my father's culture: white and male. My love for the white woman and the black woman became blurred with anger, contempt, and guilt. I did not know which of them had injured me; they became merged together

These remarks were read at the Modern Language Association, December 28, 1976, at an evening event cosponsored by the Women's Commission and the Gay Caucus. The purpose of the panel was to raise, before a large audience of teachers and scholars, the question of racism and homophobia in the teaching of literature, issues with which the Women's Commission had been struggling as a group for over a year. The other panelists were June Jordan, Audre Lorde, and Honor Moore.

in my inarticulate fury. I did not know that neither of them had had a choice. Nor did I know that what had happened between—and among—the three of us was important. It was *unspeakable*.

My father's library I felt as the source and site of his power. I was right. It contained Plutarch and Havelock Ellis, Ovid and Spinoza, Swinburne and Emerson. In that library I came to believe—a child's belief, but also a poet's—that language, writing, those pages of print, could teach me how to live, could tell me *what was possible*. But on the subject of woman-to-woman relationships, in Emily Dickinson's words: "My Classics veiled their faces." (And still, in most literature courses, most libraries, syllabi, curricula, young women are handed classics that veil, not only what might be possible, but what has been going on all along.)

In a striking essay, the novelist Bertha Harris has written of the silence surrounding the lesbian:

> The lesbian, without a literature, is without life. Sometimes pornographic, sometimes a mark of fear, sometimes a sentimental flourish, she . . . floats in space . . . without that attachment to earth where growth is composed.[1]

Reading her essay, I found she had described to me for the first time my own searches through literature in the past, in pursuit of a flickering, often disguised reality which came and went throughout women's books. That reality was nothing so simple and dismissible as the fact that two women might go to bed together. It was a sense of desiring oneself; above all, of choosing oneself; it was also a primary intensity between women, an intensity which in the world at large was trivialized, caricatured, or invested with evil.

Even before I wholly knew I was a lesbian, it was the lesbian in me who pursued that elusive configuration. And I believe it is the lesbian in every woman who is compelled by female energy, who gravi-

---

[1] Quoted from an unpublished paper, "The Purification of Monstrosity: The Lesbian as Literature," given at the MLA forum on "The Homosexual in Literature," 1974. For a further exploration of these themes, see Harris's article, "Notes toward Defining the Nature of Lesbian Literature," in *Heresies: A Feminist Publication on Art and Politics*, vol. 1, no. 3, fall 1977; available from *Heresies*, P.O. Box 766, Canal St. Station, New York, N.Y. 10013.

tates toward strong women, who seeks a literature that will express that energy and strength. It is the lesbian in us who drives us to feel imaginatively, render in language, grasp, the full connection between woman and woman. It is the lesbian in us who is creative, for the dutiful daughter of the fathers in us is only a hack.

It was the lesbian in me, more than the civil libertarian, or even the feminist, that pursued the memory of the first black woman I loved before I was taught whiteness, before we were forced to betray each other. And that relationship—mutual knowledge, fear, guilt, jealousy, anger, longing—between black and white women, I did not find, have not yet found, in literature, except perhaps, as a beginning, in Alice Walker's *Meridian*, and in some of Audre Lorde's poems. I found no black women at all in literature, only fantasies of them by whites, or by black men. But some women writers are now beginning to dare enter that particular chamber of the "unspeakable" and to breathe word of what we are finding there.

I go on believing in the power of literature, and also in the politics of literature. The experience of the black woman *as woman*, of the white and black woman cast as antagonists in the patriarchal drama, and of black and white women as lesbians, has been kept invisible for good reason. Our hidden, yet omnipresent lives have served some purpose by remaining hidden: not only in the white patriarchal world but within both the black and feminist communities, on the part both of black male critics, scholars, and editors, and of institutions like the Feminist Press. Both black studies and women's studies have shied away from this core of our experience, thus reinforcing the very silence out of which they have had to assert themselves. But it is the subjects, the conversations, the facts we shy away from, which claim us in the form of writer's block, as mere rhetoric, as hysteria, insomnia, and constriction of the throat.

∼∼∼∼∼∼∼

When I finished speaking, there was immediate reaction to my statement that "It is the lesbian in us who is creative, for the dutiful daughter of the fathers in us is only a hack." It became clear during the ensuing discussion that different women had heard this sentence in different ways. Some women asserted that they created out of their bisexuality, not their "female side"; others, that their creativity came from their commitment to black struggle; others, that they created out of love for their (male) children as much as out of love for women. One lesbian asserted that if "the lesbian in us" was to become a figurative term, she, as a woman who had been oppressed for physically expressing her love for women, wanted another name for who she was. Some women heard me as saying that all creation has simply a sexual basis (vide Freud) and that women can create only out of erotic experience with other women. My intention was, of course, to say something more complex.

I believe that I failed, in preparing my remarks, to allow for the intense charge of the word *lesbian*, and for all its deliquescences of meaning, ranging from "man-hater" and "pervert" to the concepts I was trying to invoke, of the self-chosen woman, the forbidden "primary intensity" between women, and also the woman who refuses to obey, who has said "no" to the fathers. I probably oversimplified the issue, given limits of time, and therefore obscured it. This experience made me more conscious than ever before of the degree to which, even for lesbians, the word *lesbian* has many resonances. Some of us would destroy the word altogether. Others would transform it, still others eagerly claim and speak it after years of being unable to utter it. Feminists have been made to fear that they will be "discredited" if perceived as lesbians; some lesbians have withdrawn or been forced into nonfeminist enclaves (such as the "gay" movement) which reject and denigrate "straight" women.

The lesbian/feminist lives in a complex, demanding realm of linguistic and relational distinctions. One of the tasks ahead of us is to begin trying to define those distinctions (and the overlap of female experience that is synchronymous with them). The meaning and significance of "separatism" is a case in point. Even as lesbian/feminists are beginning to create a philosophical and ethical analysis of separatism,* the word itself is frequently used by others loosely and pejoratively to imply that our politics and self-definitions proceed first out of hatred and rejection.

For us, the process of naming and defining is not an intellectual game, but a grasping of our experience and a key to action. The word *lesbian* must be affirmed because to discard it is to collaborate with silence and lying about our very existence; with the closet-game, the creation of the *unspeakable*.

* See Mary Daly, *Gyn/Ecology: The Metaethics of Radical Feminism* (Boston: Beacon, 1978), pp. 380–84; Marilyn Frye, "Some Thoughts on Separatism and Power," in *Sinister Wisdom*, no. 6, summer 1978. See also my note, pp. 229–30.

Conditions for Work: The
Common World of Women (1976)

. . . the common world is what we enter when we are born and what we leave behind when we die. It transcends our life-span into past and future alike; it was there before we came and will outlast our brief sojourn into it. It is what we have in common not only with those who live with us, but also with those who were here before and with those who will come after us. But such a common world can survive the coming and going of the generations only to the extent that it appears in public. It is the publicity of the public realm which can absorb and make shine through the centuries whatever men [sic] may want to save from the natural ruin of time.

—Hannah Arendt, *The Human Condition*

Women both have and have not had a common world. The mere sharing of oppression does not constitute a common world. Our thought and action, insofar as they have taken the form of difference, assertion, or rebellion, have repeatedly been obliterated, or subsumed under "human" history, which means the "public-

Written as the foreword to *Working It Out: 23 Women Artists, Scholars, and Scientists Talk about Their Lives and Work*, edited by Pamela Daniels and Sara Ruddick (New York: Pantheon Books, 1977). It was also published in *Heresies: A Feminist Publication on Art and Politics* (Lesbian Art and Artists Issue), vol. 1 no. 3, fall 1977.

ity of the public realm" created and controlled by men. Our history is the history of a majority of the species, yet the struggles of women for a "human" status have been relegated to footnotes, to the sidelines. Above all, women's relationships with women have been denied or neglected as a force in history.[1]

The essays in this book are parts of a much larger work, which we are still struggling to possess: the long process of making visible the experience of women. The tentativeness, the anxiety, sometimes approaching paralysis, the confusions, described in many of these essays by intelligent, educated, "privileged" women, are themselves evidence of the damage that can be done to creative energy by the lack of a sense of continuity, historical validation, community. Most women, it seems, have gone through their travails in a kind of spiritual isolation, alone both in the present and in ignorance of their place in any female tradition. The support of friends, of a women's group, may make survival possible; but it is not enough.

It is quite clear that the universities and the intellectual establishment intend to keep women's experience as far as possible invisible, and women's studies a barely subsidized, condescendingly tolerated ghetto. The majority of women who go through undergraduate and graduate school suffer an intellectual coercion of which they are not even consciously aware. In a world where language and naming are power, silence is oppression, is violence. Writing of the destruction of the civilization of Languedoc by the forces of the Church under Simon de Montfort, Simone Weil reminds us: "Nothing is more cruel to the past than the commonplace which asserts that spiritual values cannot be destroyed by force; on the strength of this belief, civilizations that have been destroyed by force of arms are denied the

---

[1] Joan Kelly suggests that a feminist view of history is not merely "compensatory history," a parallel to the accepted views of history as male. It means "to look at ages or movements of great social change in terms of their liberation or repression of woman's potential, their import for the advancement of her humanity as well as 'his.' The moment this is done—the moment one assumes that women are a part of humanity in the fullest sense—the period or set of events with which we deal takes on a wholly different character or meaning from the normally accepted one. Indeed, what emerges is a fairly regular pattern of relative loss of status for women in those periods of so-called progressive change." "The Social Relation of the Sexes: Methodological Implications of Women's History," in *Signs*, vol. 1, no. 4, summer 1976

name of civilization; and there is no risk of our being refuted by the dead."[2]

For spiritual values and a creative tradition to continue unbroken we need concrete artifacts, the work of hands, written words to read, images to look at, a dialogue with brave and imaginative women who came before us. In the false names of love, motherhood, natural law—false because they have not been defined by us to whom they are applied—women in patriarchy have been withheld from building a common world, except in enclaves, or through coded messages.

> The protection and preservation of the world against natural processes are among the toils which need the monotonous performance of daily repeated chores. . . . In old tales and mythological stories it has often assumed the grandeur of heroic fights against overwhelming odds, as in the account of Hercules, whose cleansing of the Augean stables is among the twelve heroic "labors." A similar connotation of heroic deeds requiring great strength and courage and performed in a fighting spirit is manifest in the mediaeval use of the word: labor, *travail*, *arbeit*. However, the daily fight in which the human body is engaged to keep the world clean and prevent its decay bears little resemblance to heroic deeds; the endurance it needs to repair every day anew the waste of yesterday is not courage, and what makes the effort painful is not danger but its relentless repetition.[3]

Hannah Arendt does not call this "woman's work." Yet it is this activity of world-protection, world-preservation, world-repair—the million tiny stitches, the friction of the scrubbing brush, the scouring cloth, the iron across the shirt, the rubbing of cloth against itself to exorcise the stain, the renewal of the scorched pot, the rusted knifeblade, the invisible weaving of a frayed and threadbare family life, the cleaning up of soil and waste left behind by men and children—that we have been charged to do "for love," not merely unpaid, but unacknowledged by the political philosophers. Women are not described as "working" when we create the essential conditions for the work of men; we are supposed to be acting out of love, instinct, or devotion to some higher cause than self.

[2] Simone Weil, *Selected Essays*, *1934–1943*, Richard Rees, trans. (New York: Oxford, 1962), p. 43.

[3] Hannah Arendt, *The Human Condition* (Chicago: University of Chicago, 1958), p. 55.

Arendt tells us that the Greeks despised all labor of the body neces-
sitated by biological needs. It was to spare themselves such labor that
men kept slaves—not as a means of cheaper production. "Contempt
for laboring, originally arising out of a passionate striving for freedom
from necessity and a no less passionate impatience with every effort
that left no trace, no monument, no great work worthy to remem-
brance, spread with the increasing demands of *polis* life upon the
time of the citizens [i.e., males] and its insistence on their abstention
from all but political activities."[4]

And, in the aside of a footnote: "Women and slaves belonged and
lived together . . . no woman, not even the wife of the household
head, lived among her equals—other free women—so that rank
depended much less on birth than on 'occupation' or function. . . ."
According to the index, this footnote is the last reference to women,
on page 73 of a volume of 325 pages on *The Human Condition*, written by a woman.

Every effort that left no trace . . . The efforts of women in labor,
giving birth to stillborn children, children who must die of plague or
by infanticide; the efforts of women to keep filth and decay at bay,
children decently clothed, to produce the clean shirt in which the
man walks out daily into the common world of men, the efforts to
raise children against the attritions of racist and sexist schooling,
drugs, sexual exploitation, the brutalization and killing of barely
grown boys in war. There is still little but contempt and indifference
for this kind of work, these efforts. (The phrase "wages for housework" has the power to shock today that the phrase "free love" possessed a century ago.)

II

There is a natural temptation to escape if we can, to close the door
behind us on this despised realm which threatens to engulf all
women, whether as mothers, or in marriage, or as the invisible, ill-
paid sustainers of the professionals and social institutions. There is a
natural fear that if we do not enter the common world of men, as
asexual beings or as "exceptional" women, do not enter it on its

4 Ibid., pp. 81–83.

terms and obey its rules, we will be sucked back into the realm of servitude, whatever our temporary class status or privileges. This temptation and this fear compromise our powers, divert our energies, form a potent source of "blocks" and of acute anxiety about work.

For if, in trying to join the common world of men, the professions molded by a primarily masculine consciousness, we split ourselves off from the common life of women and deny our female heritage and identity in our work, we lose touch with our real powers and with the essential condition for all fully realized work: community.

Feminism begins but cannot end with the discovery by an individual of her self-consciousness as a woman. It is not, finally, even the recognition of her reasons for anger, or the decision to change her life, go back to school, leave a marriage (though in any individual life such decisions can be momentous and require great courage). Feminism means finally that we renounce our obedience to the fathers and recognize that the world they have described is not the whole world. Masculine ideologies are the creation of masculine subjectivity; they are neither objective, nor value-free, nor inclusively "human." Feminism implies that we recognize fully the inadequacy for us, the distortion, of male-created ideologies, and that we proceed to think, and act, out of that recognition.

In the common world of men, in the professions which the writers of these essays have come to grips with, it takes more than our *individual* talent and intelligence to think and act further. In denying the validity of women's experience, in pretending to stand for "the human," masculine subjectivity tries to force us to name our truths in an alien language, to dilute them; we are constantly told that the "real" problems, the ones worth working on, are those men have defined, that the problems we need to examine are trivial, unscholarly, nonexistent. We are urged to separate the "personal" (our entire existence as women) from the "scholarly" or "professional." Several of the women who contribute to this book have described the outright insults and intellectual sabotage they encountered as women in graduate school. But more insidious may be the sabotage which appears as paternal encouragement, approval granted for internalizing a masculine subjectivity. As Tillie Olsen puts it in this book, "Not to be able to come to one's own truth or not to use it in one's writing, even when telling the truth having to 'tell it slant,' robs one of drive, of conviction, limits potential stature. . . ." Everywhere, women working in the common world of men are denied that integrity of work and life which can only be found in an emotional and intellectual connectedness with ourselves and other women.

More and more, however, women are creating community, sharing work, and discovering that in the sharing of work our relationships with each other become larger and more serious. In organizing a women's self-help clinic or law collective or a writing workshop, in editing a magazine or creating a center for women's work like the Women's Building in Los Angeles, in running a press that publishes "lost" books by women or contemporary work that may be threatening or incomprehensible to male editors, in participating in a women's prison project or a crisis center, we come to understand at first hand not only our unmet needs but the resources we can draw on for meeting them even in the face of female poverty, the hostility of institutions, the lack of documentation of our shared past. Susan Griffin has said that, for a feminist, writing may be solitary but thinking is collective. Any woman who has moved from the playing fields of male discourse into the realm where women are developing our own descriptions of the world knows the extraordinary sense of shedding, as it were, the encumbrance of someone else's baggage, of ceasing to translate. It is not that thinking becomes easy, but that the difficulties are intrinsic to the work itself rather than to the environment. In the common world of men, the struggle to make female experience visible at all—Will they take seriously a thesis on women? Will they let me teach a course on women? Can I speak bluntly of female experience without shattering the male egos around me, or being labeled hysterical, castrating?—such struggles assume the status of an intellectual problem, and the real intellectual problems may not be probed at all.

Working together as women, consciously creating our networks even where patriarchal institutions are the ones in which we have to survive, we can confront the problems of women's relationships, the mothers we came from, the sisters with whom we were forced to divide the world, the daughters we love and fear. We can challenge and inspirit each other, throw light on one another's blind spots, stand by and give courage at the birth throes of one another's insights. I think of the poet H. D.'s account of the vision she had on the island of Corfu, in the *Tribute to Freud:*

> And there I sat and there is my friend Bryher who has brought me to Greece. I can turn now to her, though I do not budge an inch or break the sustained crystal-gazing at the wall before me. I say to Bryher, "There have been pictures here—I thought they were shadows at first, but they are light, not shadow. They are quite simple objects—but of course it's very strange. I can break away from them now, if I want—it's just a matter of concentrating—what do you think? Shall I stop? Shall I go on?" Bryher says without hesitation, "Go on."
> . . . I had known such extraordinarily gifted and charming people. They had made much of me or they had slighted me and yet neither praise nor neglect mattered in the face of the gravest issues—life, death. . . . And yet, so oddly, I knew that this experience, this writing-on-the-wall before me, could not be shared with anyone except the girl who stood so bravely there beside me. This girl had said without hesitation, "Go on." It was she really who had the detachment and integrity of the Pythoness of Delphi. But it was I, battered and dissociated . . . who was seeing the pictures, and who was reading the writing or granted the inner vision. Or perhaps, in some sense, we were "seeing" it together, for without her, admittedly, I could not have gone on.[5]

Even for those who would mistrust visionary experience, the episode is revealing as metaphor. The personal relationship helps create the conditions for work (out of her vision H. D. went on to create her great, late, long poems celebrating a matriarchal world and the quests of female heroes); no less does the fact of working together deepen and sustain a personal relationship. "If Chloe likes Olivia and they share a laboratory . . . this of itself will make their friendship more varied and lasting because it will be less personal."[6] By "like" I believe Virginia Woolf (still, in that book, writing more cautiously than later in *Three Guineas*) also meant "love"; for "a laboratory" we can read "the creation of a common world."

Many women have known the figure of the male "mentor" who guides and protects his female student or colleague, tenderly opening doors for her into the common world of men. He seems willing to

[5] H. D., *Tribute to Freud* (Oxford: Carcanet Press, 1971), pp. 50–54.

[6] Virginia Woolf, *A Room of One's Own* (London: Hogarth Press, 1929), p. 126.

share his power, to conspire with her in stealing what Celia Gilbert names in this book "the sacred fire" of work. Yet what can he really bestow but the *illusion* of power, a power stolen, in any case, from the mass of women, over centuries, by men? He can teach her to name her experience in language that may allow her to live, work, perhaps succeed in the common world of men. But he has no key to the powers she might share with other women.

There is also the illusion that if you make your emotional and erotic life with women, it does not matter that your intellectual work is a collaboration with silence and lying about female experience. At a panel of lesbian writers at the Modern Language Association in San Francisco in December 1975, Susan Griffin spoke of the damage we do to ourselves and our work in censoring our own truths:

> I feel that this whole idea of the Muse, of inspiration, is a kind of cop-out. There is something very fascinating going on with a writer's psyche when you are undergoing a silence, an inability to write. Each silence and each eruption into speech constitute a kind of struggle in the life of a writer. . . . The largest struggle around silence in my life has had to do with the fact that I am a woman and a lesbian. When I recognized my feelings as a woman, when I recognized my anger as a woman, suddenly my writing was transformed—suddenly I had a material, a subject-matter. . . . And then a few years later I found myself unhappy with my writing, unhappy with the way I expressed myself, unable to speak; I wrote in a poem, *Words do not come to my mouth anymore*. And I happened also . . . to be censoring the fact that I was a lesbian. I thought that I was doing this because of the issue of child custody, and that was and still is a serious issue. But I wasn't acknowledging how important it was to me, both as a writer and as a human being, to be able to . . . write about my feelings as a lesbian.
>
> In fact, I think that writers are always dealing with taboos of one sort of another; if they are not taboos general in society, you may just have a fear in your private life of perceiving some truth because of its implications, and that will stop you from writing. . . . But when we come to the taboo of lesbianism, this is one which is most loaded for everyone, even those who are not lesbians. Because the fact of love between women . . . is one which affects every event in this society, psychic and political and sociological. And for a writer, the most savage censor is oneself.[7]

[7] *Sinister Wisdom*, vol. 1, no. 2, pp. 24–25.

The whole question of what it means or might mean to work as a lesbian might have occupied an entire essay in this book. Of past women whose thought and work have remained visible in history, an enormous number have been lesbians, yet because of the silence and denial that has enveloped lesbianism, we learn little from women's biographies about the relation of their work to their relationships with women or to the social taboos they lived among. One writer in this book mourns that "there was only one Alice B. Toklas." But in fact women's support to women *has* been there all along, lifetime or long-term comradeships. For many women, struggling for economic survival in the common world of men, these relationships have had to be dissimulated, at what cost to the work (let alone the relationships) we cannot begin to know. Every lesbian has been forced to walk past the distorting mirrors of homophobia before she could get down to the real problems of her work. Every lesbian artist knows that when she attempts to embody lesbian sexuality in her work she runs the risk of having it perceived pornographically, if it is not simply denied visibility. When a lesbian feels she may have to choose between writing or painting her truths and keeping her child, she is flung back on the most oppressive ground of maternal guilt in conflict with creative work. The question of economic survival, of keeping one's job, is terribly real, but the more terrible questions lie deeper where a woman is forced, or permits herself, to lead a censored life.

III

In thinking about the issues of women and work raised in this book, I turned to Hannah Arendt's *The Human Condition* to see how a major political philosopher of our time, a woman greatly respected in the intellectual establishment, had spoken to the theme. I found her essay illuminating, not so much for what it says, but for what it is. The issue of women as the laborers in reproduction, of women as workers in production, of the relationship of women's unpaid labor in the home to the separation between "private" and "public" spheres, of the woman's body as commodity—these questions were not raised for the first time in the 1960s and 1970s; they had already been documented in the 1950s when *The Human Con-*

dition was being written. Arendt barely alludes, usually in a footnote, to Marx and Engels's engagement with this theme; and she
writes as if the work of Olive Schreiner, Charlotte Perkins Gilman,
Emma Goldman, Jane Addams, to name only a few writers, had
never existed. The withholding of women from participation in the
vita activa, the "common world," and the connection of this with
reproductivity, is something from which she does not so much turn
her eyes as stare straight through unseeing. This "great work" is thus
a kind of failure for which masculine ideology has no name, precisely because in terms of that ideology it is successful, at the expense
of truths the ideology considers irrelevant. To read such a book, by a
woman of large spirit and great erudition, can be painful, because it
embodies the tragedy of a female mind nourished on male ideologies. In fact, the loss is ours, because Arendt's desire to grasp deep
moral issues is the kind of concern we need to build a common
world which will amount to more than "life-styles." The power of
male ideology to possess such a female mind, to disconnect it as it
were from the female body which encloses it and which it encloses,
is nowhere more striking than in Arendt's lofty and crippled book.

Women's minds cannot grow to full stature, or touch the real
springs of our power to alter reality, on a diet of masculine ideology.
This is not the same thing as saying that we can use nothing of these
ideologies, or their methods, or that we need not understand them.
But the common world of men cannot give us what we need, and
parts of it are poisoning us. Miriam Schapiro, in this book, describes
the process through which she begins to work: filling sheets of paper
with smeared paint, images created "freely, mindlessly," going back
to that place in childhood where she simply painted and was happy.
To her husband, this appeared as "deprofessionalizing" herself. Yet
the very concept of "professionalism," tainted as it is with the separation between personal life and work, with a win-or-lose mentality
and the gauging of success by public honors and market prices, needs
a thorough revaluation by women. Forty years back Virginia Woolf
was asking:

> What is this "civilization" in which we find ourselves? What are these
> ceremonies and why should we take part in them? What are these pro-

fessions and why should we make money out of them? Where in short is it leading, the procession of the sons of educated men?[8]

Her answer was that it is leading to war, to elitism, to exploitation and the greed for power; in our own time we can also add that it has clearly been leading to the ravagement of the nonhuman living world. Instead of the concept of "professionalism," we need, perhaps, a vision of work akin to that described by Simone Weil in her "Theoretical Picture of a Free Society":

> A clear view of what is possible and what impossible, what is easy and what difficult, of the labors that separate the project from its accomplishment—this alone does away with insatiable desires and vain fears; from this and not from anything else proceed moderation and courage, virtues without which life is nothing but a disgraceful frenzy. Besides, the source of any kind of virtue lies in the shock produced by the human intelligence being brought up against a matter devoid of lenience and of falsity.[9]

If we conceive of feminism as more than a frivolous label, if we conceive of it as an ethics, a methodology, a more complex way of thinking about, thus more responsibly acting upon, the conditions of human life, we need a self-knowledge which can only develop through a steady, passionate attention to *all* female experience. I cannot imagine a feminist evolution leading to radical change in the private/political realm of gender that is not rooted in the conviction that all women's lives are important; that the lives of men cannot be understood by burying the lives of women; and that to make visible the full meaning of women's experience, to reinterpret knowledge in terms of that experience, is now the most important task of thinking.

If this is so, we cannot work alone. We had better face the fact that our hope of thinking at all, against the force of a maimed and maiming worldview, depends on seeking and giving our allegiance to a

[8] Virginia Woolf, *Three Guineas* (New York: Harcourt Brace, 1966), p. 63; first published 1938.

[9] Simone Weil, *Oppression and Liberty*, Arthur Wills and John Petrie, trans. (Amherst: University of Massachusetts, 1973), p. 87.

community of women co-workers. And beyond the exchange and criticism of work, we have to ask ourselves how we can make the conditions for work more possible, not just for ourselves but for each other. This is not a question of generosity. It is not generosity that makes women in community support and nourish each other. It is rather what Whitman called the "hunger for equals"—the desire for a context in which our own strivings will be amplified, quickened, lucidified, through those of our peers.

We also, of course, need community with our past. Women's art and thought and action will continue to be seen as deviant, its true meaning distorted or buried, as long as women's work can be dismissed as "exceptional," an interesting footnote to the major texts. Or, it will be encouraged for its timidities and punished for its daring. This is obvious to women who have tried to work along seriously feminist lines in the established professions. But even before the work exists, long before praise or attack, the very form it will assume, the courage on which it can draw, the sense of potential direction it may take, require—given the politics of our lives and of creation itself—more than the gifts of the individual woman or her immediate contemporaries. We need access to the female past.

The problem, finally, is not that of who does housework and childcare, whether or not one can find a life companion who will share in the sustenance and repair of daily life—crucial as these may be in the short run. It is a question of the community we are reaching for in our work and on which we can draw; whom we envision as our hearers, our co-creators, our challengers; who will urge us to take our work further, more seriously, than we had dared; on whose work we can build. Women *have* done these things for each other, sought each other in community, even if only in enclaves, often through correspondence, for centuries. Denied space in the universities, the scientific laboratories, the professions, we have devised our networks. We must not be tempted to trade the possibility of enlarging and strengthening those networks, and of extending them to more and more women, for the illusion of power and success as "exceptional" or "privileged" women in the professions.

Husband-Right and Father-Right (1977)

In every life there are experiences, painful and at first disorienting, which by their very intensity throw a sudden floodlight on the ways we have been living, the forces that control our lives, the hypocrisies that have allowed us to collaborate with those forces, the harsh but liberating facts we have been enjoined from recognizing. Some people allow such illuminations only the brevity of a flash of sheet-lightning, that throws a whole landscape into sharp relief, after which the darkness of denial closes in again. For others, these clarifications provide a motive and impulse toward a more enduring lucidity, a search for greater honesty, and for the recognition of larger issues of which our personal suffering is a symptom, a specific example. To try to understand what has been labeled the "personal" as part of a greater political reality, has been a critical process for feminism, more critical probably for feminism than for any other movement against oppression. For fundamental to women's oppression is the assumption that we as a group belong to the "private" sphere of the home, the hearth, the family, the sexual, the emotional, out of which men emerge as adults to act in the "public" arena of power, the "real" world, and to which they return for mothering, for access to female forms of intimacy, affection, and solace unavailable in the realm of male struggle and competition.

Written as the introduction to *Legal Kidnapping* by Anna Demeter (Boston: Beacon, 1977); reprinted in *Chrysalis: A Magazine of Women's Culture*, no. 5, 1978.

When women begin to think, speak, and write in ways which challenge these dichotomies, we meet a prevailing reflex of dread. It is not simply, I think, the dread of seeing a familiar model of the world thrown into question, though this—the fear of potential change—is powerful enough. When we begin to describe sexuality, motherhood, so-called instinctual or natural behavior, as part of the public world "out there"—that is, as affected by power politics, rights, property, the institutionalized ownership by men of women and children—we encounter acute anxiety on the part of most men and many women. Even the recognition that marriage is an economic institution—a recognition which was perfectly clear to our ancestors well into the nineteenth century—severely disturbs the contemporary, liberal, middle-class facade of free choice, love and partnership, "liberated marriage"' and equality between the sexes in private life. The suggestion that motherhood is not only a core human relationship but a political institution, a keystone to the domination in every sphere of women by men, evokes outcries of distress, or of vituperative denial, from people with a heavy emotional and practical investment in leaving unexamined this "sacred calling." It is immediately assumed that the experience of maternity itself is under fire, that the maternal emotions will be invalidated if we look closely at the politics of motherhood.

The fear of change thus intersects with a fear that lucidity and love cannot coexist, that political awareness and personal intensity are contradictions, that consciousness must dissolve tenderness, intimacy, and loyalty. Lucidity, political awareness, and consciousness are equated with intellectual nihilism, with depersonalization, with the spirit of objectification. This is itself a measure of the way in which Western culture in its intense patriarchalism has polarized thought and feeling. In a society so dismembered, anonymous, and alienating, tenderness and intimacy are precious and rare and—apart from all other forces which oppose feminism—it is no wonder that people fear the loss of what emotional intensity they still have. This book, written by a woman who in her personal suffering chose lucidity and a political vision, demonstrates that this fear is a groundless one. It suggests, in fact, that only when women recognize and name as force and bondage what has been misnamed love or partnership, can we begin to love and nurture out of strength and purpose rather than out of self-annihilation and the protection of a crumbling form or fiction.

The significance of this book is much larger than its length and title might suggest. It was written to convert pain into something useful, and it has achieved that purpose to a remarkable degree. It is first of all the restrained yet highly charged account of the author's experience as a wife and mother, a wife seeking divorce and a mother whose two youngest children were kidnapped by her husband and held as hostages to force her back into the marriage. It uses that profoundly female, and feminist, genre, the journal, to carry the reader with Anna Demeter through the days and nights of her ordeal. It looks with courageous honesty at her earlier efforts to stay in a marriage which under a "gloss . . . of new forms and new sensibilities" was quite traditional, filled with unspoken and unspeakable feelings, with denial, psychic violence, and sexual bargaining. Both spouses professionals, even colleagues; the husband taking some part in the care of the youngest child; the wife a feminist who defended "liberated" marriage on public platforms; her husband taking credit for having a "liberated" wife—this network of ironies and hypocrisies will seem unnervingly familiar to many readers, and it disabled Anna Demeter for some time from acknowledging her husband's destructiveness toward her children and herself. Proud, enormously competent, running a clinic, making speeches, baking the family bread, reading aloud nightly to the children, protective of her husband's reputation both as a father and as a professional, possessed by that "sense of privacy" which is so often really the concealment of what conflicts with our self-image (and which so often cuts us off from understanding and help), believing that if she could only hold out till the children were grown she would have earned her freedom—many of us who have been characters in the fiction of a marriage can recognize ourselves in Anna Demeter, both our self-delusions and our incalculable strengths. Her passage on the "unfit mother" goes straight to the core of the experience of countless women. And I do not think I have seen rendered, even in poetry or fiction, the physical sensations of maternal longing as Anna Demeter describes them here.

Legal Kidnapping is also a kind of sourcebook for women who have to deal in their own lives with the law and the social order as they relate to parental kidnapping, specifically by the father. (This form of revenge for a proposed divorce action has become increasingly prevalent, so that many childcare centers and schools have established a "never-the-father" protocol, specifying who may and who may not pick up children after school; and legislation has recently been proposed to regularize custody and visitation among the states and to make parental kidnapping a federal crime.) In her Appendix, Anna Demeter has compiled concrete information, and a legal bibliography, based on her own experience and her research. Much of women's vulnerability both as wives and mothers comes from ignorance of the rights we have, of what recourse we can seek, and what legal power men have over us. For this information alone, Anna Demeter's book deserves a place in public libraries, legal clinics, women's centers, and the libraries of counselors and social workers dealing with women and divorce.

But finally, *Legal Kidnapping* is not a guide to one isolated problem, one exceptional aspect of divorce. In a brief space, Anna Demeter raises very large questions about the institutionalization of human relationships, and about the entity called the family—that battleground, open wound, haven and theater of the absurd, which dominates each human childhood. She attaches the issue of the rights of children to the questions feminism has raised about the possession of persons, about motherhood. The question "Mothering for what?" is essentially the question: "Into whose hands are we to deliver our children, who are we training them to obey, and for whose benefit?" It is central to the feminist critique of all economic, sexual, cultural, familial relations as patriarchally controlled, and to the radical feminist demand for change in every aspect of the social order.

The mother-child relationship can be seen as the first relationship violated by patriarchy. Mother and child, as objects of possession by the fathers, are reduced both to pieces of property and to relationships in which men can feel in control, powerful, wherever else they may feel impotent. Legally, economically, and through unwritten sanctions, including the unlegislated male-bonding network documented in this book, the mother and her child live under male control although males assume a minimal direct responsibility for children. Anna Demeter's discussion of the differences between "mother-right" and "father-right" and between the institutionalized obligations of mothers and fathers toward children, is a new step in the construction of a feminist theory of motherhood. The father's economic "obligation to support" allows him right of access to and contact with a child almost without regard to the kind of person he is; "mother-right" is legally the obligation to nurture, and can be stripped from a woman on the grounds of her personal fitness as mother.

Within the institution of patriarchal marriage, the following is true: A woman may be challenged with "unfitness" as a mother if she works outside the home and is thereby able to support her children (a threat to the economic basis of father-right). A woman who wishes to divorce her husband to marry another man is tolerated more readily than a woman who leaves a marriage in order to be separate and self-sufficient, or because she finds marriage itself an oppressive institution. An adopted child in a divorce settlement may be perceived as belonging only to the mother, while the biological child is regarded as the "seed" of the father. Thus motherhood is identified with nurture, fatherhood with the moment of conception and with economic power. A husband's vilification of his wife, with the intention and possible effect of damaging her socially and professionally, is not legally considered slander. A man cannot be legally prosecuted for raping his wife. A man's obscene telephone calls to his wife are not legally actionable as obscene, nor can she have a tap put on her telephone to locate him. Paternal custody is often sought not out of desire for the children but as a weapon of vengeance against their mother. A majority of recent cases of paternal kidnapping have been cases of kidnapping by fathers, in which the motive was to punish the mother and force her to return to the marriage. Such cases, unless a custody settlement has already been reached, are viewed as "private," a "marital dispute," and law enforcement agencies cannot be called into the search. Even where a custody settlement has been reached, the kidnapping of a child may be rewarded with a new custody hearing. The "preservation of the family" is quoted as an abstract principle without considering the quality of life within the family, or the fact that families may be held together by force, legally sanctioned terrorism, and the threat of violence.

"Father-right" must be seen as one specific form of the rights men are presumed to enjoy simply because of their gender: the "right" to

the priority of male over female needs, to sexual and emotional services from women, to women's undivided attention in any and all
situations. It would seem that a man experiences the violation of
some profound "right" when a woman leaves him: the "right" to her
services, however lacking in mutuality the relationship. Through patriarchal socialization, men learn to think in terms of their "rights"
where rights are not actually the issue: in areas like sexual behavior,
maternal behavior, which are seen, not as springing from a woman's
choice and affections but as behavior to which the male is entitled *as
a male.* The husband's "rights" over his wife are, in social terms, all-
inclusive; they can be whatever the man defines them to be at any
given moment. The patriarchal legal system, with its more limited
definition of rights of sexual access and of possession of children, in-
teracts with and augments this much larger, more diffuse area of all-
inclusive rights of men to the bodies, emotions, and services of
women.

There is much in this book that points to the need for a new psychology of male behavior. A wife's declaration that she is about to
seek divorce is a frequent occasion for a husband's violence, against
others or himself, which has been latent or contained within the
marriage. Anna Demeter suggests that a wife may be felt as a substitute for the lost mother, purchased through economic support and
assured to a man by the institution of marriage. When a wife says she
is leaving, many men are thrown back to the rage and anguish of separation from their mothers, less perhaps the "Oedipal" separation
than through the fact that the mother is expected to hand her son
over to the societal "fathers," to eject him from the female matrix,
and allow him to become a "real man"—competitive, emotionally
defended, prone to violence. Cast out from the female sphere once,
he relives that anguish when a wife divorces him or a woman "turns
him down." Michael, the husband described in this book, was a visi-
bly angry and violent man who had suffered parental kidnapping
himself as a child. (Like child abuse, kidnapping may repeat itself
from generation to generation.) But a man need not have lived
through so overt a drama in his childhood to act out primal rage and
despair when a woman seems to be depriving him of his one source
of nourishment—the maternal, female element. Because the family
has stood as the embodiment of maternal and female qualities, ab-

sent in the male-dominated society at large, it carries an unholy burden, beyond anything any actual family—or any single, actual woman—can possibly provide.

Much male fear of feminism is the fear that, in becoming whole human beings, women will cease to mother men, to provide the breast, the lullaby, the continuous attention associated by the infant with the mother. Much male fear of feminism is infantilism—the longing to remain the mother's son, to possess a woman who exists purely for him. These infantile needs of adult men for women have been sentimentalized and romanticized long enough as "love"; it is time to recognize them as arrested development, and to reexamine the ideal of preservation of "the family" within which those needs are allowed free rein even to the point of violence. Because the law and the economic and social order are heavily weighted in favor of men, the infantile needs of adult males are affirmed by a machinery of power which does not affirm or validate the needs of adult women. Institutionalized marriage and motherhood perpetuate the will of male infants as law in the adult world.

This book will undoubtedly have an illuminating effect on women contemplating divorce from physically violent men or men who seem capable of violence and kidnapping as retributory measures. This is a larger male population than is usually acknowledged. It is essential that such women see themselves as the breakers of a cycle of generational violence. It is essential for women to realize, as Anna Demeter was finally able to realize, that having acted as honestly and decently as possible we cannot take on ourselves responsibility for a husband's disordered behavior on confronting divorce. Such assumption of total responsibility is part of the mother/child pattern in which so many marriages are cast: the woman protecting the man at the expense of her and her children's selfhood and integrity; the woman as all-responsible adult, the man as irresponsible child. As more and more women refuse to be entrapped and mystified by institutional marriage and motherhood, the less likely are new generations to reenact familial tragedy.

Beyond the issues of marriage and divorce, beyond the issue of motherhood, lies the implacable political necessity for women to gain control of our bodies and our lives. We must do this for ourselves and for each other; we can also believe that as we do so, the generational sickness will repeat itself more and more rarely. Clearly, Anna Demeter and her children have not been destroyed by their ordeal but strengthened in their mutual bonds; her relationship with the world is clearer, more honest than it ever was; her sense of integrity reconstituted through her refusal to give in to terrorism. We do not "save" men by bending to violence, nor do we "save" our children by letting them see, in their own homes, their first community, violence prevailing as the ultimate recourse in human relations, and victimization accepted in the name of "love." The children of mothers who are able to take their lives in hand and confront the institutions that oppress them, are our best hope for a future in which human existence will no longer be ruled by hypocrisy and force.

The Meaning of Our Love for Women Is What We Have Constantly to Expand (1977)

The summer of 1977 was a summer of militant, media-scrutinized "Gay Pride" marches, responding to the antihomosexual campaign whose media symbol was a woman, Anita Bryant. The male gay movement had embraced Bryant as a target for its anger with an alacrity suggestive of the movement's unexamined, underlying gynephobia. "Anita" was equated with Hitler, or viciously lampooned in terms of her female anatomy; while the husband and pastor at her shoulders, the corporate interests financing "her" crusade, the churches and American Legion chapters that swelled it, were erased as the image of a woman became the simplistic focus of the gay movement.

Many lesbian/feminists walked in those marches feeling torn and alienated; we understood that a strong presence of women was necessary to raise public awareness that women are a significant group denied civil rights by antihomosexual laws; yet the woman-hating tone of large sections of the marches reasserted to us that we could find no real "brotherly" solidarity in the gay movement. Our understanding of the meaning of Anita Bryant, and the meaning of woman-identification, was of necessity more complex. This speech, read to a small group of women who had chosen to separate from the Gay Pride demonstration in Central Park's Sheep Meadow and hold our own rally, was later printed as the first in a series of pamphlets on lesbian/feminism by Out & Out Books, Brooklyn, New York.

〰〰〰〰〰〰

I want to talk about some connections which I believe it is urgent for us to make at this time—connections which demand of us, not only pride, anger, and courage, but the willingness to think, and to face our own complexity.

A concerted attack is now being waged against homosexuality, by the church, by the media, by all the forces in this country that need a scapegoat to divert attention from racism, poverty, unemployment, and utter, obscene corruption in public life.[1] It is not a bit surprising that this attack has created a new popular and infamous image of feminine evil: Anita Bryant. It should be obvious to us all that no woman in male-dominated society can wield the public influence ascribed to Anita Bryant, unless men say she shall do so, and unless male power networks give her, as they have given Phyllis Schlafly of the anti-ERA campaign, access to the media, free publicity, and financial support.

Last weekend in Los Angeles, these forces joined to attempt a take-over of the International Women's Year Conference in the state of California. Only a mass turnout of feminists prevented the passing of resolutions for the essential overturn of every gain made by the feminist movement over the past eight years. It should be clear that Anita Bryant and Phyllis Schlafly are the masks behind which the system of male dominance is attacking, not just lesbians, or "gay" men, but women, and the feminist movement even in its most moderate form; that the attack is being fueled and fostered by the only people in America with the resources to do so: men.

We also know that in the rhetoric of Anita Bryant, as in the rhetoric of the male "gay" movement, "homosexuality" is viewed through a male lens, as a male experience. I have stopped believing that this is because lesbians are simply perceived as "not threatening." Much as the male homophobe hates the male homosexual, there is a far deeper—and extremely well-founded—dread in patriarchy of the mere existence of lesbians. Along with persecution, we have met with utter, suffocating silence and denial: the attempt to wipe us out of history and culture altogether. This silence is part of the totality of silence about women's lives. It has also been an effective way of obstructing the intense, powerful surge toward female community and woman-to-woman commitment, which threatens patriarchy far

[1] And, of course, from the psychic and physical destruction of thousands of women by institutionalized heterosexuality, in marriage and the pursuit of "normal" sexuality.

worse than the bonding of male homosexuals does, or the plea for equal rights. And finally, there is an even deeper threat now being posed by lesbian/feminism, which is a wholly new force in history.

Before any kind of feminist movement existed, or could exist, lesbians existed: women who loved women, who refused to comply with the behavior demanded of women, who refused to define themselves in relation to men. Those women, our foresisters, millions of whose names we do not know, were tortured and burned as witches, slandered in religious and later in "scientific" tracts, portrayed in art and literature as bizarre, amoral, destructive, decadent women. For a long time, the lesbian has been a personification of feminine evil. At the same time, as male homosexual culture developed, the lives of men have, as ever, been seen as the "real" culture. Lesbians have never had the economic and cultural power of homosexual men; and those parts of our lives which homosexual men could not relate to—our faithful and enduring relationships, our work as social activists on behalf of women and children, our female tenderness and strength, our female dreams and visions—have only begun to be portrayed, in literature and scholarship, by lesbians.

Lesbians have been forced to live between two cultures, both male-dominated, each of which has denied and endangered our existence. On the one hand, there is the heterosexist, patriarchal culture, which has driven women into marriage and motherhood through every possible pressure—economic, religious, medical, and legal—and which has literally colonized the bodies of women. Heterosexual, patriarchal culture has driven lesbians into secrecy and guilt, often to self-hatred and suicide.

On the other hand, there is homosexual patriarchal culture, a culture created by homosexual men, reflecting such male stereotypes as dominance and submission as modes of relationship, and the separation of sex from emotional involvement—a culture tainted by profound hatred for women. The male "gay" culture has offered lesbians the imitation role-stereotypes of "butch" and "femme," "active" and "passive," cruising, sado-masochism, and the violent, self-destructive world of "gay" bars. Neither heterosexual nor "gay" culture has offered lesbians a space in which to discover what it means to be self-defined, self-loving, woman-identified, neither an imitation man nor his objectified opposite. In spite of this, lesbians throughout history have survived, worked, supported each other in community, and passionately loved.

There have been self-conscious, political feminists for nearly two hundred years;[2] there has been a homophile movement for nearly a century; and many of the most uncompromising and heroic activists in all movements for social change have been lesbians. We are now for the first time at a point of fusing lesbianism and feminism. And this is precisely the thing that patriarchy has most to dread, and will do all in its power to keep us from grasping.

I believe that a militant and pluralistic lesbian/feminist movement is potentially the greatest force in the world today for a complete transformation of society and of our relation to all life. It goes far beyond any struggle for civil liberties or equal rights—necessary as those struggles continue to be. In its deepest, most inclusive form it is an inevitable process by which women will claim our primary and central vision in shaping the future.

We can, however, be turned aside, by the same strategy that has kept us powerless for centuries. The strategy takes many forms but its purpose is always the same: to divide us from each other, to tell us we may not work and love together. Patriarchy has always split us into virtuous women and whores, mothers and dykes, madonnas and medusas. The present-day male Left has steadily refused to work on women's issues, to deal with sexual oppression in any but the most shallow, hypocritical terms, to confront its own fear and hatred of women. Instead, it continues to attempt to divide lesbians and "straight"-identified women, black and white women, to represent lesbianism as bourgeois decadence and feminism as counterrevolutionary, middle-class trivia, just as men in the black movement have tried to define lesbianism as a "white woman's problem." (In this connection, I love to think of the independent women silk-workers of China, whom Agnes Smedley described in the 1930s, who refused to marry, lived in female communities, celebrated the births of daughters with joy, formed secret women's unions in the factories,

---

[2] A cautious estimate. The witch-burnings of the fourteenth–seventeenth centuries in Europe were undoubtedly a form of antifeminist backlash; and as we unbury female history in earlier centuries we find more and more individual female-identified, politically conscious women.

and were openly attacked as lesbians.)[3] The male-defined "sexual revolution" of pornography, a multi-billion-dollar industry which asserts rape as pleasurable, humiliation as erotic, is also a message to women who relate sexually to men, that they can still be "normal" whatever degradations they may undergo in the name of heterosexuality. Better to collaborate in male fantasies of sexual violence than be a lesbian; better to be battered than queer.

Today, lesbians are being urged by the male "gay" movement to bond with men against a common enemy, symbolized by a "straight" woman; to forget that we are women and define ourselves again as "gay." It is important for lesbian voices to be heard there, insisting on our lesbian reality; we cannot afford to reject or dismiss our sisters who are attending the "gay" rally today, although we *can* hope that they are insisting that the "gay" movement confront its own vicious sexism, if it shall continue to expect even occasional support from lesbians. For without a pervasive, insistent feminist consciousness, the "gay" movement is as little a source of change as the Socialist Workers party.

There is another appeal, coming not from men but out of the most intense pain, rage, and frustration that we have experienced—the appeal to a simplistic dyke separatism: the belief that to withdraw from the immense, burgeoning diversity of the global women's movement will somehow provide a kind of purity and energy that will advance our freedom. All lesbians know the anger, grief, disappointment, we have suffered, politically and personally, from homophobia in women we hoped were too aware, too intelligent, too feminist, to speak, write, or act, or to remain silent, out of heterosexual fear and blindness. The gynephobia of men does not touch us nearly so deeply or shatteringly as the gynephobia of women. Many times I have touched the edge of that pain and rage, and comprehended the impulse to dyke separatism. But I believe it is a temptation into sterile "correctness," into powerlessness, an escape from radical complexity. When abortion—a right which the Supreme Court has just effectively denied, most effectively to poor women—when abortion can be labeled a "straight" issue, we are

[3] See Agnes Smedley, *Portraits of Chinese Women in Revolution* (Old Westbury, N.Y.: Feminist Press, 1976).

simply not dealing with the fact that thousands of women are still forced, by rape or economic necessity, to have sex with men; that among these women there are an unquantifiable number of lesbians; that *whatever* their sexual orientation, freedom of reproduction is an issue urgently affecting the lives of poor and nonwhite women, and that to turn our backs upon millions of our sisters in the name of loving women is to deceive ourselves most grievously. Racism is not a "straight" issue, motherhood and childcare are not "straight" issues, while there is one black or Third World lesbian, or one lesbian mother, in the world. Violence against women takes no note of class, color, age, or sexual preference. Lesbians and straight-identified women alike are victims of enforced sterilization, indiscriminate mastectomy and hysterectomy, the use of drugs and electroshock therapy to tame and punish our anger. There is no way we can withdraw from these issues by calling them "man-connected problems." There is no way we can afford to narrow the range of our vision.

In this country, as in the world today, there is a movement of women going on like no other in history. Let us have no doubt: it is being fueled and empowered by the work of lesbians. Lesbians are running presses, starting magazines and distribution systems, setting up crisis centers and halfway houses for rape victims and battered women; creating political dialogues; changing our use of language; making a truly lesbian and female history available for us for the first time; doing grassroots organizing and making visionary art. I want to name just a few institutions that exist in this city alone thanks to lesbian/feminists: the journal *13th Moon*; Out & Out Books, a publishing house; Virginia Woolf House, a collective now raising funds to open a center for lesbians in stress, which will also provide referrals for straight-identified women; the Lesbian Herstory Archives, the first library devoted entirely to documenting our lives, past and present; the magazine *Conditions*, publishing writing by women "with an emphasis on writing by lesbians." These women, and many like them, are trying to reveal and express and support our female complexity, acting *towards* rather than reacting *against*; moving us forward. These projects are not "reformist." We are engaged today in trying to change not one or two, but every aspect of women's lives.

We need much, much more: we need women's centers and coffeehouses throughout the five boroughs, not just one or two spaces where women can seek community away from the bars; we need women's places of healing, shelters for old women now roaming the streets, shelters for battered women, whether housewives or prostitutes; halfway houses for women in transition from prison; self-health clinics, childcare centers, counselling and therapy that is genuinely lesbian and feminist, yet trained and experienced and not a rip-off. We need the brains, the hands, the backbone of every lesbian, in all her love, skill, courage, and anger.

We come from many pasts: out of the Left, out of the ghetto, out of the holocaust, out of the churches, out of marriage, out of the "gay" movement, out of the closet, out of the darker closet of long-term suffocation of our love of women. To the historic feminist demand for equal humanity, for a world free of domination through violence, lesbian/feminism has joined the more radical concept of woman-centered vision, a view of society whose goal is not equality but utter transformation. In the last few years, lesbian/feminism has taken enormous strides, and it has done so because lesbian/feminists have steadily taken leadership and responsibility in issues which affect all women. When we are totally, passionately engaged in working and acting and communicating with and for women, the notion of "withdrawing energy from men" becomes irrelevant: we are already cycling our energy among ourselves.[4] We must remember that

---

[4] The danger of some ironic forms of "false transcendence" should be noted here. True separatism has yet to be adequately defined. Some "separatists" expend a major portion of energy on fantasies of violence against men, while actively trashing women who work in male-dominated institutions, publish in the male-controlled media, or even hold meetings and cultural events in spaces open to men. The "separatism" expressed in psychic and physical harassment of women who have not severed all ties with men (including their male children) may be a diversion from the more serious and difficult problem, the lifelong process of separating ourselves from the patriarchal elements in our own thinking, such as the use of phallic language and the fear of any difference from our own "correct" positions. The woman whose psyche is still heavily involved with a father, brother, teacher, or other male figures out of her past, and who denies the power these figures still exert in her, may refuse to sleep, eat, or speak with men, yet still be psychically enthralled to maleness. The movement of the self away from male-identification, dependence on male ideology, involves genuine psychic struggle. Therefore it is continually being reduced to and dealt with as a rigid political position, a program, an act of will.

A. R., 1978: A separatism which is neither simplistic nor rigid is beginning to be

we have been penalized, vilified, and mocked, not for hating men, but for loving women. The meaning of our love for women is what we have constantly to expand.

Thinking about today and its significance has forced me to place myself and my feelings absolutely on the line. This rally and some of my sisters, women I love, have created the conditions in which I have had to try and think my way through the complexities of being alive, a lesbian, and a feminist in America today. I wish for each of you the kind of challenge, argument, and critical support I have drawn upon, and for all of us, the kind of love we all deserve.

----

defined, e.g., by Mary Daly in *Gyn/Ecology: The Metaethics of Radical Feminism*, and by such writers as Marilyn Frye in "Some Thoughts on Separatism and Power," in *Sinister Wisdom*, no. 6, summer 1978.

Claiming an Education
(1977)

For this convocation, I planned to separate my remarks into two parts: some thoughts about you, the women students here, and some thoughts about us who teach in a women's college. But ultimately, those two parts are indivisible. If university education means anything beyond the processing of human beings into expected roles, through credit hours, tests, and grades (and I believe that in a women's college especially it *might* mean much more), it implies an ethical and intellectual contract between teacher and student. This contract must remain intuitive, dynamic, unwritten; but we must turn to it again and again if learning is to be reclaimed from the depersonalizing and cheapening pressures of the present-day academic scene.

The first thing I want to say to you who are students, is that you cannot afford to think of being here to *receive* an education; you will do much better to think of yourselves as being here to *claim* one. One of the dictionary definitions of the verb "to claim" is: *to take as the rightful owner; to assert in the face of possible contradiction.* "To receive" is *to come into possession of; to act as receptacle or container for; to accept as authoritative or true.* The difference is that between acting and being acted-upon, and for women it can literally mean the difference between life and death.

This talk was given at the Douglass College Convocation, September 6, 1977, and first printed in *The Common Woman*, a feminist literary magazine founded by Rutgers University women in New Brunswick, New Jersey.

One of the devastating weaknesses of university learning, of the store of knowledge and opinion that has been handed down through academic training, has been its almost total erasure of women's experience and thought from the curriculum, and its exclusion of women as members of the academic community. Today, with increasing numbers of women students in nearly every branch of higher learning, we still see very few women in the upper levels of faculty and administration in most institutions. Douglass College itself is a women's college in a university administered overwhelmingly by men, who in turn are answerable to the state legislature, again composed predominantly of men. But the most significant fact for you is that what you learn here, the very texts you read, the lectures you hear, the way your studies are divided into categories and fragmented one from the other—all this reflects, to a very large degree, neither objective reality, nor an accurate picture of the past, nor a group of rigorously tested observations about human behavior. What you can learn here (and I mean not only at Douglass but any college in any university) is how *men* have perceived and organized their experience, their history, their ideas of social relationships, good and evil, sickness and health, etc. When you read or hear about "great issues," "major texts," "the mainstream of Western thought," you are hearing about what men, above all white men, in their male subjectivity, have decided is important.

Black and other minority peoples have for some time recognized that their racial and ethnic experience was not accounted for in the studies broadly labeled human; and that even the sciences can be racist. For many reasons, it has been more difficult for women to comprehend our exclusion, and to realize that even the sciences can be sexist. For one thing, it is only within the last hundred years that higher education has grudgingly been opened up to women at all, even to white, middle-class women. And many of us have found ourselves poring eagerly over books with titles like: *The Descent of Man; Man and His Symbols; Irrational Man; The Phenomenon of Man; The Future of Man; Man and the Machine; From Man to Man; May Man Prevail?; Man, Science and Society; or One-Dimensional Man*—books pretending to describe a "human" reality that does not include over one-half the human species.

Less than a decade ago, with the rebirth of a feminist movement in this country, women students and teachers in a number of universities began to demand and set up women's studies courses—to *claim* a woman-directed education. And, despite the inevitable accusations of "unscholarly," "group therapy," "faddism," etc., despite backlash and budget cuts, women's studies are still growing, offering to more and more women a new intellectual grasp on their lives, new understanding of our history, a fresh vision of the human experience, and also a critical basis for evaluating what they hear and read in other courses, and in the society at large.

But my talk is not really about women's studies, much as I believe in their scholarly, scientific, and human necessity. While I think that any Douglass student has everything to gain by investigating and enrolling in women's studies courses, I want to suggest that there is a more essential experience that you owe yourselves, one which courses in women's studies can greatly enrich, but which finally depends on you, in all your interactions with yourself and your world. This is the experience of *taking responsibility toward yourselves*. Our upbringing as women has so often told us that this should come second to our relationships and responsibilities to other people. We have been offered ethical models of the self-denying wife and mother; intellectual models of the brilliant but slapdash dilettante who never commits herself to anything the whole way, or the intelligent woman who denies her intelligence in order to seem more "feminine," or who sits in passive silence even when she disagrees inwardly with everything that is being said around her.

Responsibility to yourself means refusing to let others do your thinking, talking, and naming for you; it means learning to respect and use your own brains and instincts; hence, grappling with hard work. It means that you do not treat your body as a commodity with which to purchase superficial intimacy or economic security; for our bodies and minds are inseparable in this life, and when we allow our bodies to be treated as objects, our minds are in mortal danger. It means insisting that those to whom you give your friendship and love are able to respect your mind. It means being able to say, with Charlotte Brontë's *Jane Eyre:* "I have an inward treasure born with me, which can keep me alive if all the extraneous delights should be withheld or offered only at a price I cannot afford to give."

Responsibility to yourself means that you don't fall for shallow and easy solutions—predigested books and ideas, weekend encounters guaranteed to change your life, taking "gut" courses instead of ones you know will challenge you, bluffing at school and life instead of doing solid work, marrying early as an escape from real decisions, getting pregnant as an evasion of already existing problems. It means that you refuse to sell your talents and aspirations short, simply to avoid conflict and confrontation. And this, in turn, means resisting the forces in society which say that women should be nice, play safe, have low professional expectations, drown in love and forget about work, live through others, and stay in the places assigned to us. It means that we insist on a life of meaningful work, insist that work be as meaningful as love and friendship in our lives. It means, therefore, the courage to be "different"; not to be continuously available to others when we need time for ourselves and our work; to be able to demand of others—parents, friends, roommates, teachers, lovers, husbands, children—that they respect our sense of purpose and our integrity as persons. Women everywhere are finding the courage to do this, more and more, and we are finding that courage both in our study of women in the past who possessed it, and in each other as we look to other women for comradeship, community, and challenge. The difference between a life lived actively, and a life of passive drifting and dispersal of energies, is an immense difference. Once we begin to feel committed to our lives, responsible to ourselves, we can never again be satisfied with the old, passive way.

Now comes the second part of the contract. I believe that in a women's college you have the right to expect your faculty to take you seriously. The education of women has been a matter of debate for centuries, and old, negative attitudes about women's role, women's ability to think and take leadership, are still rife both in and outside the university. Many male professors (and I don't mean only at Douglass) still feel that teaching in a women's college is a second-rate career. Many tend to eroticize their women students—to treat them as sexual objects—instead of demanding the best of their minds. (At Yale a legal suit [*Alexander* v. *Yale*] has been brought against the university by a group of women students demanding a stated policy against sexual advances toward female students by male professors.) Many teachers, both men and women, trained in the male-centered tradition, are still handing the ideas and texts of that tradition on to students without teaching them to criticize its antiwoman attitudes, its omission of women as part of the species. Too often, all of us fail to teach the most important thing, which is that clear thinking, active discussion, and excellent writing are all necessary for intellectual freedom, and that these require *hard work*. Sometimes, perhaps in discouragement with a culture which is both antiintellectual and antiwoman, we may resign ourselves to low expectations for our students before we have given them half a chance to become more thoughtful, expressive human beings. We need to take to heart the words of Elizabeth Barrett Browning, a poet, a thinking woman, and a feminist, who wrote in 1845 of her impatience with studies which cultivate a "passive recipiency" in the mind, and asserted that "women want to be made to *think actively*: their apprehension is quicker than that of men, but their defect lies for the most part in the logical faculty and in the higher mental activities." Note that she implies a defect which can be remedied by intellectual training; *not* an inborn lack of ability.

I have said that the contract on the student's part involves that you demand to be taken seriously so that you can also go on taking yourself seriously. This means seeking out criticism, recognizing that the most affirming thing anyone can do for you is demand that you push yourself further, show you the range of what you *can* do. It means rejecting attitudes of "take-it-easy," "why-be-so-serious," "why-worry-you'll-probably-get-married-anyway." It means assuming your share of responsibility for what happens in the classroom, because that affects the quality of your daily life here. It means that the student sees herself engaged *with* her teachers in an active, ongoing struggle for a real education. But for her to do this, her teachers must be committed to the belief that women's minds and experience are intrinsically valuable and indispensable to any civilization worthy the name; that there is no more exhilarating and intellectually fertile place in the academic world today than a women's college—*if* both students and teachers in large enough numbers are trying to fulfill this contract. The contract is really a pledge of mutual seriousness about women, about language, ideas, methods, and values. It is our shared commitment toward a world in which the inborn potentialities of so many women's minds will no longer be wasted, raveled-away, paralyzed, or denied.

Taking Women Students Seriously
(1978)

I see my function here today as one of trying to create a context, delineate a background, against which we might talk about women as students and students as women. I would like to speak for awhile about this background, and then I hope that we can have, not so much a question period, as a raising of concerns, a sharing of questions for which we as yet may have no answers, an opening of conversations which will go on and on.

When I went to teach at Douglass, a women's college, it was with a particular background which I would like briefly to describe to you. I had graduated from an all-girls' school in the 1940s, where the head and the majority of the faculty were independent, unmarried women. One or two held doctorates, but had been forced by the Depression (and by the fact that they were women) to take secondary school teaching jobs. These women cared a great deal about the life of the mind, and they gave a great deal of time and energy—beyond any limit of teaching hours—to those of us who showed special intellectual interest or ability. We were taken to libraries, art museums, lectures at neighboring colleges, set to work on extra research projects, given extra French or Latin reading. Although we sometimes felt "pushed" by them, we held those women in a kind of respect

The talk that follows was addressed to teachers of women, as the one preceding was spoken to women students. It was given for the New Jersey College and University Coalition on Women's Education, May 9, 1978.

which even then we dimly perceived was not generally accorded to women in the world at large. They were vital individuals, defined not by their relationships but by their personalities; and although under the pressure of the culture we were all certain we wanted to get married, their lives did not appear empty or dreary to us. In a kind of cognitive dissonance, we knew they were "old maids" and therefore supposed to be bitter and lonely; yet we saw them vigorously involved with life. But despite their existence as alternate models of women, the *content* of the education they gave us in no way prepared us to survive as women in a world organized by and for men.

From that school, I went on to Radcliffe, congratulating myself that now I would have great men as my teachers. From 1947 to 1951, when I graduated, I never saw a single woman on a lecture platform, or in front of a class, except when a woman graduate student gave a paper on a special topic. The "great men" talked of other "great men," of the nature of Man, the history of Mankind, the future of Man; and never again was I to experience, from a teacher, the kind of prodding, the insistence that my best could be even better, that I had known in high school. Women students were simply not taken very seriously. Harvard's message to women was an elite mystification: we were, of course, part of Mankind; we were special, achieving women, or we would not have been there; but of course our real goal was to marry—if possible, a Harvard graduate.

In the late sixties, I began teaching at the City College of New York—a crowded, public, urban, multiracial institution as far removed from Harvard as possible. I went there to teach writing in the SEEK Program, which predated Open Admissions and which was then a kind of model for programs designed to open up higher education to poor, black, and Third World students. Although during the next few years we were to see the original concept of SEEK diluted, then violently attacked and betrayed, it was for a short time an extraordinary and intense teaching and learning environment. The characteristics of this environment were a deep commitment on the part of teachers to the minds of their students; a constant, active effort to create or discover the conditions for learning, and to educate ourselves to meet the needs of the new college population; a philosophical attitude based on open discussion of racism, oppression, and the politics of literature and language; and a belief that learning in the classroom could not be isolated from the student's experience as a member of an urban minority group in white America. Here are some of the kinds of questions we, as teachers of writing, found ourselves asking:

(1) What has been the student's experience of education in the inadequate, often abusively racist public school system, which rewards passivity and treats a questioning attitude or independent mind as a behavior problem? What has been her or his experience in a society that consistently undermines the selfhood of the poor and the nonwhite? How can such a student gain that sense of self which is necessary for active participation in education? What does all this mean for us as teachers?

(2) How do we go about teaching a canon of literature which has consistently excluded or depreciated nonwhite experience?

(3) How can we connect the process of learning to write well with the student's own reality, and not simply teach her/him how to write acceptable lies in standard English?

When I went to teach at Douglass College in 1976, and in teaching women's writing workshops elsewhere, I came to perceive stunning parallels to the questions I had first encountered in teaching the so-called disadvantaged students at City. But in this instance, and against the specific background of the women's movement, the questions framed themselves like this:

(1) What has been the student's experience of education in schools which reward female passivity, indoctrinate girls and boys in stereotypic sex roles, and do not take the female mind seriously? How does a woman gain a sense of her *self* in a system—in this case, patriarchal capitalism—which devalues work done by women, denies the importance and uniqueness of female experience, and is physically violent toward women? What does this mean for a woman teacher?

(2) How do we, as women, teach women students a canon of literature which has consistently excluded or depreciated female ex-

perience, and which often expresses hostility to women and validates violence against us?

(3) How can we teach women to move beyond the desire for male approval and getting "good grades" and seek and write their own truths that the culture has distorted or made taboo? (For women, of course, language itself is exclusive: I want to say more about this further on.)

In teaching women, we have two choices: to lend our weight to the forces that indoctrinate women to passivity, self-depreciation, and a sense of powerlessness, in which case the issue of "taking women students seriously" is a moot one; or to consider what we have to work against, as well as with, in ourselves, in our students, in the content of the curriculum, in the structure of the institution, in the society at large. And this means, first of all, taking ourselves seriously: Recognizing that central responsibility of a woman to herself, without which we remain always the Other, the defined, the object, the victim; believing that there is a unique quality of validation, affirmation, challenge, support, that one woman can offer another. Believing in the value and significance of women's experience, traditions, perceptions. Thinking of ourselves seriously, not as one of the boys, not as neuters, or androgynes, but *as women*.

Suppose we were to ask ourselves, simply: What does a woman need to know? Does she not, as a self-conscious, self-defining human being, need a knowledge of her own history, her much-politicized biology, an awareness of the creative work of women of the past, the skills and crafts and techniques and powers exercised by women in different times and cultures, a knowledge of women's rebellions and organized movements against our oppression and how they have been routed or diminished? Without such knowledge women live and have lived without context, vulnerable to the projections of male fantasy, male prescriptions for us, estranged from our own experience because our education has not reflected or echoed it. I would suggest that not biology, but ignorance of our selves, has been the key to our powerlessness.

But the university curriculum, the high-school curriculum, do not provide this kind of knowledge for women, the knowledge of Womankind, whose experience has been so profoundly different from that of Mankind. Only in the precariously budgeted, much-condescended-to area of women's studies is such knowledge available to women students. Only there can they learn about the lives and work of women other than the few select women who are included in the "mainstream" texts, usually misrepresented even when they do appear. Some students, at some institutions, manage to take a majority of courses in women's studies, but the message from on high is that this is self-indulgence, soft-core education: the "real" learning is the study of Mankind.

If there is any misleading concept, it is that of "coeducation": that because women and men are sitting in the same classrooms, hearing the same lectures, reading the same books, performing the same laboratory experiments, they are receiving an equal education. They are not, first because the content of education itself validates men even as it invalidates women. Its very message is that men have been the shapers and thinkers of the world, and that this is only natural. The bias of higher education, including the so-called sciences, is white and male, racist and sexist; and this bias is expressed in both subtle and blatant ways. I have mentioned already the exclusiveness of grammar itself: "The student should test himself on the above questions"; "The poet is representative. He stands among partial men for the complete man". Despite a few half-hearted departures from custom, what the linguist Wendy Martyna has named "He-Man" grammar prevails throughout the culture. The efforts of feminists to reveal the profound ontological implications of sexist grammar are routinely ridiculed by academicians and journalists, including the professedly liberal *Times* columnist, Tom Wicker, and the professed humanist, Jacques Barzun. Sexist grammar burns into the brains of little girls and young women a message that the male is the norm, the standard, the central figure beside which we are the deviants, the marginal, the dependent variables. It lays the foundation for androcentric thinking, and leaves men safe in their solipsistic tunnel-vision.

Women and men do not receive an equal education because outside the classroom women are perceived not as sovereign beings but as prey. The growing incidence of rape on and off the campus may or may not be fed by the proliferations of pornographic magazines and X-rated films available to young males in fraternities and student unions; but it is certainly occurring in a context of widespread images of sexual violence against women, on billboards and in so-called high art. More subtle, more daily than rape is the verbal abuse experienced by the woman student on many campuses—Rutgers for example—where, traversing a street lined with fraternity houses, she must run a gauntlet of male commentary and verbal assault. The undermining of self, of a woman's sense of her right to occupy space and walk freely in the world, is deeply relevant to education. The capacity to think independently, to take intellectual risks, to assert ourselves mentally, is inseparable from our physical way of being in the world, our feelings of personal integrity. If it is dangerous for me to walk home late of an evening from the library, *because I am a woman and can be raped,* how self-possessed, how exuberant can I feel as I sit working in that library? how much of my working energy is drained by the subliminal knowledge that, as a woman, I test my physical right to exist each time I go out alone? Of this knowledge, Susan Griffin has written:

> . . . more than rape itself, the fear of rape permeates our lives. And what does one do from day to day, with *this* experience, which says, without words and directly to the heart, *your existence, your experience, may end at any moment.* Your experience may end, and the best defense against this is not to be, to deny being in the body, as a self, to . . . avert your gaze, make yourself, as a presence in the world, less felt.[1]

Finally, rape of the mind. Women students are more and more often now reporting sexual overtures by male professors—one part of our overall growing consciousness of sexual harassment in the workplace. At Yale a legal suit has been brought against the university by a group of women demanding an explicit policy against sexual advances toward female students by male professors. Most young women experience a profound mixture of humiliation and intellectual self-doubt over seductive gestures by men who have the power to award grades, open doors to grants and graduate school, or extend special knowledge and training. Even if turned aside, such gestures

[1] Quoted from the manuscript of her forthcoming book, *Rape: The Power of Consciousness;* to be published in 1979 by Harper & Row.

constitute mental rape, destructive to a woman's ego. They are acts of domination, as despicable as the molestation of the daughter by the father.

But long before entering college the woman student has experienced her alien identity in a world which misnames her, turns her to its own uses, denying her the resources she needs to become self-affirming, self-defined. The nuclear family teaches her that relationships are more important than selfhood or work; that "whether the phone rings for you, and how often," having the right clothes, doing the dishes, take precedence over study or solitude; that too much intelligence or intensity may make her unmarriageable; that marriage and children—service to others—are, finally, the points on which her life will be judged a success or a failure. In high school, the polarization between feminine attractiveness and independent intelligence comes to an absolute. Meanwhile, the culture resounds with messages. During Solar Energy Week in New York I saw young women wearing "ecology" T-shirts with the legend: CLEAN, CHEAP AND AVAILABLE; a reminder of the 1960s antiwar button which read: CHICKS SAY YES TO MEN WHO SAY NO. Department store windows feature female mannequins in chains, pinned to the wall with legs spread, smiling in positions of torture. Feminists are depicted in the media as "shrill," "strident," "puritanical," or "humorless." and the lesbian choice—the choice of the woman-identified woman—as pathological or sinister. The young woman sitting in the philosophy classroom, the political science lecture, is already gripped by tensions between her nascent sense of self-worth, and the battering force of messages like these.

Look at a classroom: look at the many kinds of women's faces, postures, expressions. Listen to the women's voices. Listen to the silences, the unasked questions, the blanks. Listen to the small, soft voices, often courageously trying to speak up, voices of women taught early that tones of confidence, challenge, anger, or assertiveness, are strident and unfeminine. Listen to the voices of the women and the voices of the men; observe the space men allow themselves, physically and verbally, the male assumption that people will listen, even when the majority of the group is female. Look at the faces of the silent, and of those who speak. Listen to a woman groping for language in which to express what is on her mind, sensing that the terms of academic discourse are not her language, trying to cut down her thought to the dimensions of a discourse not intended for her (*for it is not fitting that a woman speak in public*); or reading her paper aloud at breakneck speed, throwing her words away, deprecating her own work by a reflex prejudgment: *I do not deserve to take up time and space.*

As women teachers, we can either deny the importance of this context in which women students think, write, read, study, project their own futures; or try to work with it. We can either teach passively, accepting these conditions, or actively, helping our students identify and resist them.

One important thing we can do is *discuss* the context. And this need not happen only in a women's studies course; it can happen anywhere. We can refuse to accept passive, obedient learning and insist upon critical thinking. We can become harder on our women students, giving them the kinds of "cultural prodding" that men receive, but on different terms and in a different style. Most young women need to have their intellectual lives, their work, legitimized against the claims of family, relationships, the old message that a woman is always available for service to others. We need to keep our standards very high, not to accept a woman's preconceived sense of her limitations; we need to be hard to please, while supportive of risk-taking, because self-respect often comes only when exacting standards have been met. At a time when adult literacy is generally low, we need to demand more, not less, of women, both for the sake of their futures as thinking beings, and because historically women have always had to be better than men to do half as well. A romantic sloppiness, an inspired lack of rigor, a self-indulgent incoherence, are symptoms of female self-depreciation. We should help our women students to look very critically at such symptoms, and to understand where they are rooted.

Nor does this mean we should be training women students to "think like men." Men in general think badly: in disjuncture from their personal lives, claiming objectivity where the most irrational passions seethe, losing, as Virginia Woolf observed, their senses in the pursuit of professionalism. It is not easy to think like a woman in a man's world, in the world of the professions; yet the capacity to do that is a strength which we can try to help our students develop. To think like a woman in a man's world means thinking critically, refusing to accept the givens, making connections between facts and ideas which men have left unconnected. It means remembering that every mind resides in a body; remaining accountable to the female bodies in which we live; constantly retesting given hypotheses against lived experience. It means a constant critique of language, for as Wittgenstein (no feminist) observed, "The limits of my language are the limits of my world." And it means that most difficult thing of all: listening and watching in art and literature, in the social sciences, in all the descriptions we are given of the world, for the silences, the absences, the nameless, the unspoken, the encoded—for there we will find the true knowledge of women. And in breaking those silences, naming our selves, uncovering the hidden, making ourselves present, we begin to define a reality which resonates to *us*, which affirms *our* being, which allows the woman teacher and the woman student alike to take ourselves, and each other, seriously: meaning, to begin taking charge of our lives.

Power and Danger: Works of a Common Woman (1977)

The necessity of poetry has to be stated over and over, but only to those who have reason to fear its power, or those who still believe that language is "only words" and that an old language is good enough for our descriptions of the world we are trying to transform.

For many women, the commonest words are having to be sifted through, rejected, laid aside for a long time, or turned to the light for new colors and flashes of meaning: *power, love, control, violence, political, personal, private, friendship, community, sexual, work, pain, pleasure, self, integrity* . . . When we become acutely, disturbingly aware of the language we are using and that is using us, we begin to grasp a material resource that women have never before collectively attempted to repossess (though we were its inventors, and though individual writers like Dickinson, Woolf, Stein, H. D., have approached language as transforming power). Language is as real, as tangible in our lives as streets, pipelines, telephone switchboards, microwaves, radioactivity, cloning laboratories, nuclear power stations. We might hypothetically possess ourselves of every recognized technological resource on the North American continent, but as long as our language is inadequate, our vision remains formless, our

Originally appeared as the introduction to *The Work of a Common Woman: The Collected Poetry of Judy Grahn*, published by and available from Diana Press, 4400 Market St., Oakland, Ca. 94608.

thinking and feeling are still running in the old cycles, our process may be "revolutionary" but not transformative.

For many of us, the word "revolution" itself has become not only a dead relic of Leftism, but a key to the deadendedness of male politics: the "revolution" of a wheel which returns in the end to the same place; the "revolving door" of a politics which has "liberated" women only to use them, and only within the limits of male tolerance. When we speak of *transformation* we speak more accurately out of the vision of a process which will leave neither surfaces nor depths unchanged, which enters society at the most essential level of the subjugation of women and nature by men. We begin to conceive a planet on which both women and nature might coexist as the She Who we encounter in Judy Grahn's poems.

Poetry is, among other things, a criticism of language. In setting words together in new configurations, in the mere, immense shift from male to female pronouns, in the relationships between words created through echo, repetition, rhythm, rhyme, it lets us hear and see our words in a new dimension:

> I am the wall at the lip of the water
> I am the rock that refused to be battered
> I am the dyke in the matter, the other
> I am the wall with the womanly swagger . . .

Poetry is above all a concentration of the *power* of language, which is the power of our ultimate relationship to everything in the universe. It is as if forces we can lay claim to in no other way, become present to us in sensuous form. The knowledge and use of this magic goes back very far: the rune; the chant; the incantation; the spell; the kenning; sacred words; forbidden words; the naming of the child, the plant, the insect, the ocean, the configuration of stars, the snow, the sensation in the body. The ritual telling of the dream. The physical reality of the human voice; of words gouged or incised in stone or wood, woven in silk or wool, painted on vellum, or traced in sand.

Forces we can lay claim to in no other way . . . Think of the deprivation of women living for centuries without a poetry which spoke of

women together, of women alone, of women as anything but the
fantasies of men. Think of the hunger unnamed and unnameable,
the sensations mistranslated.

In January 1974, struggling with flu and a rising temperature, I lay
in bed and turned the pages of a magazine to a poem called "A
Woman Is Talking to Death." Its first three or four lines possessed an
uncanny urgency, rare even among the strong poems that *Amazon
Quarterly*—the magazine I held in my hands—had been publishing.[1] When I finished the poem, I realized I had been weeping; and I
knew in an exhausted kind of way that what had happened to me was
irreversible. All I could do with it at that point was lie down and
sleep, let the flu run its course, and the knowledge that was ac-
cumulating in my life, the poem I had just read, go on circulating in
my bloodstream.

A week or two later I heard that Judy Grahn was giving a reading
in New York. I went. A woman, looking both slight and strong, got
up in the darkish clutter of the Westbeth Artists' Project and started
speaking in a low voice, first about the Oakland Women's Press Collective, which she had helped to found, then briefly about her own
work. She read some poems from a pamphlet-sized book called *The
Common Woman* and then, apologizing unapologetically for her difficulty in reading the poem aloud, she read "A Woman Is Talking to
Death." She read very quietly. I have never heard a poem encom-
passing so much violence, grief, anger, compassion, read so quietly.
There was absolutely no "performance." It was clear that many in
the audience, like myself, had already discovered the poem for
themselves.

That evening she also read "A Plain Song from an Older Woman
to a Younger Woman"—utterly different from, yet as extraordinary
in its way as "A Woman Is Talking to Death": a poem of tender, bitter, lamentation, its rhymes and rhythms strung in a very old form,
but its direction a new one for poetry: the "new words" which are
written by women writing entirely to and for women. (The point, by
the way, in case it need be made here in this book which so many

---

[1] I want here to pay tribute to that journal, which provided, in its brief life, a space
in which thinking as a woman, loving women, and creating for women became fused,
made more possible, in essay after essay, poem after poem, vision after vision.

will hold in their hands, is not the "exclusion" of men; it is that *primary presence of women to ourselves and each other* first described in prose by Mary Daly, and which is the crucible of a new language.)

Much later, some of us went out to get something to eat; and I was able to speak to Judy Grahn, rather haltingly, of the effect of her work on me. We were strangers, she even shyer than I, perhaps instinctively shy of New York. I remember her saying that writing "A Woman Is Talking to Death" had frightened her enough that she'd decided to stop writing poetry for a while and work on a novel. But of course she didn't stop writing poetry. She continues work on the novel; but this collection shows that she has chosen to acknowledge the importance of her poetry as a body of work and as a path into the future.

I felt I could understand why she said writing the long poem had frightened her; it wasn't simply the routine hype of the traveling poet who is expected to give back provocative responses to compliments. I think any poet lives in both terror and longing for the poem which will bring together—at least for the time being—everywhere she has been, everything her work to date has been a preparation for. "A Woman Is Talking to Death" feels like such a poem. Flashes of the poet's experience (*testimony in trials that never got heard*) intersect with images of death at work: historical violence against women, ranging from the feudal wife through the witches to the aging or teenaged rape victim; the reduction of black people, poor people, and women to nonhuman status; the violence—of neglect, of rejection, of outright brutality or accidental cruelty—that the powerless inflict on ourselves and each other; the sapping-away of female spirit and flesh by the culture of patriarchy. There is nothing more unnerving and yet empowering than the making of connections, and "A Woman Is Talking to Death" makes connections first for the poet, among events in her own life; then for us who live intensely, through the power of her language, what she has lived and seen. It is in the language of the poem that the fragments come together, echoing off each other in repetitions, in rhythms, in an intricate structure which may not be obvious on a first reading or hearing, but which works like the complexity of a piece of music. Nothing less complex could do justice to the "contradictions" of the games we play with death in a culture which not only blames the victim but sets the victim to blaming other victims, keeps the wheel of powerlessness spinning, dead motorcyclist to black motorist to white women outside the law fleeing the bridge in fear, the repetitions of history:

> keep the women small and weak
> and off the street, and off the
> bridges, that's the way, brother,
> one day I will leave you there,
> as I have left you there before,
> working for death.

Under the pressure of these contradictions, which are transformed into connections, words are forced to yield up new meanings in the poem: *lovers; I wanted her; indecent acts*. The word *lover*, purged of romantic-sentimental associations, becomes a name for what human beings might mean to each other in a world where each person held both power and responsibility. There are poems which, as we write them, we know are going to change the ways in which it is possible for us to see and act. Perhaps "A Woman Is Talking to Death" was this kind of poem for Judy Grahn.

It has been this kind of poem for me, and I think for a great many of its readers. And I think it is a pivotal poem in this book.

"A Woman Is Talking to Death" is both a political poem and a love poem. I mean, that it is a political poem to the extent that it is a love poem, and a love poem insofar as it is political—that is, concerned with powerlessness and power. No true political poetry can be written with propaganda as an aim, to persuade others "out there" of some atrocity or injustice (hence the failure, as poetry, of so much anti-Vietnam poetry of the sixties). As *poetry*, it can come only from the poet's need to identify her relationship to atrocities and injustice, the sources of her pain, fear, and anger, the meaning of her resistance. Nor are we likely to write good love poems because, having "fallen in love" we want to lay a poem in the lover's lap. The gift-poem is usually unmeaningful to anyone but the recipient. The most revealing and life-sustaining love poetry is not "about" the lover but about the poet's attempt to live with her experience of love, to fathom how she can order its chaos and ride out its storms, to ask what *loving* an individual can mean in the face of death, cruelty, famine, violence, taboo. For the lesbian poet it means rejecting the entire convention of love-poetry and undertaking to create a new tradition. She is forced by the conditions under which she loves, and the conditions in which all women attempt to survive, to ask questions that did not occur to a Donne or a Yeats, or even to an Elizabeth Barrett Browning (whose love sonnets are conventional, though her political poems are not); questions about taboo, integrity, the fetishization of the female body, the worldwide, historical violence against women by men, what it means to be "true to one another" when we are women, what it means to love women when that love is denied reality, treated as perversion, or, even more insidiously, "accepted" as a mirror-image or parallel to heterosexual romance. Judy Grahn, more than any other poet today, has taken up that challenge.

The book begins, interestingly, with a very early warning against the romantic convention. "Edward the Dyke" is a satire on the psychoanalysts and their "scientific" diagnosis and cures for lesbianism; but it is also a satire on lesbian romanticism. Edward indeed has a "problem," but it is not her "homosexuality"; rather it's that she has only a sentimental and rhetorical language in which to describe her experience: "Love flowers pearl, of delighted arms. Warm and water. Melting of vanilla wafer in the pants. Pink petal roses trembling overdew on the lips, soft and juicy fruit. . . . Cinnamon toast poetry. Justice equality higher wages. Independent angel song. It means I can do what I want." The reverse of all this is her capitulation before the psychoanalyst's bullying: "I am vile! I am vile!" Because Edward has no sense of her love for women as anything but utopian, individual, and personal, she has no resistance to "treatment," in fact seeks it out; she is easily turned against herself. The warning of "Edward the Dyke" (and it is a serious one, couched in an apparently witty and light-hearted fable) is that if you unquestioningly accept one piece of the culture that despises and fears you, you are vulnerable to other pieces. Language is the key. Dr. Knox doesn't listen to anything Edward is saying; but Edward herself fails to examine both the breathless language of her love *and* the language of the analyst's version: "sordid . . . depraved . . . clandestine . . . penis envy . . . narcissism . . . mother substitute." Only as we begin to ask ourselves whether terms like "penis envy," "masochism," even "homosexual" have any meaning, or what they are actually describing, do we begin to create a language and worldview of our own, to perceive the vast landscape of woman-hating and male envy of women, underlying the haze of heterosexual romance, the domestic idyll, and the jargon of "pathology" and "deviance."

Over and over Grahn calls up the living woman against the manufactured one, the manmade creation of centuries of male art and literature. *Look at me as if you had never seen a woman before . . . Our lovers teeth are white geese flying above us/Our lovers muscles are rope-ladders under our hands.* Marilyn Monroe's body, in death, becomes a weapon, her bone a bludgeon to beat the voyeurs, the fetishists, the poets and journalists vampirizing off the "dumb-blonde" of the centerfolds. *There were two long-haired women/holding back the traffic just behind me/with their bare hands, the machines came down like mad bulls . . .* Loving women means loving not a fantasy but women as we are, a woman as she is:

> wanting, wanting
> am I not   broken
> stolen   common
>
> am I not crinkled cranky poison
> am I not glint-eyed and frozen
>
> am I not   aged
> shaky   glazing
> am I not   hazy
> guarded   craven. . . .
>
> was I not   over
> over   ridden?   ("Plain Song")

She keeps her mind the way men
keep a knife—keen to strip the game
down to her size. She has a thin spine,
swallows her eggs cold, and tells lies . . .

> ("Ella in a square apron . . .")

And it means above all asking questions about power:

> if Love means protect then whenever I cannot
> protect you

I cannot call my name Love.
if Love means rebirth then when I see us
dead on our feet
I cannot call my name Love.
if Love means provide & when I cannot
provide for you
why would you call my name Love?

Powerless, women have been seduced into confusing love with false
power—the "power" of mother-love, the "power" of gentle influence, the "power" of nonviolence, the "power" of the meek who are
to inherit the earth. Grahn conjures up other meanings of power:

> . . . Many years back
> a woman of strong purpose
> passed through this section
> and everything else tried to follow.
>
> • • •
>
> was I not   ruling
> guiding   naming
> was I not   brazen
> crazy   chosen
>
> even the stones would do my bidding?
>
> • • •
>
> Carol and her
> crescent wrench
> work bench
> wooden fence
> side stance . . .
> Carol and her
> hack saw
> well worn
> torn back
> bad spine
> never-mind
> timberline
> clear mind . . .

The power and danger of the lesbian converge in "A Woman Is
Talking to Death." *This woman is a lesbian, be careful.* When, after

leaving the bridge where the motorcyclist was killed, the narrator looks in the mirror, she sees:

> . . . nobody was there to testify
> how clear, an unemployed queer woman
> makes no witness at all,
> nobody at all was there for
> those two questions: what does
> she do, and who is she married to?

Power and powerlessness: the original "Common Woman" sequence is a study in this theme, besides being the most vivid and clear-honed series of portraits of women in any poetry I know. Each of these women is fighting in her own way to gain a little control over her life: Helen trying to grasp it at the price of "spite and malice," a "metallic" respectability, a life in which "details take the place of meaning"; Ella who "turns away the smaller tips, out of pride" and who "shot a lover who misused her child" thereby losing the child; Nadine who "holds things together, collects bail . . . pokes at the ruins of the city/like an armored tank . . ."; Carol, forced to hide her strength on the job, who "walks around all day/quietly, but underneath it/she's electric:angry energy inside a passive form"; Annie who "when she smells danger . . . spills herself all over/like gasoline, and lights it"; Margaret, "fired for making/strikes, and talking out of turn/. . . Lusting for changes, she laughs through her/teeth, and wanders from room to room"; Vera with her "religion which insisted that people/are beautiful golden birds and must be preserved."

The "Common Woman" is far more than a class description. What is "common" in and to women is the intersection of oppression and strength, damage and beauty. It is, quite simply, the *ordinary* in women which will "rise" in every sense of the word—spiritually and in activism. For us, to be "extraordinary" or "uncommon" is to fail. History has been embellished with "extraordinary," "exemplary," "uncommon," and of course "token" women whose lives have left the rest unchanged. The "common woman" is in fact the embodiment of the extraordinary will-to-survival in millions of obscure women, a life-force which transcends childbearing: unquenchable, chromosomatic reality. Only when we can count on this force in each other, everywhere, know absolutely that it is there for us, will we cease abandoning and being abandoned by "all of our lovers." Judy Grahn reclaims "the common woman" as a phrase from vulgar Marxist associations, or such political clichés as "the century of the common man."[2]

I think this passion for survival is the great theme of women's poetry (How interesting that male critics have focused on our suicidal poets, and on their "self"-destructiveness rather than their capacity for hard work and for staying alive as long as they did. How expectable, yet how nauseating, the vogue for Julie Harris's sugared impersonation of Emily Dickinson as *The Belle of Amherst*, depicting as a neurasthenic, "feminine" little eccentric the poet whose major themes were power and anger.). The poetry of female survival has its own history, but in it must be mentioned Juana de la Cruz, Louise Labé, the women troubadours, Emily Dickinson, Elizabeth Barrett Browning, Emily Brontë, H. D.—"Every woman who writes is a survivor," Tillie Olsen has said. Literacy, the time and space to make literature, were stolen from women by the patriarchal order. And when we could make literature, it has been lost, misread, kept from us. In my college years we studied the "great" long poems of modernism: Eliot's "The Waste Land," Hart Crane's "The Bridge," Pound's "Cantos"; and later William Carlos Williams's "Paterson," Allen Ginsberg's "Howl." But we did not read, and courses in modern poetry still do not teach, H. D.'s epic poem, "Trilogy," in which she confronted war, nationalist insanity, the ruin of the great cities, not mourning the collapse of Western civilization but turning back for her inspiration to prehistory, to a gynocentric tradition. H. D. insisted that the poet-as-woman should stop pouring her energies into a ground left sterile by the power-mongers and death-cultists: *Let us leave / the place-of-a-skull / to them that have made it*. Nor did we know that H. D.'s life had been literally saved by a woman, Bryher, who took her off to Greece after her near-death in childbirth in the

---

[2] She also reclaims the lesbian from the stereotyping images of male Decadent painters such as Egon Schiele, Aubrey Beardsley, Gustav Klimt, who perceived the lesbian as an exotic hothouse flower, elegantly and evilly erotic, and essentially predatory; also from the historical stereotype derived from such actual women as Natalie Barney, Renée Vivien, Radclyffe Hall, Romaine Brooks, or Gertrude Stein (who would certainly have rejected the term "common woman" as applied to herself, but who also suffered acutely from her sense of herself as a loner).

1917 flu epidemic, and stood beside her while the poet underwent the hallucination, or vision, out of which her mature work was to flower. For women, the "breakdown" of Western "civilization" between the wars and after the holocaust has never seemed as ultimate and consequential as it has for men; Lillian Smith remarks in an essay that what Freud "mistook for her lack of civilization is woman's lack of *loyalty* to civilization."[3] What the male poets were mourning and despairing over had never *been* ours, and, as H. D. saw, what we have yet to create does not depend on their institutions; would in fact rather be free of them. She saw that for her as a woman poet, "the walls do not fall"—there are living sources for her that transcend the death-spiral of patriarchy. Judy Grahn is a direct inheritor of that passion for life in the woman poet, that instinct for true power, not domination, which poets like Barrett Browning, Dickinson, H. D., were asserting in their own very different ways and voices.

The last section in this book, "Confrontations with the Devil in the Form of Love," are astringent, low-key, variations on the theme of love as personal solution, salvation, false control, false power. Some of them have the acid taste of wild apples, the sting of the unforgettable, as:

> Love came along and saved
> no one
> Love came along, went broke
> got busted, was run out of
> town and desperately needs—
> something. Don't tell her it's Love.

I find myself wishing I could see these "Confrontations" inscribed every which way on a wall—not hung together in linear sequence—for each takes on new meaning read with the others, and the apparently innocent and casual in Grahn's work is often the most subversive, ironic, and shrewd. The "devil" is always that which wants us to settle for less than we deserve, for panaceas, handouts, temporary safety; and for women, the devil has most often taken the form of

[3] "Autobiography as a Dialogue between King and Corpse," in *The Winner Names the Age: A Collection of Writings by Lillian Smith*, Michelle Cliff, ed. (New York: Norton, 1978), p. 191.

love rather than of power, gold, or learning. So the apparent lightness of these poems had better be taken very seriously, and we might well call to mind, as we read these latest poems, the redefinition of "lovers" that Grahn has offered us in "A Woman Is Talking to Death."

The necessity of poetry has to be stated over and over, but only to those who have reason to fear its power, or those who still believe that language is "only words" and that an old language is good enough for our descriptions of the world we are trying to transform.

Motherhood: The Contemporary Emergency and the Quantum Leap (1978)

I want to begin by saying something that has been on my mind ever since I was asked to participate in this conference. I hope, and believe, that every woman in this room knows that on the subject of motherhood there are no experts. What we need, in any case, as women, is not experts on our lives, but the opportunity and the validation to name and describe the truths of our lives, as we have known them. Whatever you hear from me, from Jessie Bernard, from Dorothy Dinnerstein, from Tillie Olsen, [the three other invited speakers at the conference] remember that it is your own sense of urgency, your own memories, needs, questions, and hopes, your own painfully gathered knowledge of daughterhood and motherhood, which you must above all trust. Listen to us, then, as to four women who through certain kinds of luck, privilege, struggle, exceptional status, and at certain kinds of cost, have been able not only to live the experience of daughterhood and motherhood, but also to reflect and write about it. But listen even more closely to yourselves.

One of the most powerful social and political catalysts of the past decade has been the speaking of women with other women, the telling of our secrets, the comparing of wounds and the sharing of

Talk for Columbus, Ohio, conference on the Future of Mothering, sponsored by the Women's Resource and Policy Development Center, June 2, 3, 4, 1978.

words. This hearing and saying of women has been able to break many a silence and taboo; literally to transform forever the way we see. Let this be a time, then, for hearing and speaking together, for breaking silences, not only within yourselves but among all our selves: the daughter and the mother; the black woman and the white; the lesbian mother and the married housewife; the woman who has chosen single or communal motherhood and the woman who has chosen to use her life in ways which do not include the raising of children; the woman who has given up custody of her children and the woman who is fighting to keep hers; the step-daughter, the foster-mother, the pregnant woman; the daughter who has never known her mother, the mother who has no daughters. What we all, collectively, have lived, as the daughters of women, as the mothers of children, is a tale far greater than any three or four of us can encompass: a tale only beginning to be told. I hope that here, speaking to and hearing one another, we can begin to fling cables of recognition and attention across the conditions that have divided us. And so I begin tonight by urging each of you to take responsibility for the voicing of her experience, to take seriously the work of listening to each other and the work of speaking, whether in private dialogue or in larger groups. In order to change what is, we need to give speech to what *has been*, to imagine together what *might be*.

I have seen massive sculpturelike weavings, of jute, hemp, and wool, in which many varicolored strands are quickly visible like vines or striations; but when you come closer and try to touch this or that strand, your hand enters a dense, bristling mesh, thick with knotted and twisted filaments, some harsh and rough to the fingers, others surprisingly silky and strong. In writing *Of Woman Born*, and in thinking about motherhood ever since, I have felt a similar sensation, of elemental exploration and of complex discovery. Let us try then to do justice to the complexity of this immense weaving, even as we single out particular strands or finger particular knots that seem to account for the whole. For motherhood is the great mesh in which all human relations are entangled, in which lurk our most elemental assumptions about love and power.

If we speak of motherhood at all, we are inevitably speaking of something far more than the relationship of a woman with her children. And even this relationship has been shaped long before the first child's birth. All women are daughters of women—is this an obvious, a simple-minded statement? or does it reach through the layers of the weaving to inner chambers only now beginning to be explored by women? It has been suggested by Margaret Mead that possibly a deep chemical affinity exists, of which we as yet know nothing, between the body of the mother and her still unborn female child. It has been affirmed by Nancy Chodorow, that through the intense mother-daughter relationship women come into a deep and richer inner life than men, and, even when heterosexual, tend to be more deeply attached to women than to men, and more capable than men of relationship.[1] Both Chodorow and Dorothy Dinnerstein feel strongly that the solution to sexual inequality would be a radical change in the system of parenting, that is, that parenting must be shared equally between women and men. I wish here to suggest other forces which sit in wait in the birth-chamber as a woman completes her first nine months of mothering.

Historically, cross-culturally, a woman's status as childbearer has been the test of her womanhood. Through motherhood, every woman has been defined from outside herself: mother, matriarch, matron, spinster, barren, old maid—listen to the history of emotional timbre that hangs about each of these words. Even by default motherhood has been an enforced identity for women, while the phrases "childless man" and "nonfather" sound absurd and irrelevant to us.

And so this woman in labor is on the one hand, even perhaps in terror and pain, doing what history has told her it was her duty and destiny to do; while at the same time doing what her mother did, reenacting a scene, which both separates her from her own mother (for now she is, supposedly, herself a woman and no longer a child) and creates her more intensely in her mother's image.

Motherhood is also, of course, at the crux of the self-determination of women over our bodies. Many of you need no reminding that here in Ohio we meet on soil already shaken by the fire-bombing and burning of four women's health clinics within the past four months, part of a nationwide pattern of terrorism against the hard-won and fragile right of women to make the invariably difficult

[1] *The Reproduction of Mothering* (Berkeley: University of California, 1978), p. 198.

choice to end an unwanted pregnancy. But these attacks on the grassroots, spreading movement of women to repossess our bodies are only one small piece of the larger picture to which I allude, in the title of this talk, as "the contemporary emergency." Sometimes referred to as "the backlash," this emergency is many-pronged, and I believe it is important to grasp it as clearly and as realistically as we can.

Motherhood, the family, are still too often relegated to the realm of the "private and personal." "For love," women are assumed to provide unflagging emotional care, not only to children but to men; while in terms of the physical work we do, our enormous, unpaid contribution to every economy is everywhere dismissed as only the natural service of women to men and children. We would rightly be skeptical of a feminism which denied the value and dignity of traditional women's work in the home. But in fact it is not feminists who have belittled and devalued the work of the housewife and mother: It is the statisticians, the political scientists, the economists, the image-makers of television and other advertising, the professionals, who depict the woman at home as "not working," as invisible, as an empty-headed consumer. Listen to the idiotic baby-voices allotted to women in canned radio commercials, look at the grimacing smiles of housewives and mothers as depicted on television, observe the obscene patronizing of women on game shows, read the childraising and sex manuals, equally patronizing, written by the male doctor experts.[2] The feminist movement has from the first demanded choice as each women's right, respect for each woman's being; feminist artists, historians, anthropologists have been the first to show concern and respect for the crafts of the midwives and grandmothers, the anonymous work of women's hands, the oral culture of women sitting in kitchens, the traditional arts and remedies passed on from mother to daughter, the female culture never granted the reverence accorded to "high art." A recognition of women's unquenchable creativity—contained so often within domestic limits, yet astounding

[2] For a detailed documentation and analysis of the creation of "the woman problem" by postindustrial science, especially medicine, see B. Ehrenreich and D. English, *For Her Own Good: 150 Years of the Experts' Advice to Women* (New York: Doubleday/Anchor, 1978), a brilliant study marred only by its failure to deal with heterosexuality itself as a primary mandate to women.

in its diversity—has been one of the deep perceptions of a feminism which looks with fresh eyes on all that has been trivialized, devalued, forbidden, or silenced in female history. And so we can both take pride in all that women have done for "love"—including the resourceful, heroic coping of ordinary women everywhere—and also ask: "Why should women, and women only, work for love only? And what kind of love is this, which means always to be for others, never for ourselves?"

But the dismissal of the traditional work of women as nonwork, of our art as mere "decoration" or "craft" or "scribbling," the condescension to the housewife and mother, the long and violent campaign against voluntary motherhood, the suspect status of women who are neither wives nor mothers—these are merely symptoms of the much larger phenomenon of *gynephobia*—fear and hatred of women—which in its less virulent and savage forms we have called "sexism." Much is being written these days about gender-identity—and about how we can change the restricting images of self that both girls and boys learn so early, as the chief lessons of culture. I believe that the issue of gender-identity may well mask a reality much deeper and more terrifying to contemplate than the superstitions which impose one set of qualities upon one sex and another set on the other.

Beneath sexism, beneath socially enforced gender-identity and stereotype, lies *gynephobia*. It is an ancient and well-documented phenomenon,[3] and it is not a simple one, neither in its origins nor in the many faces it wears in the present day. Certainly male contempt and loathing for women and for women's bodies is embedded in language, art, folklore, and legend; the need to contain and restrict women's creativity and power within the mothering role is an insistent theme in all social institutions; what has been called "the backlash" is, I think, only an intensification of the long assault upon every effort by women to repossess ourselves, to lay hold on our integrity, to refuse to hate ourselves as we have been hated.

There has been a basic contradiction throughout patriarchy: be-

[3] See H. R. Hays, *The Dangerous Sex: The Myth of Feminine Evil* (New York: Pocket Books, 1972), first published 1964; Katherine M. Rogers, *The Troublesome Helpmate: A History of Misogyny in Literature* (Seattle: University of Washington, 1966); Andrea Dworkin, *Woman Hating* (New York: Dutton, 1974); Mary Daly, *Gyn/Ecology: The Methaethics of Radical Feminism* (Boston: Beacon, 1979).

tween the laws and sanctions designed to keep women essentially powerless, and the attribution to mothers of almost superhuman power (of control, of influence, of life-support). The other side of the contradiction, of course, is the negation of women who are not mothers, or who are woman-identified. The unmarried or childless woman may be more acceptable today than when she was perceived as so threatening that she was burned as a witch. But the socialization of every girl toward heterosexual romance and childbearing is still probably the most intense socialization practiced by society as a whole. At the same time, once a woman has borne a child she is viewed as the primary and uttermost source of that child's good and evil, its survival, health, sanity, and selfhood. A society which penalizes some children because they are not white, others because they are not male, indoctrinating in them a sense of worthlessness, can still lay the blame for the waste of its young on the "bad" mothers who have somehow failed to be superhuman, who have somehow failed to rear, in a callous and ruthless social order, well-adjusted, obedient, achieving, nonalienated children.

Gynephobia supposes the eternal, universal guilt of women, and most women carry in us a learned, internalized version of that guilt. Maternal guilt is perhaps the most familiar to many of us; but many also know the guilt leveled at the woman who affirms herself, who is centered-in-herself, and who, in a woman-hating environment, dares to love herself and other women. It is ironic, to say the least, that the first verbal attack slung at the woman who demonstrates a primary loyalty to herself and other women is *man-hater*. The fear of appearing or being named as a man-hater still causes many women to deny the reality of gynephobia, the concrete evidences of woman-hating embedded in our culture, in language, image, and act.

Gynephobia is an old historical reality; what creates an emergency today is the fusion of gynephobia with technology. To deal fully with the implications of this—the acceleration of technological change over the past century, the rapidly increasing complexity of systems and the training of elite males who will decide how and for what technology is to be used—this would take several volumes, and some of these are already written. In response to this crisis, a strong feminist ecology movement is beginning to take shape, as exemplified by the Women's Conference on the Environment in Albany, June

17–18, 1978, and by the publication of two major books on women, manmade technology, and nature: Susan Griffin's *Woman and Nature* and Mary Daly's *Gyn/Ecology*.[4] What I want to do here is look at some things that are happening with respect to the control of motherhood, the exploitation of women's reproductive power by male-dominated institutions and systems.

The Supreme Court decision leading to state withdrawal of Medicaid funds for abortion is a legal attack upon a hard-won freedom for women. It is also directly linked with the growing use of sterilization as a population-control device—first in Latin America and other Third World areas, but soon to be attempted in the States as a major form of "family planning." If poor women cannot afford abortion, and cannot afford to raise their children, they are more likely to give what is often cynically termed "informed consent" to sterilization.[5] Already by 1968, 35.3 per cent of Puerto Rican women of childbearing age, two-thirds of them under thirty, had been sterilized—under funding by the department cynically termed Health, Education, and Welfare. Experimental contraceptives are tested by AID in Puerto Rico for dissemination in the Third World although they fail to meet the admittedly low standards of the United States drug industry. Sterilization is being used on poor women and women of color in the continental United States, even where abortion is legal and has been requested.

[4] Susan Griffin, *Woman and Nature: The Roaring Inside Her* (New York: Harper & Row, 1978); Mary Daly, op. cit. For an analysis of a specific application of technology, see Janice Raymond, *The Transsexual Empire: The Making of the She-Male* (Boston: Beacon, 1979).

[5] The importance of "guidelines" in the performance of elective sterilization is unquestionable. But, as we examine the social and economic conditions under which women give consent, and the absence of alternatives, it becomes clear that "the question of poverty is inseparable from reproductive freedom for women" and the meaning of "voluntary" becomes inseparable from a woman's entire life-situation, the actual range of her choices, her view of sterilization as "an escape from abject poverty." For an excellent overview of the issue, with emphasis on Puerto Rico, see *Workbook on Sterilization and Sterilization Abuse* (Ad Hoc Women's Studies Committee Against Sterilization Abuse, Women's Studies, Sarah Lawrence College, Bronxville, N.Y. 10708). See also "Who Controls Reproduction: Birth Control, Population Control, Sterilization Abuse" in *Isis* International Bulletin no. 7, spring 1978 (Case Postale 301, 1227 Carouge/Geneva, Switzerland).

Here are some examples quoted from an article on sterilization of Native American women from the Denver, Colorado, feminist newspaper, *Big Mama Rag*:

> Sterilization of women in this country has increased 300% since 1970. . . . An estimated 32% of all black women under thirty have been sterilized. . . . Over 25% of all American Indian women of childbearing age have been sterilized since 1973, leaving only about 100,000 women of childbearing age who can have children. Among those sterilized, 10% were under the age of 21. . . . Many Indian women are coerced into signing forms agreeing to sterilization. It is frequently insinuated that they will lose welfare payments and benefits if they refuse. A large number of women agree to sterilization operations because they are afraid that their children will be taken away from them if they don't. To avoid this type of misunderstanding government agencies are now required to inform women that there are other forms of birth control available to them and that other benefits may not be withheld if they refuse. However, there is no indication that these laws are being followed or enforced.[6]

The agencies implementing sterilization policies here and abroad are among those which present a "humanitarian" image to the public: HEW, VISTA, the Peace Corps, AID.[7] But women must be deeply skeptical of apparent solutions to human distress which may deprive any woman or group of women of the decision as to how their bodies are to be used. The assumptions justifying coercive sterilization are part of the objectification and exploitation of women's bodies that we see in pornography and in cultural imagery everywhere that degrades women. And no woman, or group of women, is finally exempt from these attitudes.

[6] Judy Barlow, "Sterilization of Native American Women," *Big Mama Rag*, vol. 6, no. 5, May 1978.

[7] "Humanitarian" at least in name. " 'The United States plans to sterilize one-quarter of the world's women,' said Dr. R. T. Ravenholt, director of AID's office on population control. According to Ravenholt, population control is necessary to maintain 'the normal operation of commercial interests around the world.' 'Without our trying to help these countries with their economic and social development, the world would rebel against the strong U.S. commercial presence,' " he said. (Liberation News Service, quoted in *Akwesasne Notes*, September 1977, p. 31.)

Meanwhile, in underdeveloped countries, the multinational corporations manufacturing commercial infant formula have been aggressively marketing their products as a better, Western replacement for breast milk. In Africa, the Caribbean, Latin America, the Philippines, areas where protein-calorie malnutrition can be an acute problem, and where mothers have successfully breastfed their children for centuries, samples of formula are given away at prenatal clinics, pushed by company employees costumed as "milk nurses," while clinic walls are plastered with posters alleging the superiority of powdered formula. Hospitals are bribed to permit advertising and sales with free gifts of medical equipment and other largesse. Very large numbers of children are dying from malnutrition—the mothers want to do the best, the most modern thing, for their infants, cannot afford to feed them the full formula, have in any case no refrigeration or sterile water supply, and often dilute or reduce the formula to save money.[8] When we hear of "population control" as a solution to famine, we must not forget starvation caused by the ruthlessness of "free" enterprise, and by a profound indifference to the lives of women and children.

I believe—as my poem "Hunger" attempts to delineate in a different kind of language—that the problem of world hunger is a central issue for women, that it is inextricably bound up with motherhood, and with the control of women's bodies by male-dominated interests. We hear a great deal about the "population explosion," but little about the withholding of resources, the waste and misuse of protein, the use of food as a tool of international pressure. "Population control" is targeted at women from groups considered expendable or "unfit" on the basis of income, class, and race. Instead of finding ways of supporting human life humanely on the planet, instead of controlling the expansion of corporate power and profiteering in agriculture, such male-dominated, and utterly nonfeminist, groups as Zero Population Growth and International Planned Parenthood seek to remove all choice from women as to the use of their potential for motherhood; sterilization is to replace contraception or

---

[8] See *Isis* International Bulletin no. 2, "Breast-Feeding: A Political Issue"; also "Baby Food Politics" in *Isis* no. 7; and Jane Cottingham, ed., *Bottle Babies: A Guide to the Baby Foods Issue*, published by *Isis*, December 1976.

abortion. Obviously, sterilization itself is no evil, so long as women have real psychological and economic choices. It is the *uses* of technology for both genocidal and gynecidal purposes which more and more women now view as a major emergency.

Another example: the sudden rise of 50 percent in the number of Caesarean operations performed in U.S. hospitals has attracted the attention of feminists in health work and childbirth education, as well as of some male physicians. Here again low-income women stand a higher chance of being viewed as "poor risks" in pregnancy and given Caesareans—using Medicaid money to pay the higher costs of this kind of delivery.[9] It is increasingly clear that medical technology has, in U.S. hospitals, but also in other parts of the world, become a means of alienating women from the act of giving birth, hence from their own bodies, their own procreative powers, and of keeping birth itself so far as possible in male control. It has also become a major industry. The story of this male "theft of childbirth" has been told and documented by Ehrenreich and English, by Suzanne Arms, and by myself;[10] and there is an active feminist health and home-birth movement dedicated to the project of "taking our bodies back." But the effort to seize the process of birth from women is now abetted by a technology far more developed than when in the seventeenth century the Chamberlen family hid the secret of the forceps for three generations. This new level of technology and medical research can create female genitals in a male-to-female transsexual; it can offer "restructured vaginas" as a solution for heterosexual sex problems; it can project mammal cloning as a realistic possibility; yet it has been unable to produce a truly safe and effective contraceptive device. The enormous complexity of sex-change surgery, as Janice Raymond has exhaustively shown, is now a major medical industry, aimed at solving the problems of gender-suffering through technology rather than through profound societal changes which would do away with sex roles altogether.[11]

[9] Maritza Arrastia, "Epidemic of Caesareans," *Seven Days*, May 5, 1978.

[10] B. Ehrenreich and D. English, *Witches, Midwives, and Nurses: A History of Women Healers* (Old Westbury, N.Y.: Feminist Press, 1973); Suzanne Arms, *Immaculate Deception* (Boston: Houghton Mifflin, 1975); Adrienne Rich, *Of Woman Born: Motherhood as Experience and Institution* (New York: Norton, 1976).

[11] Raymond, op cit.

Finally, while a powerful corporate state works to remove the right of motherhood from thousands of poor and Third World women, a powerful Church and other corporate interests agitate as "friends of the fetus." As Alice Rossi has pointed out,

> There are now far more fetuses in the American work-place than there ever were children in our mines and factories in the whole history of American child labor; yet there have been no large-scale investigations of the potential influence on the fetus of the vast array of new chemicals and synthetic substances in the environments in which employed women work. In one of the few studies in this area, [Vilma] Hunt found a significant correlation between severe air pollution and the incidence of fetal distress, prematurity, and stillbirths.[12]

Both the Right-to-Life and the Population Control movements are obsessed with direct control of women's bodies—not with discovering and creating conditions which would make life more livable for the living. In the middle-class United States, a veneer of "alternate life-styles" disguises the reality that, here as everywhere, women's apparent "choices" whether to have or not have children are still dependent on the far from neutral will of male legislators, jurists, a male medical and pharmaceutical profession, well-financed lobbies, including the prelates of the Catholic Church, and the political reality that women do not as yet have self-determination over our bodies, and still live mostly in ignorance of our authentic physicality, our possible choices, our eroticism itself.

We are undermined and subverted, not simply by precarious and whimsical abortion laws, precarious and fallible birth-control devices; but also by laws and conventions protecting a husband's right to rape and batter his wife or kidnap his children; by pornographic advertising which tells us we love to submit to sexual violence; by the victim-imagery of the Christian Church, which extols passive motherhood in the person of the Virgin Mary; by the very manner in which we give birth in hospitals, surrounded by male experts, su-

[12] Alice Rossi, "Children and Work in the Lives of Women," paper delivered at the University of Arizona, Tucson, February 7, 1976. See Chapter IV, "Work, Reproduction and Health," in Jeanne Mager Stellman, *Women's Work, Women's Health, Myths and Realities* (New York: Pantheon, 1977).

pinely drugged or stirruped against our will, our babies taken from us at birth by other experts who will tell us how often to feed, when we may hold, our newborns. And, finally, by the whispering voice of the culture, internalized in us, that says *we* are forever guilty; guilty of living in a woman's body, guilty of getting pregnant, guilty of refusing the mother-role altogether. A male-dominated technological establishment and a male-dominated population-control network view both the planet and women's bodies as resources to be seized, exploited, milked, excavated, and controlled. Somehow, in the nightmare image of an earth overrun with starving people because feckless, antisocial women refuse to stop breeding, we can perceive contempt for women, for the children of women, and for the earth herself.

I have often asked myself whether the experience of motherhood under patriarchy is finally radicalizing or conservatizing. In attempting to give our children the security, the stability, we know they need, do we become more obedient to a social order we know is morally bankrupt; do we give in to the pressures of convention, of schools, of jobs; are our children our hostages to the State, its real safeguard—and escape-valve—against the anger of women? Or do we discover, in motherhood, the coarse, bitter, bedrock truth of the way things are, the callousness of patriarchy, its hatred of women, its indifference to new life, even to youth itself, that supposed idolatry of American life? In motherhood we are often separated from other women, enclosed in the home, and like paid domestic workers, we find it difficult to organize. Yet mothers *do* organize: to start cooperative childcare, to get broken glass cleaned off a playground, to keep schools open. In Brooklyn there is a Sisterhood of Black Single Mothers, surely one of the most beleaguered of all groups between the twin grindstones of gynephobia and racism. The Lesbian Mothers' National Defense Fund, based in Seattle, has helped a number of women to fight for and win custody of their children. The Welfare Mothers' Movement is a growing force across the country. These groups and others like them consist of women considered marginal to society, women who through color, poverty, and sexual preference already have reason to be politicized, in addition to their status as mothers. If they have organized under the daily, hourly emergency of their situations, mothers everywhere can organize. But we will need to disabuse ourselves of the myths of motherhood, of the idea of its sacredness, its protected status, its automatic validation of us as women.

The right to have or not have children; the right to have both children and a selfhood not dependent on them; these are still being fought for, and this fight threatens every part of the patriarchal system. We cannot afford to settle for individual solutions. The myth that motherhood is "private and personal" is the deadliest myth we have to destroy, and we have to begin by destroying it in ourselves. The institution of motherhood—which is maintained by the law, by patriarchal technology and religion, by all forms of education—including pornography—has, by the most savage of ironies, alienated women from our bodies by incarcerating us in them.

The "quantum leap" of my title is of course a leap of the imagination. When I chose that title, I was thinking a great deal about time. I am a woman of forty-nine, a lesbian/feminist, mother of three adult sons who still sometimes appear as young children in my dreams. The feminist movement of this half-century surfaced "just in time" for me; I had been a solitary feminist for too long. I know that the rest of my life will be spent working for transformations I shall not live to see realized. I feel daily, hourly impatience, and am pledged to the active and tenacious patience that a lifetime commitment requires: there can be no resignation in the face of backlash, setback, or temporary defeat; there can be no limits on what we allow ourselves to imagine. Because the past ten years of feminist thinking and action have been so full, so charged with revelations, challenges, as well as with anger and pain, we sometimes think of that decade as if it had been fifty years, not ten. *Why haven't we come further?* But in the great evolution of woman that this century's radical feminism envisions, we have only begun. And yet this longer historical view seems unbearable to me when I consider the urgency of each woman's life that may be lost, poured away like dishwater, because history does not move fast enough for her.

So the "quantum leap" implies that even as we try to deal with backlash and emergency, we are imagining the new: a future in which women are powerful, full of our own power, not the old patriarchal power-over but the power-to-create, power-to-think, power-to-articulate and concretize our visions and transform our lives and those of our children. I believe still, as I wrote in the afterword to *Of Woman Born*, that this power will begin to speak in us more and more as we repossess our own bodies, including the decision to mother or not to mother, and how, and with whom, and when. For the struggle of women to become self-determining is rooted in our bodies, and it is an indication of this that the token woman artist or intellectual or professional has so often been constrained to deny her female physicality in order to enter realms designated as male domain.

It has never been my belief that mothering could, under different circumstances, become easy. As I wrote at the end of my book:

> To destroy the institution is not to abolish motherhood. It is to release the creation and sustenance of life into the same realm of decision, struggle, surprise, imagination, and conscious intelligence, as any other difficult, but freely chosen, work.

This means, among other things, that a woman could choose motherhood freely, not just because safe and effective birth control was universally available, but because she would have no need to prove her adequacy as a woman by getting pregnant; that a woman need not look for economic security to a man, getting pregnant as a by-product; that no false necessity would dictate a choice between a woman's uterus and her brain; that the woman mothering her child was a being with dignity in the world, who respected her body, who had as much power as any other individual person to act upon and shape her society, and who possessed the wherewithal to meet her own needs and those of her children, whether she chose to live with a man, with a woman, with other parents and children, or in a separate household with her children. These are minimal conditions; but implied in them are enormous social and political changes.

What would it mean to mother in a society where women were deeply valued and respected, in a culture which was woman-affirming? What would it mean to bear and raise children in the fullness of our power to care for them, provide for them, in dignity and pride? What would it mean to mother in a society which had truly addressed the issues of racism and hunger? What would it mean to mother in a society which was making full use of the spiritual, intellectual, emotional, physical gifts of women, in all our difference and diversity? What would it mean to mother in a society which laid no stigma upon lesbians, so that women grew up with real emotional and erotic options in the choice of life companions and lovers? What would it mean to live and die in a culture which affirmed both life and death, in which both the living world and the bodies of women were released at last from centuries of violation and control? This is the quantum leap of the radical feminist vision.

I believe we must cope courageously and practically, as women have always done, with the here and now, our feet on this ground where we now live. But nothing less than the most radical imagination will carry us beyond this place, beyond the mere struggle for survival, to that lucid recognition of our possibilities which will keep us impatient, and unresigned to mere survival.

Disloyal to Civilization: Feminism, Racism, Gynephobia (1978)

The text that follows grew—over nearly a year—out of talks I prepared for two occasions. The first was a panel conceived and moderated by Julia P. Stanley, and sponsored by the Women's Commission and the Gay Caucus of the Modern Language Association under the title: "The Transformation of Silence into Language and Action." Other participants were Mary Daly, Audre Lorde, and Judith McDaniel.* The second occasion was a talk I gave a few weeks later for the Turning Point Project of the University of Massachusetts, Boston, a group doing advocacy work for the women's prison at Framingham, publishing an excellent magazine of art and writing by women prisoners, and working in the outside community to lessen the gap of separation between women in prison and women who are "free." One goal of the project has been to educate women outside to the political realities that create a female prison population of which the majority are poor women and women of color.

In both of these talks my themes were silence and separation: the silence surrounding the lives of lesbians and black women, the separation of black and white women from each other. As I worked on revising the MLA talk for publication in the lesbian/feminist journal *Sinister Wisdom*, I felt a pressing need to work out the ideas sketched there in a longer and more reflective essay. The subject, of course, deserves a book; many books. And they will be, are undoubtedly being, written. These notes, as I finally think of them, are an attempt to suggest some of the geography I see, lying half in shadow, waiting to be mapped and recorded.

The following women read earlier drafts of this essay and gave generously

* For a transcript of this panel, see *Sinister Wisdom*, no. 6, summer 1978.

of both support and critical challenge: Maureen Brady, Michelle Cliff, Mary Daly, Sarah Hoagland, June Jordan, Lisa Leghorn, Audre Lorde, Judith McDaniel, Barbara Smith, Laura Sperazi. In acknowledging my debt to them for helping me clarify my thought and push it further, I do not imply that any or all of them necessarily agree with everything I have written here.

The essay was first published in *Chrysalis: A Magazine of Women's Culture*, no. 7.

But no matter whether my probings made me happier or sadder, I kept on probing to know.

—Zora Neale Hurston, *Dust Tracks on a Road* (1942)

I have seen a Negro woman sold upon the block at auction . . . . I felt faint, seasick. . . . She was magnificently gotten up in silks and satins . . . sometimes ogling the bidders, sometimes looking quite coy and modest . . . I dare say the poor thing knew who would buy her. My very soul sickened . . . I tried to reason. "You know how women sell themselves and are sold in marriage, from queens downward, eh? You know what the Bible says about slavery, and marriage. Poor women, poor slaves."

—Diary of Mary Boykin Chestnut, March 1861

. . . of this class of women, I am constrained to say . . . that their education is miserably deficient; that they are taught to regard marriage as the one thing needful, the only avenue to distinction; hence to attract the notice and win the attentions of men, by their external charms, is the chief business of fashionable girls. . . . Fashionable women regard themselves, and are regarded by men, as pretty toys or mere instruments of pleasure; and the vacuity of mind, the heartlessness, the frivolity which is the necessary result of this false and debasing estimate of women, can only be understood by those who have mingled . . . in fashionable life . . .

—Sarah Grimké, *Letters on the Equality of the Sexes* (1838)

They said we had no souls, that we were animals.

> —Unidentified Savannah black woman, 1865 (quoted in Herbert Gutman, *The Black Family in Slavery and Freedom*)

How did woman first become subject to man, as she now is all over the world? By her nature, her sex, just as the negro is and always will be to the end of time, inferior to the white race, and, therefore, doomed to subjection; but she is happier than she would be in any other condition, just because it is the law of her nature . . .

> —*The New York Herald*, 1852

The investigation of the rights of the slave has led me to a better understanding of our own. I have found the Anti-Slavery cause to be the high school of morals in our land— the school in which *human rights* are more fully investigated and better understood and taught, than in any other. . . . These rights may be wrested from the slave, but they cannot be alienated; his title to himself . . . is stamped on his moral being and is, like it, imperishable. Now if rights are founded in the nature of our moral being, then the *mere circumstance of sex* does not give to man higher rights and responsibilities, than to woman.

> —Angelina Grimké, *Letters to Catherine Beecher* (1836)

. . . the police had arrested a large group of women— white, black, mixed color—while they were gathered for a Voodoo dance. Those making the arrests said the women were acting "indecent and orgiastic."

> —*New Orleans Weekly Delta*, July 1850

I was to walk with the storm and hold my power, and get my answers to life and things in storms. The symbol of lightning was painted on my back. This was to be mine forever.

> —Zora Neale Hurston (on her initiation into voodoo); *Dust Tracks on a Road* (1942)

Freud said once that woman is not well acculturated; she is, he stressed, retarded as a civilized person. I think what he

mistook for her lack of civilization is woman's lack of *loyalty*
to civilization. Southern women have never been as loyal to
the ideology of race and segregation as have southern men.
. . . Many of them have been betraying White Supremacy
for two hundred years but most who have done so could not
reason with you as to why.

> —Lillian Smith: "Autobiography as a Dialogue between
> King and Corpse" (1962)

Shall we press the old word "freedom" once more into
service? . . . Let "freedom from unreal loyalties" then stand
as the fourth great teacher of the daughters of educated
men.

> —Virginia Woolf, *Three Guineas* (1938)

. . . In the past, I don't care how poor this white woman
was in the South she felt like she was more than us. In the
North, I don't care how poor or how rich this white woman
has been, she still felt like she was more than us. But coming to the realization of the thing, her freedom is shackled
in chains to mine, and she realizes for the first time that she
is not free until I am free. The point about it, the male influence in this country—you know the white male didn't go
and brainwash the black man and the black woman, he
brainwashed his wife too. . . . He made her think that she
was an angel.

> —Fannie Lou Hamer, "The Special Plight and Role of
> Black Women" (1971)

I have not been able to touch the destruction
within me
But unless I learn to use
the difference between poetry and rhetoric
my power too will run corrupt as poisonous mold
or lie limp and useless as an unconnected plug
and one day I will take my teenaged plug
and connect it to the nearest socket
raping an 85-year-old white woman
who is somebody's mother
and as I beat her senseless and set a torch to her bed
a greek chorus will be singing in 3/4 time

"Poor thing. She never hurt a soul. What beasts they are."

—Audre Lorde, "Power" (1976)

My hope is that our lives will declare
this meeting
open

   —June Jordan, "Metarhetoric" (1976)

It is difficult to begin writing the words that will carry my thoughts
on feminism and racism beyond the confines of my own mind, this
room. It is difficult because I wish to be understood, because I write
at a crossroads which is mined with pain and anger, and because I do
not want my words to lend themselves to distortion or expropriation,
either by apologists for a shallow and trivial notion of feminism,[1] or
by exponents of a racial politics that denies the fundamental nature
of sexual politics and gender-oppression.

Throughout this paper, I shall be assuming that black and white
feminists have in common a commitment, not to some concept of
civil rights within the old framework of capitalism and misogyny, not
to an extension of tokenism to include more women in existing
social structures, but to a profound transformation of world society
and of human relationships; and that we agree that such a transformation requires minimally that every woman be self-identifying and
self-defining, with the right to determine how, when, and for whom
she will exercise her sexuality and her reproductive powers.

As a lesbian/feminist, my nerves and my flesh as well as my intellect tell me that the connections between and among women are
the most feared, the most problematic, and the most potentially
transforming force on the planet. I conceive this paper as one strand
in a meditation and colloquy among black and white feminists, an
intercourse just beginning, and charged with a history that touches

[1] E.g.: Feminists who don't think racism is "their problem" ("My field is Modernism, after all"); women who see "feminism" as a new road to inclusion within a white
male order; feminists who would deny the histories of real differences between and
among women.

our nerve-ends even though we are largely ignorant of it.[2] I begin by stating that I was born into a racist and patriarchal home, a racist and patriarchal city and culture; and because in those early years deemed so crucial in a child's education in love, the most unconditional, tender, and, I now believe, intelligent love I received was given to me by a black woman. (By "unconditional" I do not mean foolishly indulgent. But my own parents saw me as instrumental for them, an item on their agenda, as she did not, or so it feels at this lapse of time.)

This personal history is not unique; many white women have been mothered by black women, a connection we sentimentalize at our peril. Nor do I consider it (as one or two white women have suggested to me) the "cause" for my concern with the issues in this paper. It simply adds to the sense of urgency that has prompted me to enter the colloquy. I have written of this relationship elsewhere, and I do not wish to belabor it here.[3]

Throughout this text I say "black" and not "First (or Third) World," because although separation by skin color and class is by no means confined to that between black and white women, black women and white women in this country have a special history of polarization, as well as of shared oppression and shared activism, and I address myself to that history here.

This paper has as its most recent impulse two articles: Barbara Smith's "Toward a Black Feminist Criticism," which first appeared in *Conditions*, no. 2 (P.O. Box 56, Van Brunt Station, Brooklyn, N.Y. 11215); and "The Combahee River Collective: A Black Feminist Statement," published in *Capitalist Patriarchy: A Case for Socialist Feminism*, edited by Zillah Eisenstein. But I must also acknowledge the earlier impact of "A Historical and Critical Essay for Black Women in the Cities," by Pat Robinson and group, in Toni Cade's anthology, *The Black Woman*, which I read in 1970, and which seems to me still a generative piece of feminist thinking.

[2] See "Breaking the Silence: A Dialogue between Barbara Smith and Laura Sperazi" in *Equal Times: Boston's Newspaper for Women*, March 26, 1978.

[3] See *Of Woman Born: Motherhood as Experience and Institution* (New York: Norton, 1976), pp. 253–55. See also above, "It Is the Lesbian in Us," pp. 199–200.

I

The mutual history of black and white women in this country is a realm so painful, resonant, and forbidden that it has barely been touched by writers either of political "science" or of imaginative literature. Yet until that history is known, that silence broken, we will all go on struggling in a state of deprivation and ignorance. It is not that white feminists have simply ignored or discounted the experience, the very existence, of black women, though, as Barbara Smith points out, much feminist scholarship has been written as if black women did not exist, and many a women's studies course or text pays token reference, if any, to black women's lives and work. Even where racism is acknowledged in feminist writings, courses, conferences, it is too often out of a desire to "grasp" it as an intellectual or theoretical concept; we move too fast, as men so often do, in the effort to stay "on top" of a painful and bewildering condition, and so we lose touch with the feelings black women are trying to describe to us, their lived experience *as women*. It is far easier, especially for academically trained white women, to get an intellectual/political "fix" on the *idea* of racism, than to identify with black female experience: to explore it emotionally as part of our own.

Beneath all this, I believe, lies a deeper, more insidious problem: a great deal of white feminist thinking and writing, where it has attempted to address black women's experience, has done so laboring under a massive burden of guilt feelings and false consciousness, the products of deeply inculcated female self-blame, and of a history we have insufficiently explored. (There is a profound difference between actual guilt—or accountability—and guilt feelings.) We have also been laboring under feelings of ignorance of, and therefore inadequacy toward, the real lives of black women. This ignorance is, of course, actual. It is bred by what passes for education, which takes white experience as normative, and it is bolstered by the very fear and anxiety it creates. It is time that we shed these unuseful burdens and look with fresh eyes at the concept of female racism. For true accountability is a serious question for the feminist ethic—and indeed for any lasting and meaningful feminist action.

Women did not create the power relationship between master and slave, nor the mythologies used to justify the domination of men over women: such as, that the master is "called by nature" or "destiny" to rule because of his inherent superiority; that he alone is "rational" while the Other is emotion-swayed, closer to the animal, an embodiment of the "dark" unconscious, dangerous and therefore needing to be controlled; that women and slaves are creatures without immortal souls; that the enslaved really love their masters (that women love sexual violence and humiliation), that the oppressed "accept" or even are happy with their lot till "outside agitators" stir them to discontent. Women did not create this relationship, but in the history of American slavery and racism white women have been impressed into its service, not only as the marriage-property and creature-objects of white men, but as their active and passive instruments.

> My new mistress proved to be all she appeared when I first met her at the door,—a woman of the kindest heart and the finest feelings. She had never had a slave under her control previously to myself, and prior to her marriage she had been dependent upon her own industry for a living. She was by trade a weaver; and by constant application to her business, she had been in a good degree preserved from the blighting and dehumanizing effects of slavery. I was utterly astonished at her goodness. . . . She was entirely unlike any other white woman I had ever seen. . . . The crouching servility, usually so acceptable a quality in a slave, did not answer when manifested toward her. Her favor was not gained by it; she seemed to be disturbed by it. . . . The meanest slave was put fully at ease in her presence, and none left without feeling better for having seen her . . .

> But alas! this kind heart had but a short time to remain such. The fatal poison of irresponsible power was already in her hands, and soon commenced its infernal work. That cheerful eye, under the influence of slavery, soon became red with rage . . .

> Very soon after I went to live with Mr. and Mrs. Auld, she very kindly commenced to teach me the A, B, C. After I had learned this, she assisted me in learning to spell words of three or four letters. Just at this point of my progress, Mr. Auld found out what was going on, and at once forbade Mrs. Auld to instruct me further, telling her, among other things, that it was unlawful, as well as unsafe, to teach a slave to read. . . . "A nigger should know nothing but to obey his master. . . . Learn-

ing would *spoil* the best nigger in the world. . . . It would make him discontented and unhappy . . ." (*Narrative of the Life of Frederick Douglass*)[4]

This independent woman artisan had entered the institutions of marriage and of slavery simultaneously. In marrying, she took on the corruptions both of the male/female and of the master/slave relationship. She was not, I suggest, corrupted by "irresponsible power" in the sense that a male tyrant or patriarchal despot could be so described; but rather, torn and maddened by false power and false loyalty to a system against which she had at first instinctively revolted, and which was destroying her integrity. Powerless in the institution of marriage, the institution of slavery *did* give her near-absolute power over another human being, her only outlet for rage and frustration being the control she had over that person. Ironically, one power she did not possess was the power of manumission (to free her slaves), which she lost in marriage.[5]

White women in revolt against the ideologies of slavery and segregation have most often worked from positions of powerlessness, or from a false sense of our own power and its uses; while men in power have called our sense of justice "emotionalism," our humanity "irresponsible," dismissing our voices and acts of protest because we have had no collective leverage of our own to bring to the struggles we undertook on behalf of others. It would have made a great difference if more American women could have understood from the first that slavery and segregation were not conditions peculiar only to institutionalized racism, but dominant practices of patriarchy.[6] Such an understanding might have impelled us toward a politics more func-

[4] (1845; reprint ed., New York: Signet, 1968) pp. 48–49. It is more than suggestive that in the nineteenth-century education was seen as spoiling both the slave for slavery, and the woman for marriage and motherhood.

[5] See Linda Brent, *Incidents in the Life of a Slave Girl*, ed. by Lydia Maria Child (1861; reprint ed., New York: Harcourt Brace, 1973), pp. 50–51. "Linda Brent" was the pseudonym of Harriet Brent Jacobs, a black woman reared in slavery who became a fugitive, went into hiding for seven years in her grandmother's house, finally escaped to the North and joined the antislavery movement in New York.

[6] According to Linda Brent, the term "patriarchal" was used in the South as a defense of slavery—"a beautiful patriarchal institution."

tional both for ourselves and for those who, like women, have been
defined as "the Other."

The passive or active instrumentality of white women in the practice of inhumanity against black people is a fact of history. (So, also,
is the passive or active instrumentality of women of the same race
against each other: the African woman excising and mutilating the
clitoris and vulva of the young girl; the Chinese mother crushing her
daughter's feet into tiny "lotus hooks" to make her marriageable; the
token woman betraying her sisters in exchange for her place in a
male establishment: loyalty to masculine civilization.)[7] But beneath
that indisputable fact—or overarching it—there are other facts.
White women, like black women and men, have lived from the
founding of this country under a constitution drawn up and still in-
terpreted by white men, and under which, even if the Equal Rights
Amendment should finally pass, there would still, given the composition of the courts, be no guarantee to *any* woman even of equal
rights under the law.[8] Women, like black people, are still regarded as
inferior in intellectual quality: marginal: guilty victims. Women,
like black people, know what it means to live in fear of violence
against which the sanctions of the community and the legal system
offer no protection: rape, woman-beating, sexual abuse by adult
male relatives, the violence of male medical practice. And it is important for white feminists to remember that, despite lack of constitutional citizenship, educational deprivation, economic bondage to
men, laws and customs forbidding women to speak in public or to
disobey fathers, husbands, and brothers, our white foresisters have,
in Lillian Smith's words, repeatedly been "disloyal to civilization,"
and have "smelled death in the word 'segregation,' "[9] often defying

[7] See Mary Daly, *Gyn/Ecology: The Metaethics of Radical Feminism* (Boston: Beacon, 1978).

[8] The opinion of Justice Powell in the Supreme Court decision on *University of
California* v. *Bakke* expresses clearly the attitude that gender discrimination is viewed
as less repugnant than racial or ethnic discrimination: ". . . the perception of racial
classifications as inherently odious stems from a lengthy and tragic history that gender-
based classifications do not share. In sum, the Court has never viewed such classifica-
tion as inherently suspect or as comparable to racial or ethnic classifications for the
purpose of equal protection analysis."

[9] "Autobiography as a Dialogue between King and Corpse" in Lillian Smith, *The
Winner Names the Age*, Michelle Cliff, ed., (New York: Norton, 1978), p. 191.

patriarchy for the first time, not on their own behalf but for the sake of black men, women, and children. We have a strong antiracist female tradition, despite all efforts by the white patriarchy to polarize its creature-objects, creating dichotomies of privilege and caste, skin-color and age and condition of servitude. It is that tradition—rather than guilt feelings or "liberal" politics—that I wish to invoke in this paper.

II

White feminists have a particular historical relationship to the concept of racism itself. The nineteenth-century movement for women's rights was bred in the activism of the abolitionist movement in which Lucretia Mott, Elizabeth Cady Stanton, Susan B. Anthony, and many others first found their voices. After the Civil War the suffrage movement was deeply impaired by the split over the issue of whether black males should receive the vote before white and black women. The "Negro's hour" (as the issue of manhood suffrage was described) was, as Sojourner Truth vehemently noted, "a great stir about colored men getting their rights, but not a word about the colored women." If the drive for women's enfranchisement had remained united and radically feminist, it would have been articulated in Sojourner Truth's and Susan B. Anthony's terms, as a drive for the enfranchisement of *all* citizens, black and white, native and foreign-born, middle-class and poor, but in the heated pressures over whether black men, or white and black women, should first be enfranchised, a classist, racist, and even xenophobic rhetoric crept in.[10] It is easy to see from this distance that the old patriarchal strat-

[10] At the National American Woman's Suffrage Convention held in New Orleans, 1903, a Mississippi suffragist argued for the enfranchisement of women on the grounds that it "would insure immediate and durable white supremacy, honestly attained, for upon unquestioned authority it is stated that in every Southern State but one there are more educated women than all the illiterate voters, white or black, native and foreign, combined" (Ida Husted Harper, *History of Woman Suffrage*, vol. V, 1922, pp. 82–83). Compare this with Susan B. Anthony, at the first annual meeting of the American Equal Rights Association In 1867: "As I understand the difference between Abolitionists, some think this is harvest time for the black man, and seed-sowing time for woman. Others, with whom I agree, think we have been sowing the seed of individual rights, the foundation idea of a republic for the last century, and that this

egy was at work: *either* black men *or* women (black and white) might
be enfranchised, but not both—thus playing off sex against race, in a
false historical necessity, as has been done and is being done to this
day.

The historian Barbara Berg offers an earlier version of white feminist origins in America: the "female benevolent societies" or voluntary agencies that grew up under the pressures of urbanization in
the first half of the nineteenth century. Often contemptuously dismissed as Lady Bountifuls indulging in "do-goodism," the urban
female organizers worked, according to Berg, from a strong sense of
solidarity with all women, in revolt against middle-class ideologies of
female frailty and dependency, and

> formed hundreds of associations dedicated to helping the aged, infirm,
> impoverished, and deviant female in cities across the nation. Woman's
> vaguely perceived needs, drives and wishes found definition in the
> collage of the city. . . . The reality of her own oppression became ines-
> capable . . .

> Female benevolent societies in the years between 1800 and 1860 trans-
> formed the imprecise perceptions of women throughout America into a
> compelling feminist ideology. [Berg means, of course, but fails to state,
> *white* women.]

> The members postulated a community of women. They continually
> emphasized the similarities between themselves and Black, Indian, and
> immigrant women . . .

Berg goes on to comment:

> . . . In their fight for the vote, women both ignored and compromised
> the principles of feminism. The complexities of American society at the

---

is the harvest time for all citizens who pay taxes, obey the laws and are loyal to the government" (Susan B. Anthony, et al., *History of Woman Suffrage*, vol. II, 1881, p.
220).

We need more study of the dynamic between misogyny in the abolitionist movement and racism in the movement for women's rights. The rhetoric of the nineteenth-
century women's movement—both the inherently radical demands and protests, and
the language of manipulative argument—went through significant changes between
Seneca Falls and World War I; this rhetoric too needs to be better understood. Not to
exonerate the nineteenth-century white feminists of racism, but to see further into the
tangle of sex and race, to shed light on our own mistakes, and to stop repeating them.

turn of the century induced the suffragists to change the basis of their demand for franchise. They had originally argued that it was the natural right of *every woman*, as well as every man, to participate in the legal system that would govern them . . . the later suffrage movement denied the basic human rights of lower-class women. . . .

. . . The woman's movement that developed between the years 1800 and 1860 was a probing body of thought. *It stood on the threshold of recognizing that the liberation of one class of women depended upon the freedom of all others* [italics mine]. It has, indeed, been the misfortune of the twentieth century to have remembered only the suffrage campaign while forgetting the origins of American feminism.[11]

The nascent antiracist, class-transcending feminism which Berg discerns in the early nineteenth-century women's reform movement—and which Anthony constantly affirmed in the suffrage movement—would always be under pressure from the patriarchal strategy of divide and conquer. This strategy has repeatedly fed on the capacity of privileged women to delude themselves as to where their privilege originates, and what they are having to pay for it, and as I shall try to show further on, on the use of women—black and white—as the buffer between the powerful and their most abject victims. But it has also fed on the fact that women—privileged or not—are trained to identify with men, whether with the males in power to whom they may be attached, or—as emotional sympathizers—with the men of an oppressed group. Identification with women *as women*, not as persons similar in class or race or cultural behavior, is still profoundly problematic. The constraints that have demanded of white women that to keep our respectability or advantages we must deny our sisters (and our sisters in ourselves) have also seemed to require black women to deny either their sex or their race in political alignments. The charge of deviance, always leveled at women who bond together, especially across racial and class lines, has been used against black and white feminists alike. We all know the changes rung in that vocabulary: from "strong-minded woman" in the nineteenth century to "castrating bitch," "man-

[11] *The Remembered Gate: Origins of American Feminism* (New York: Oxford, 1978), pp. 246–50.

hater," "matriarch," "bulldagger," "dyke," and "counterrevolutionary."[12]

The attempt by white women to formulate a radical feminist politics in the face of intense negative pressures by the male-dominated
Left in the 1960s is, perhaps, a history already blurred and dimmed,
in our antihistorical era, by the desire either to forget the sixties or to
relegate them to "nostalgia." (Many black feminists, undoubtedly,
were then in their conscious politics trying to deal with the contradictions of the black nationalist movement.) That feminist struggle
against the politics of guilt has been documented by Kathleen Barry,
Barbara Burris, Joanne Parrent, et al., in "The Fourth World Manifesto" (1972), a piece of our history and a piece of radical feminist
theory which also documents the efforts of the male dominated Left

[12] In an article, "Scratching the Surface: Some Notes on Barriers to Women and
Loving," Audre Lorde notes:

> . . . on the campus of a New York college recently, where black women sought
> to come together around feminist concerns . . . violently threatening phone calls
> were made to those black women who dared to explore the possibilities of a
> feminist connection with non-black women. . . . When threats did not prevent
> the attempted coalition of black feminists, the resulting hysteria left some black
> women beaten and raped . . . (the *Black Scholar*, vol. 9, no. 7, April 1978.)

See also Ishmael Reed (described in the *New York Times*, October 28, 1977, as
"perhaps the best black poet writing today"):

> The feminists jumped on me like hell, they didn't like the characters, especially
> the black ones, they didn't like my black characters. . . . There's one woman at
> *Newsweek*, who's been giving me a lot of problems like, Margo Jefferson, a real
> fair-skinned woman who's like *Newsweek*'s house black, house feminist, house
> creole. . . . She called me a misogynist. You got this thing now where if you
> don't create a character to their liking, to the party line, then you get banished,
> like they banished Norman Mailer from public life because he made some
> remarks about women. They got a lot of power now . . . these *types* are well
> known in everybody's folklore; the shrew, the *bitch*. I mean there must *be* one,
> people been talking about in different cultures for thousands of years, you
> know—all of a sudden these people gonna come along, these feminist intellec-
> tuals or whatever you call them, and they're gonna change the whole thing,
> they're gonna change biology. . . . People been fucking 50,000 years without
> using dildos . . . (*Boston Real Paper*, February 25, 1978, pp. 25 and 26.)

to recapture the emerging feminist movement of the early seventies.[13]

If a shallow, "life-style" brand of feminism can shrug off the issue of racism altogether, it is also true that more "political" white feminists still often feel vulnerable to the charge that "white middle-class women" or "bourgeois feminists" are despicable creatures of privilege whose oppression is meaningless beside the oppression of black, Third World, or working-class women and men. That charge, of course, resolutely avoids the central fact of male gynephobia and violence against all women.[14] It also diverts energy into the ludicrous and fruitless game of "hierarchies of oppression," which has the savor of medieval theology. To bow to it, in a reflex of liberal guilt, is to blur and distort real issues of difference among women and the selective treatment of women under patriarchy and racism.

The fact that white or middle-class women's "privilege" has been a lethal toy has been recognized by some black feminists from early on.[15] Such writers have been quick to perceive the insulting and idiotic forms that white middle-class female "privilege" has taken: the "doll's house," the enforced childishness and helplessness imposed by institutionalized heterosexuality and marriage on perfectly competent, intelligent women; the degrading games the economically dependent white woman has had to play in order to buy her privileges; the moral and legal and theological sanctions used to keep her from exercising initiative and judgment. If black women have sometimes viewed the middle-class white woman with a mixture of envy and contempt, they have also perceived with anguish how middle-class black culture attempts to replicate the achieving white culture, including the turning of intelligent, capable women into "parlor entertainers."

[13] First published in "Notes from the Third Year"; reprinted in Anne Koedt, Ellen Levine, and Anita Rapone, eds., *Radical Feminism* (New York: Quadrangle, 1978).

[14] *Gynephobia:* the age-old, cross-cultural male fear and hatred of women, which women too inhale like poisonous fumes from the air we breathe daily.

[15] See Gwen Patton, "Black People and the Victorian Ethos"; Toni Cade, "On the Issue of Roles"; Pat Robinson, et al., "A Historical and Critical Essay for Black Women in the Cities"; in Cade, ed., *The Black Woman* (New York: New American Library, 1970).

The charge of "racism" flung at white women in the earliest groupings of the independent feminist movement was a charge made in the most obscene bad faith by white "radical" males (and by some Leftist women) against the daring leap of self-definition needed to create an autonomous feminist analysis. That leap, as group after group, woman after woman, has discovered, often involves feelings of extreme dislocation, "craziness," and terror. For many white feminists, the cynical and manipulative use of the charge of "racism" as a deterrent to feminist organizing was one bitter source of disenchantment with the male-dominated Left (along with the visible male supremacism both of the Left and of men in the black movement). It corresponded, for us, to the charges black feminists have had to withstand, of "fragmenting" the black struggle or "castrating" the black man. In other words, and ironically, the more deeply a woman might recognize and hate the fact of racist oppression (and many of the first white independent feminists had learned its realities in the civil rights movement in the South), the more vulnerable she felt in her struggle to define a politics which would, for once, take the position of women as central, and which would perceive the oppression of women both as a political reality embedded in every institution, and as a permeating metaphor throwing light on every other form of domination. These feelings, along with the need to reject false guilt and false responsibility for the bedrock racism of American society, may have evoked a kind of retreat from anything resembling rhetorical demands that white feminists "deal with our racism" as a first priority. But surely such demands have a different meaning and imperative when they come in bad faith from the lips of white—or black—males, whose intention is to discredit feminist politics; and when they are articulated by black feminists, who are showing themselves, over time, unflagging and persistent in their outreach toward white women, while refusing to deny—or to have denied—an atom of their black reality.

I can easily comprehend that when black women have looked at the present-day feminist movement, particularly as caricatured in the male-dominated press (both black and white), and have seen blindness to, and ignorance of, the experience and needs of black women, they have labeled this "racism," undifferentiated from the racism endemic in patriarchy. But I hope that we can now begin to differentiate and to define further, drawing both on a deeper understanding of black and white women's history, and on an unflinching view of patriarchy itself.

III

It is only within the past fifty years, and with many interruptions and obstacles, that we have begun to rediscover and reevaluate the history of women, always omitted, distorted, or banalized in the writings of male (and some token female) scholars. The mere effort to challenge the misogyny and heterocentrism of school and college texts, to "include" women in the historical canon at all, is still an uphill struggle. As early as 1972, Gerda Lerner, a white feminist historian, published her documentary anthology, *Black Women in White America*; yet ignorance of the political leadership, resource networks, art, and community-sustaining work of black women still pervades most courses and writings on women. A great deal of contemporary social and political documentation was to be found in Toni Cade's anthology, *The Black Woman*, published in 1970, a collection of essays which signaled the stirrings of black feminism even though some of its authors were still largely concerned with querying the role of women within the black nationalist movement. But the polarization of black and white women in American life is clearly reflected in a historical method which, if it does not dismiss all of us altogether, or subsume us vaguely under "mankind," has kept us in separate volumes, or separate essays in the same volume.

I say "polarization"; but, as always under the conditions of patriarchy, we need to look beneath what is apparent for what has been simultaneously true, though unseen. In the psyche of the white masters (and of their black imitators), the splitting of the female image has served the purposes both of sexual and racial domination: white goddess/black she-devil; chaste virgin/nigger whore; the blonde, blue-eyed doll/the exotic, "mulatto" object of sexual craving. The blonde, blue-eyed woman, the "pure" southern lady of the antebellum era, was also male property just as she is today. Whiteness

did not preserve any woman from ownership by men; it did bestow a
skin-deep privilege that could delude her as to her fundamental ob-
ject-status as woman, unenfranchised and dominated.

> The stories that have come down to us by word of mouth from our slave
> great-grandmothers tell of stag pens throughout Virginia and South
> Carolina where "black bucks" were made to copulate with indentured
> females from England.
>
> This arrangement was a good basis for establishing faithful house slaves
> to look to the physical comfort and entertainment of the master and his
> family, since the master controlled the children from all Black unions.
> He usually allowed these lighter-skinned Blacks in the big house and
> slowly created another class of slaves in addition to the house slaves.
> This one was based on color as well as on social hierarchy. The chil-
> dren from the master's union with the slave women were a part of this
> class. Many from this group became educated, multi-lingual parlor en-
> tertainers . . .
>
> . . . The female slave subtly transferred much of her feeling of depriva-
> tion in this patriarchal society to the benign Protestant male God pro-
> vided by the conquerors to support their system. Aping 'Miss Anne'
> gave some comfort but no strong reflection of human worth, for the
> white woman was a female and every female was dangerous to male
> rule.[16]

The "black stud" made to rape the indentured white woman servant. The history of lynching, of antimiscegenation laws. The history of "the master's union with" (read intensive raping of) the slave
women. The hierarchy of color (blue-eyed blonde, light-skinned
house slave, dark "nigger" perceived as closer to animal than
human). The indentured white woman servant raped under com-
mand by the black slave. The white mistress as entertainer. The
upper-class white woman, presumed to have no sexual longings.
The hierarchy of slaves. The hierarchy among white women:
young/beautiful/marriageable to a well-to-do man; plain/"old
maid"/barren; poor white trash; indentured servant and breeder;
whore. For any woman, class shifts with shade of skin color, but also

[16] Robinson, et al., op cit., pp. 206–8.

with age, marrige, or spinsterhood, with a hundred factors all relating to what kind of man she is—or is not—attached to. Class breaks
down over color, then is reconstituted within color lines. Rape everywhere: in the master bedroom, the slave cabins, niggertown.
Marital rape, legal to this day. Black men lynched for the alleged
rape of white women; white and black women (though differently)
viewed as inciters to rape, guilty victims; black women raped daily by
black men, unavenged.

> I hate slavery. You say there are no more fallen women on a plantation
> than in London, in proportion to numbers; but what do you say to this?
> A magnate who runs a hideous black harem with its consequences
> under the same roof with his lovely white wife and beautiful and ac-
> complished daughters? He holds his head as high and poses as the
> model of all human virtues to these poor women whom God and the
> laws have given him. . . . You see, Mrs. Stowe did not hit the sorest
> spot. She makes Legree a bachelor.

> . . . His wife and daughters, in their purity and innocence, are sup-
> posed never to dream of what is plain before their eyes as the sunlight.
> And they play the parts of unsuspecting angels to the letter. They
> profess to adore their father as the model of all earthly goodness.
> (Diary of Mary Boykin Chesnut, August 1861)[17]

Mary Chesnut's diaries are a painful study in one white southern
woman's instinctive, undeveloped awareness of the connections between sexuality and racism under slavery. Like some intelligent
women today, whose writings reveal a partial, yet blocked, feminism, she seems to pace back and forth, tormented, seeing and articu-
lating just so far, helpless finally within the limitations of her vision.
Married to a high-ranking Confederate aide, she is bitter against
women and men alike. Her hatred of slavery proceeds directly from
the humiliation and hypocrisy it inflicts on white women, whom she
also sees as collaborators in an obscene patriarchal charade. If her
life and the life of the black woman on the auction block ever connect for her, it is only in oblique flashes of insight, never in a coher-
ent vision. To her, the black woman remains Other.

[17] Ben Ames Williams, ed., A *Diary from Dixie* (Boston: Houghton Mifflin,
1949), p. 122.

I hate slavery. I even hate the harsh authority I see parents think it their duty to exercise toward their children. [She does not mention the authority of husband over wife.]

. . . I have before me a letter I wrote to Mr. Chesnut while he was on our plantation in Mississippi in 1842. It is the most fervid abolitionist document I have ever read. I came across it while burning letters the other day, but that letter I did not burn . . .

Yes, how I envy those saintly Yankee women, in their clean cool New England homes, writing books to make their fortunes and shame us. The money they earn goes to them. Here every cent goes to pay the factor who supplies the plantation. (Diary of Mary Boykin Chesnut, November 1861)[18]

Scathing the northern abolitionist woman; turning and turning in her cage of bitter knowledge, contempt, defensiveness, consciousness of collusion: the white southern woman, part and parcel of a sexual, racial, and economic tangle she had not created.

And the tangle gripped both black and white women at the heart of their female existence. Linda Brent gives a detailed account of the black/white female cathexis in a house where the master obsessively pursued his aim of making the young black woman his concubine:

No matter whether the slave girl be as black as ebony or as fair as her mistress. In either case, there is no shadow of law to protect her from insult, from violence, or even from death. . . . The mistress, who ought to protect the helpless victim, has no other feelings towards her but those of jealousy and rage . . .

Even the little child, who is accustomed to wait on her mistress and her children, will learn, before she is twelve years old, why it is that her mistress hates such and such a one among the slaves. Perhaps the child's own mother is among those hated ones. She listens to violent outbreaks of jealous passion, and cannot help understanding what is the cause . . .[19]

Of her mistress, who cross-examined her as to what had actually happened, Linda Brent notes that "she felt that her marriage vows were

[18] Ibid., p. 164.

[19] Brent, op cit., pp. 26–27.

desecrated, her dignity insulted; but she had no compassion for the poor victim of her husband's perfidy . . . I was an object of her jealousy, and, consequently of her hatred." She describes Mrs. Flint as a woman who "had not enough strength to superintend her household affairs; but her nerves were so strong, that she could sit in her easy chair and see a woman whipped, till blood trickled from every stroke of the lash."[20] Brutality was the order of the day in this household, restrained chiefly by the fear of community scandal.

If the white married woman had any status or identity, it was by virtue of her wifehood and motherhood (though her children were the property of their father). Yet she was forced into impotent jealousy of black women both as the preferred sexual objects of her husband, and as mother-surrogates for her children. The sources of her value as a woman, patriarchally defined, were constantly in question no matter the height of her "pedestal." In this intolerable yet everyday situation we can see the roots of a later assumption prevalent among white women, that the black woman was by nature immoral and lascivious. However the slave might struggle to fend off her own rape, she was defined as the guilty victim, the permissible scapegoat for the anger of her rapist's wife. And when her children too obviously resembled her rapist, they might be sold away as an embarrassment or an exacerbation of the conjugal disgust between white wife and white paterfamilias.

Disloyalty to civilization: one other image from the nineteenth century. In an essay on the female origins of jazz, the sociologist Susan Cavin quotes from accounts of the "voodoo Queens" of New Orleans, in whose cults and congregations African and European musical elements first began to fuse. Despite a law against "the assembling of white women and slaves" the communal and ecstatic experience of voodoo ceremonies was one shared by black and white women, under the tutelage and authority of the "mamaloi" or black vodun queen, in a cult of which "women seem . . . to have made up at least eighty per cent of the cultists, and it was always the female of the white race who entered the sect . . ." The origins of vodun were Dahomeyan, from a culture charged with female power. The newspapers described the dances of the women as "orgiastic and in-

[20] Ibid., p. 10.

decent"; in 1895 an arrest in a "dilapidated tenement" was depicted
in the vocabulary of Victorian and racist sexual prudery and disgust:

> The women, having cast off their everyday apparel, had put on white
> camisoles. . . . Blacks and whites were circling around promiscuously,
> writhing . . . panting, raving and frothing at the mouth. But the most
> degrading and infamous feature of this scene was the presence of a very
> large number of ladies (?) moving in the highest walks of society, rich
> and hitherto respectable, that were caught in the dragnet.[21]

These women would undoubtedly have shocked and horrified the
white churchwomen Lillian Smith describes, who, in 1930, organized the Association of Southern Women for the Prevention of
Lynching:

> The lady insurrectionists gathered together in one of our southern cit-
> ies. . . . They said calmly that they were not afraid of being raped; as for
> their sacredness, they could take care of it themselves; they did not need
> the chivalry of a lynching to protect them and did not want it. Not only
> that, . . . they would personally do everything in their power to keep
> any Negro from being lynched and furthermore, they squeaked bravely,
> they had plenty of power.

> They had more than they knew. They had the power of spiritual black-
> mail over a large part of the South. . . . No one, of thousands of white
> men, had any notion how much or how little each woman knew about
> his private goings-on . . .[22]

There are many forms of disloyalty to civilization.

[21] Susan Cavin, "Missing Women: On the Voodoo Trail to Jazz," *Journal of Jazz
Studies*, vol. 3, no. 1, fall 1975.

[22] *Killers of the Dream* (New York: Norton, 1961, rev. ed.), pp. 145–46. Lillian
Smith mentions the background influences of this group, including "the Negroes
themselves, led by courageous men like Walter White of Atlanta and W. E. B. Du
Bois": she fails to mention Ida B. Wells, founder of the *Memphis Free Speech*, whose
one-woman crusade against lynchings exposed her to mob violence, and who organized black women in several northern and western cities. For an account of her career,
including her exchanges with Frances Willard and Susan B. Anthony on racism, see
Crusade for Justice: the Autobiography of Ida B. Wells, edited by her daughter, Alfreda
B. Duster (Chicago: University of Chicago, 1972).

IV

The images we have of each other. The complementarity that developed between many white women and the black women who "coped" for them as enslaved or underpaid workers in their homes, a complementarity so often defined by the white woman's infantilization. The "privileges" of economically dependent white married women have traditionally demanded as their price enforced "feminine" helplessness, idleness, denial of competency and physical strength, and the kind of little-girlishness Ibsen depicted in the first act of A Doll's House. A woman with white middle-class "privilege" (access to resources, some education, mobility, physical comforts, etc.) would be held in check from real power by the crippling norms of "femininity" (as well as by property and other laws). This "femininity" (or infantilism), though mandated by male requirements, was experienced not just in contrast to men, but to black women. While the black domestic worker laundered, ironed, cooked, cleaned floors, polished silver, watched over the white woman's children, she could also—and, I suspect, did—become a receptacle for the white woman's fantasies of being mothered—even when the two were of the same age; and, if the white woman had in childhood been cared for by a black woman, the transference would be an easy one. But what this meant was that the relative power available to the white middle-class woman was never really tapped, whether on her own behalf or that of the black woman who, most ironically, was forced to embody female strength, competence, and emotional stability in many a white household. "Privilege" for the white woman included the privilege of falling apart—in societally encouraged hypochondria, withdrawal, breakdown—especially where a black woman could be counted on to keep the household running and hold things together.[23] Meanwhile, the emotional and psychic strengths which black women developed and transmitted to each

[23] The same black woman might, of course, also be "infantilized" in a different sense by her white female employer, condescended to as one of an "irresponsible, lazy, intellectually childlike" race.

other in the struggle to survive, were kept utterly disconnected from any access to economic or social power.[24]

The images we have of each other. How black woman and white move as myths through each other's fantasies, myths created by the white male psyche including its perverse ideas of beauty.[25] How have I handed my own sexuality, my sense of myself as deviant, over to black women, not to speak of my own magic, my own rage? What illusions do we harbor still, of our own or each other's Amazon power or incompetence, glamor or disability, "smart-ugliness" or cerebral coolness, how do we play the mother or the daughter, how do we use each other to keep from touching our own power? (Frances Dana Gage, describing the effect of Sojourner Truth's "Ain't I a Woman" speech: "She had taken us up in her strong arms and carried us safely over the slough of difficulty, turning the whole tide in our favor." Powerful black mother of us all, the most politically powerless woman in that room: *She had taken us up in her strong arms.*) What caricatures of bloodless fragility and broiling sensuality still imprint our psyches, and where did we receive these imprintings? What happened between the several thousand northern white women and southern black women who together taught in the schools founded under Reconstruction by the Freedmen's Bureau, side by side braving Ku Klux Klan harassment, terrorism, and the hostility of white communities?[26] How to estimate the loss incurred when white women's organizations at the turn of the century excluded black women, kept them in separate units of the Women's Christian Temperance Union and the Young Women's Christian Association—"on the ground of the immorality of these women" (division and conquest); how to analyze the sexual wounds, the identification with men, which could cause white women to protest lynchings but still ascribe "low moral standards" to black women— both poor ex-slaves and college-educated, middle-class women like

---

[24] And privilege has proven no substitute for the kinds of power middle-class women have actually been able to tap *on condition we are willing to bond together as women—* risking the loss of respectability and privilege thereby.

[25] See Lillian Smith, "Woman Born of Man," in *The Winner Names the Age*, op. cit., especially pp. 204–5, 207.

[26] See Nancy Hoffman, " 'Missis Comes Fur Larn We': Yankee Schoolmarms in the Civil War South" (unpublished paper).

themselves? How did the old sexual wounds between black and white women break open yet again in the 1960s civil rights movement? How has the white man, how has the black man, stood to gain from pitting *white bitch* against *nigger cunt*, "yellow gal" against black?

Taught to deny my longings for another female body, taught that dark skin was stigma, shame, I look at you and see your flesh is beautiful; different from my own, but taboo to me no longer. Whether we choose to act on this or not (and whatever pain we may explore in touching one another) if we both have this knowledge, if my flesh is beautiful to you and yours to me, because it belongs to us, in affirmation of our similar and different powers, in affirmation of scars, stretch-marks, life-lines, the mind that burns in each body, we lay claim to ourselves and each other beyond the most extreme patriarchal taboo. We take each other up in our strong arms. We do not infantilize each other; we refuse to be infantilized. We drink at each other's difference. We begin to fuse our powers.

V

Racism. *Active domination:* Enslavement. Lashings. Rape. Lynching: not only of men but of pregnant women.[27] Burning of living bodies, of houses, of buses, of crosses in front of homes. Fire-bombing of churches. *Enforced segregation:* in shelter, in eating, in toilets and water-fountains, in churches and schoolrooms. Antimiscegenation laws. *Institutional violence:* the Department of Welfare. The public school system. The prison and bail systems. The control of information and communications. The myth of the First Amendment. The "I.Q." test. Enforced sterilization. *Justification:* mythologizing; dehumanization through language; fragmentation (the token exception to "prove" the rule).

Passive collusion: Snow-blindness. White solipsism: To think, imagine, and speak as if whiteness described the world. Mythic misperception: Mammy, superwoman, Black Amazon, her breasts like

[27] If the term "lynching" by any chance sounds abstract, see Ida B. Wells's *Crusade for Justice,* op. cit.; Lura Beam's *He Called Them by the Lightning: A Teacher's Odyssey in the Negro South, 1908–1919* (New York: Bobbs-Merrill, 1967), especially pp. 171–75; and, for a contemporary account, June Jordan, "In the Valley of the Shadow of Death: The Meaning of Crown Heights," in *Seven Days,* August 1978.

towers; foxy, fly, (*where did we receive these imprintings?*) *Male-directed fragmentation:* I am ugly if you are beautiful; you are ugly if I am beautiful. (Always the reference being, neither to me nor to you but to the man—black or white—who will judge us, find one of us wanting.) *Internalized gynephobia:* if I despise myself as woman I must despise you even more, for you are my rejected part, my antiself.

Your body or mine, depending on neighborhood: stretched out, above the street, the subway platform, uptown or downtown, vodka or Scotch, in velvet or satin, mistress or concubine, black or white. Lips curved or pouting in the semblance of the doll. Black pussy, piece of white ass, ball-buster, floozy, chippie, nympho, sweathog, two-bit whore, pipe-cleaner, nutcracker, cunt.

VI

I used to envy the "colorblindness" which some liberal, enlightened, white people were supposed to possess; raised as I was, where I was, I am and will to the end of my life be acutely, sometimes bitterly, aware of color. Every adult around me in my childhood, white or black, was aware of it; it was a sovereign consciousness, a hushed and compelling secret. But I no longer believe that "colorblindness"—if it even exists—is the opposite of racism; I think it is, in this world, a form of naiveté and moral stupidity. It implies that I would look at a black woman and see her as white, thus engaging in white solipsism to the utter erasure of her particular reality. But in moving further and further out of the worldview into which I was born, something else happened: I began to perceive women as women. I began to see what separations by class, race, and age did not wish me to see; but above all, what patriarchal fragmentation did not intend for me to see, or for us to see in each other. That we are different, that we are alike; that we have been together by miracle and against the law; that we have been disconnected by violence; that we still dread and mistrust each other; that we long for and are necessary to each other; that to make a primary commitment to women is to break a primary taboo, for which we often go on paying through self-punishment as well as through the penalties imposed by the taboo-keepers.

VII

If black and white feminists are going to speak of female account-ability, I believe the word *racism* must be seized, grasped in our bare hands, ripped up out of the sterile or defensive consciousness in which it so often grows, and transplanted so that it can yield new in-sights for our lives and our movement. An analysis that places the guilt for active domination, physical and institutional violence, and the justifications embedded in myth and language, on white women not only compounds false consciousness; it allows us all to deny or neglect the charged connections among black and white women from the historical conditions of slavery on; and it impedes any real discussion of women's instrumentality in a system which oppresses all women, and in which hatred of women is also embedded in myth, folklore, and language.[28]

There is a dead weight which can be felt in many discussions of racism in the white feminist movement, a stale and stifling smell, the presence of guilt and self-hatred. I believe that black feminists recognize the uselessness, the stagnancy, of those emotions. The black feminists who have asserted that "sexual politics in patriarchy is as pervasive in black women's lives as are the politics of class and race"[29] have each had to examine and discard a great deal of female guilt and self-hatred on their own account in order to make such a declaration.

[28] In describing the self-derogatory "black" humor of her childhood, Zora Neale Hurston observes:

> I found the Negro, and always the blackest Negro, being made the butt of all jokes—particularly black women.
>
> They brought bad luck for a week if they came to your house of a Monday morning. They were evil. They slept with their fists balled up ready to fight and squabble even when they were asleep. They even had evil dreams. White, yellow and brown girls dreamed about roses and perfume and kisses. Black gals dreamed about guns, razors, ice-picks, hatchets, and hot lye. I heard men swear they had seen women dreaming and knew these things to be true. (Hurston, *Dust Tracks on a Road* [Philadelphia: Lippincott, 1971], p. 225; first published 1942.)

[29] "The Combahee River Collective: A Black Feminist Statement," in Zillah Ei-senstein, ed., *Capitalist Patriarchy: A Case for Socialist Feminism* (New York: Monthly Review Press, 1978), p. 365.

Responsibility for instrumentality—accountability—is a profound and continuing question. Mary Daly, in *Gyn/Ecology*, relentlessly depicts how in Africa and Asia—not only in white, western culture—women have been made into "token torturers" for other women. Each culture teaches women specific requirements for "survival" (which may be merely a living death)—demonstrations of loyalty to patriarchal civilization. One of these has been the passing-on from generation to generation of a mutilation endured because there seemed no other choice (although we know that mothers have taught daughters subversion and rebellion as well as loyalty to patriarchy). When, in an oppressive hierarchy, women are trained for and given access only to certain "service" positions (mother, nurse, teacher, social worker, day-care center worker—ill-paid, sentimentalized roles) it is chiefly women who find themselves facing, in the actual presence of living individuals (children, welfare clients, the sick, the aging), the consequences of the cruelty and indifference of powerful males who control the professions and institutions. It is women who are supposed to absorb the anger, the hunger, the unmet needs, the psychic and physical pain of the human lives which become statistics and abstractions in the hands of social scientists, government officials, administrators; or poetic material in the hands of "humanist scholars," who (like the recently canonized Robert Coles)[30] vampirize the lives of the oppressed.

Many such women are not particularly political; they are holding down the kind of jobs for which they were told they were eligible; they are underpaid or nonpaid, and if they make common cause with their clients they are usually fired. Many *have* heroically sought to subvert "the system" in large or small ways; many others suffer the damges inherent in all professional training. Their instrumentality is one consequence of the way they, as women, have been "tracked" or chosen for one kind of work but not for others; one indication of the huge gaps in their training, the lies they were taught, how they learned to swallow dissent in order to pass, to graduate, to get a job, to keep it. Racism, misogyny, are of the very texture of the professions, white male supremacism the thread of which they are woven. But a black first-grader, or that child's mother, or a black patient in a

---

[30] See the *New York Times Magazine*, March 26, 1978.

hospital, or a family on welfare, may experience racism most directly in the person of a white woman, who stands for those "service" professions through which white male supremacist society controls the mother, the child, the family, and all of us. It is *her* racism, yes, but a racism learned in the same patriarchal school which taught her that women are unimportant or unequal, not to be trusted with power; where she learned to mistrust and fear her own impulses for rebellion: to become an instrument. The question of accountability remains alive, nonetheless; since some women in "service" jobs find ways of being less instrumental, more disloyal to civilization, than others.

But what of women who consider themselves politicized, as feminists? What of those of us who have, as feminists, asked with Virginia Woolf:

> . . . Let us never cease from thinking,—what is this "civilization" in which we find ourselves? What are these ceremonies and why should we take part in them? What are these professions and why should we make money out of them? Where in short is it leading us, the procession of the sons of educated men?[31]

The concept of racism itself is often intellectualized by white feminists. For some, a conscientious, obligatory mention of "racism-and-classism" allows it to be assumed that deep qualitative differences in female experience have been taken into account, where in fact intellectual analysis has been trusted to do the work of emotional apprehension, *which it cannot do*. (We all recognize that phenomenon where male analyses of sexism are concerned.) It is possible to make obeisance to the abstract existence of racism, even to work politically on issues of immediate concern to black and Third World women, such as sterilization abuse, out of an intellectual right-mindedness which actually distances us from the point where black and white women have to begin together. I have more than once felt anger at abstractly "correct" language wielded by self-described political feminists: a language, it seemed to me, which sprang from learned analysis rather than from that synthesis of reflec-

[31] *Three Guineas* (New York: Harcourt Brace, 1966), pp. 62–63; first published 1938.

tion and feeling, personal struggle and critical thinking, which is at the core of feminist process. My anger has been aroused in part by the distancing effect of such rhetoric, which leaves me feeling out of touch with some vital center I need to experience in order not to feel powerless. But it was—and is—also anger at the reduction to formula of the still unexplored movements and gestures, silences and dialogues, between women—in this case, between black women and white.

(Yet, I, also, have done this: pronounced the word "racism" while withholding my body and soul from the reality that word could evoke for me, if I would let it: half a lifetime's layered experience, lived in ambiguity and double-vision, peripheral vision, memories swept under the rug.)

Racism. The sound of the word itself: short, sharp, suitably ugly; how easy to speak it if you are white, feeling justice has been done to the realities it represents. But it can also mask those realities. Charged as it is—"That's a racist thing to say" hurled into a women's group: anger, tears, denial, rebuttal, ensuing conversations— charged as it is, it is at the same time mechanized, like any abstraction: a button we can press, if we are white, and go on living as always.

We have to go on using the word, however. When I began writing this paper I wanted to annihilate it; I thought it carried too much of a burden of shame on the one hand and pure abstraction on the other, to be of use to us. I thought of trying to claim other language in which to describe, specifically, the white woman's problem in encountering the black woman; the differences that have divided black and white women; the misnaming or denial of those differences in everyday life. But I am convinced that we must go on using that sharp, sibilant word; not to paralyze ourselves and each other with repetitious, stagnant doses of guilt, but to break it down into its elements, comprehend it as a *female* experience, and also to understand its inextricable connections with gynephobia. Our stake, as women, in making those connections, is not abstract justice; it is integrity and survival.

One of the useful things about the past is its safe distance: I mean, because we feel a certain detachment from it, we can allow ourselves to perceive in history ways of behaving which continue into the present, and afflict our actions still. Frances Kemble's *Journal of a Residence on a Georgian Plantation* is a case in point. I knew the book by hearsay as the work of an Englishwoman, married to an American slaveholder, who was appalled by the institution of slavery and whose convictions led to the breakup of her marriage and the loss of her children. To read it is to experience the full impact of racist language and cliché embedded in a passionate and unrelenting indictment of slavery. Black people are "good-natured, childish human beings, whose mental condition is kin in its simplicity and proneness to impulsive emotion" to that of white children; the features of adult black men and women are "displeasing" and "ugly" though "I have seen many babies on this plantation who were quite as pretty as white children"; black people are "sooty" with "dazzling grinders," their eyeballs and teeth gleam in the dark, etc., etc. Yet her perceptions of the workings of the institution are politically incisive, such as her comments on the Georgia pinelanders, or poor whites: "To the crime of slavery, though they have no profitable part or lot in it, they are fiercely accessory, because it is the barrier that divides the black and white races, at the foot of which they lie wallowing in unspeakable degradation, but immensely proud of the base freedom which still separates them from the lash-driven tillers of the soil."

Or, observing the self-congratulation of southerners on "the degree of license to which they capriciously permit their favorite slaves occasionally to carry their familiarity" she remarks: "It is only the degradation of the many that admits of this favoritism to the few—a system of favoritism which, as it is perfectly consistent with the profoundest contempt and injustice, degrades the object of it quite as much, though it oppresses him less, than the cruelty practiced upon his fellows."[32]

I found reading Fanny Kemble an enlightening experience; for she knew what racism was, analyzing with sensitivity its effects upon the morale and psyche of free black people in the North, while unconscious of the extent to which her own language reflected her lingering allegiance to white racist culture. It is precisely her in-

[32] Frances Kemble, *Journal of a Residence on a Georgian Plantation in 1838–1839*, John A. Scott, ed. (New York: New American Library, 1975).

telligence and depth of feeling, the authenticity of her anger and
pain, which throw into unintentional relief the forms of racism she
has *not* explored or encompassed in her defense of black people and
her indictment of slavery.[33]

VIII

Racism is often alluded to as if it were monolithic or uniform: in
fact it is multiform. As women we need to develop a language in
which to describe the forms that directly affect our relations with
each other. I believe that white feminists today, raised white in a
racist society, are often ridden with *white solipsism*—not the consciously held *belief* that one race is inherently superior to all others,
but a tunnel-vision which simply does not see nonwhite experience
or existence as precious or significant, unless in spasmodic, impotent
guilt-reflexes, which have little or no long-term, continuing mo-
mentum or political usefulness. I believe also that we have been ridden with *mythic misperceptions* of black women and other women of
color, and that these misperceptions have flourished in the combined soil of racism and gynephobia, the subjectivity of patriarchy.
In choosing to examine female racism from a feminist perspective, I
can more accurately perceive the white solipsism which surrounds
me and which I have partly internalized and helped to perpetuate;
the mythic misperceptions I have held, first about black women but
also about other women who seemed to me to have some special
access to truth, magic, and transforming power, some right *to take
their condition seriously*, which I was denying to myself.

It also seems to me that guilt feelings—so easily provoked in
women that they have become almost a form of social control—can
also become a form of solipsism, a preoccupation with our own feelings which prevents us from ever connecting with the experience of
others. Guilt feelings paralyze, but paralysis can become a conve-
nient means of remaining passive and instrumental. If I cannot even

[33] Lura Beam touches upon the racism which cannot see beyond the aesthetics of
the dominant culture: "I have known Negro women who said they minded their looks
more than any other burden they bore. I know white men and women who had spent
a lifetime among them, who would have died for them as a matter of principle, yet
called them 'an ugly race.' " (*He Called Them by the Lightning*, op. cit., p. 212).

approach you because I feel so much guilt towards you, I need never listen to what you have actually to say; I need never risk making common cause with you as two women with choices as to how we might exist and act. Accountability might begin with a serious effort to separate the strands of patriarchally induced female self-hatred from our honest recognition of instrumentality in the past, a recognition which is not mere self-accusation, which is truly historical and usable.

White feminists are not going to transcend the past through the careful "inclusion" of one or more black women in our projects and imaginings; nor through false accountability to some shadowy "other," the Black Woman, the Myth. Real transcendence—and use—of the past demands more difficult work. But it also brings into play that lightning-rod conductor between women which I think of as pulsing at the core of lesbian/feminism: love experienced as identification, as tenderness, as sympathetic memory and vision, as appreciation perhaps of some little detail, how this old woman wears her hat or that young girl takes off down a street—a nonexploitative, non-possessive eroticism, which can cross barriers of age and condition, the sensing our way into another's skin, if only in a moment's apprehension, against the censure, the denial, the lies and laws of civilization.

(Lest any think I am offering woman-identification as a simple solution, let me say here that I believe love, integrity, and survival all depend, in the face of our history as part of American racism, on the continuing question: *How are black and white women going to name, to found, to create, justice between us?* For even making love together we can, and often do, perpetuate injustice.)

If then we begin to recognize what the separation of black and white women means, it must become clear that it means separation from ourselves. For white women to break silence about our past means breaking silence about what the politics of skin color, of white and black male mythology and sexual politics, have meant to us, and listening closely as black women tell us what it has meant for them. Why, for example, should we feel more alien to the literature and lives of black women than to centuries of the literature and history of white men? Which of those two cultures—black and female, or white and male—is more vital for us to know as we strive to claim a female vision of reality? We cannot hope to define a feminist culture, a gynecentric vision, on racist terms, because a part of ourselves will remain forever unknown to us.

The past ten years of feminist writing and speaking, saying our own words or attempting to, have shown us that it is the realities civilization has told us are unimportant, regressive or unspeakable which prove our most essential resources. Female anger. Love between women. The tragic, potent bond between mother and daughter. The fact that a woman may rejoice in creating with her brain and not with her uterus. The actualities of lesbian motherhood. The sexuality of older women. The connections—painful, oblique, and often bitter—between black and white women, including shame, manipulation, betrayal, hypocrisy, envy, and love. If we have learned anything in our coming to language out of silence, it is that what has been kept unspoken, therefore *unspeakable,* in us is what is most threatening to the patriarchal order in which men control, first women, then all who can be defined and exploited as "other." All silence has a meaning.

IX

To take our condition seriously: Black women as well as white women know that the oppression most readily acknowledged by both black and white people in America—even by those who justify and practice racism—is racial and/or class oppression. To assert womanhating as a constant fact of life both within the black community and as a fact of white women's lives has meant, for both black and white feminists, taking an immense and courageous step beyond past political positions, old analyses of power and powerlessness. The dismissal or postponement of "women's issues" (as if "women's issues" were not central human issues) by "radical" and "revolutionary" groups is part of the mass psychology of male supremacism; that women have accepted it at all is a measure of our indoctrinated self-denial. It is that same self-denial which has allowed us to endure without protest the spiritual nausea induced in us by jokes about old maids, mothers-in-law, Jewish mothers, dykes, prostitutes; by pornography; by the daily bulletins of male violence against women; by our knowledge that men we have nurtured, supported, and done time for were not our spiritual and emotional equals, and that our selfhood, our womanhood itself, has been contemptible or terrifying to them. The anger and pain aroused in us by language, images, acts that defame and destroy women has taken three forms: compassion (for our rapists and batterers, not for each other); denial and laughter (boys *will* be boys; a sense of humor is *so* important); or the old, entangled rage of woman vs. woman. To permit ourselves to acknowledge the depth of woman-hatred encountered, tolerated, and justified in everyday life is frightening; yet somewhere, we all know it, and I believe that as this fear becomes more conscious it also becomes healthier. Unanalyzed pain leads us to numbness, subservience, or to random and ineffectual bursts of violence. As separate individuals, women have rarely been in a position to use our pain and anger as a creative force for change. Most women have not even been able to touch this anger, except to drive it inward like a rusted nail.

To the extent that I can imagine being a black woman, a black feminist, I can imagine carrying a particular fear in me: that white feminists, and other white women who have "changed their lives" in the light of the feminist movement, might still possess the capacity to delude themselves into some compromise of inclusion into patriarchy, into the white male order. That they (we) would not emotionally believe what they (we) intellectually profess as to the need for an end to patriarchy. That their (our) physical, genetic knowledge would fail to rise like warning nausea where selective treatment of women offers money, prizes, "life-style liberation," personal solutions, to the few—and those few, overwhelmingly white. That they (we) would not recognize the forms of suicide we have practiced in the past, under their newest guises. (The First Woman to be Cloned? The First Lesbian Secretary of State? The First Mother on the Moon?) That, unable or unwilling to fathom the destructiveness of racism as black people live it, they (we) will also fail to fathom the violence of gynephobia as they (we) are living it.

But this, of course, is not solely a black feminist's nightmare.

The contradictions, the taboos, of difference. They said to us: *That flesh, darker or lighter than your own, encloses a foreign country. You cannot know it. It speaks another language, it is alien territory: otherness.* At the same time they told us: *You cannot find wholeness with one whose body is formed like your own, one who like you has only a clitoris, only a vulva, one who like you is in a state of lack. You must seek the Opposite, the Other, Him whose difference from you means power, means mastery. Without Him you are powerless, unfinished. With her you can only be two halves, unbalanced, multilated, contemptible.*

But in you I seek both difference and identity. We both know that women are not identical: the movement of your mind; the pulse of your orgasm; the figures in your dreams; the weapons you received from your mothers, or had to invent; the range of your hungers—I cannot intuit merely because we both are women. And yet, there is so much I can know. What has stopped me short, what fuses my anger now, is that we were told we were utterly different, that the difference between us must be everything, must be determinative, *that from that difference we each must turn away; that we must also flee from our alikeness.*

As a lesbian/feminist, what can passive subservience to those orders mean to me, but that I passively consent to remain an instrument of men, who have always profited from slavery, imperialism, enforced heterosexuality and motherhood, organized prostitution and pornography, and the separation of women from each other? What can obedience to those orders mean, but that my woman-identification is mere "sexual preference," my erotic self still distorted and constrained?

As I thrust my hand deeper into the swirl of this stream—history, nightmare, accountability—I feel the current angrier and more multiform than the surface shows: There is fury here, and terror, but there is also power, power not to be had without the terror and the fury. We need to go beyond rhetoric or evasion into that place in ourselves, to feel the force of all we have been trying—without success—to skim across.

ALSO BY ADRIENNE RICH

OF WOMAN BORN
Motherhood as Experience and Institution
Adrienne Rich

Of Woman Born is a memoir of the author's experiences as the mother of three sons, and an analysis of women's role as mother throughout history. Drawing on anthropology, medicine, psychology, literature and history, this brilliant poet has distilled her research into a book which is sometimes angry, often painful, always memorable. It is also a celebration of motherhood and a work of great imaginative force – one of those rare books which stretch the imagination and change one's thinking.

'Fierce and urgent and rare. . . Rich cuts deep, her tools those of thinking and feeling, her intention to expose and heal' – NANCY MILFORD, author of *Zelda*

'She reaches moments of great poignancy and eloquence' – FRANCINE DU PLESSIX GRAY, *New York Times Book Review*

'There are pitifully few books as yet that touch the subject, and it is one aspect of femininity that is essential male reading too . . . Rich's chapter on the relationship between mothers and daughters would alone be enough to cherish her book' – JILL TWEEDIE

LESBIAN PEOPLES
Materials for a Dictionary
Monique Wittig & Sande Zeig

This delightful dictionary redefines selected historical
and mythical persons, places, countries, flowers and animals,
celebrating the primitive, exotic and sexual powers of women.
With wit and verbal magic, the authors present a fascinating world
where women are the sole inhabitants, weaving words and
wonders of their own.

SILENCES
Tillie Olsen

Drawing on the lives, letters, diaries and testimonies of
many writers, Tillie Olsen examines the needs and work of
creation and those circumstances which obstruct it –
circumstances of sex, colour, class, the times and climate into
which a writer is born. A testament to the struggle of all artists to
defy the enemies of their promise.

Like A *Room of One's Own* it will be quoted wherever there is
talk of the circumstances in which literature is possible' –
ADRIENNE RICH

THINKING ABOUT WOMEN
Mary Ellmann

A witty analysis of sexual stereotypes in literature,
delicately demolishing the proposition that a woman's biology
determines her way of thinking.

'Acute, witty. . . with the omnivorousness of a scholar. . . Mrs
Ellmann tries to startle us out of our tired sexual analogies' –
CAROLYN HEILBRUN, *The New York Book Review*

A LITERATURE OF THEIR OWN
British Women Novelists from Brontë to Lessing
Elaine Showalter

A remarkable study of women novelists from 1880 to
the present day – their lives, their writings, the world of fiction

they created, including not only famous names such as
Eliot, Austen, Woolf and Drabble, but many less famous but
equally fascinating contemporaries.

'Required reading for anyone who cares about women or the
history of the novel' – ERICA JONG

PATRIARCHAL ATTITUDES
Eva Figes

With Germaine Greer's *The Female Eunuch* and Kate
Millett's *Sexual Politics*, *Patriarchal Attitudes* was a book which
changed the consciousness of a generation, and has established
itself as an outstanding contribution to the debate on women's
position in society

'The only one whose work can be set beside John Stuart Mill's
celebrated review of the subject and not seem shoddy or
self-serving.' – GORE VIDAL, *The New York Review of Books*

SEXUAL POLITICS
Kate Millett

Devastatingly witty and brilliantly researched, this
passionately argued work of literary and cultural analysis is one of
the most famous critical works of our time.

'A book which must take its place at a single leap in the ranks of
the best modern polemical literature' – MICHAEL FOOT, *Evening
Standard*

NOT IN GOD'S IMAGE
Women in History
eds. Julia O'Faslain and Lauro Martines

Through the words of contemporary writers this invaluable
souce book explores the lives women have led throughout
European history, illuminating the position of women over the
centuries.

'It adds a whole new dimension to the study of history, from
antiquity to the present' – *New Society*

THE PARADISE PAPERS
The Suppression of Women's Rites
Merlin Stone

The Paradise Papers tells the fascinating story of the most ancient religion, the religion of the Goddess, from its origins to its final suppression, and shows how this suppression laid the foundation of women's subservient position in society.

'It makes a beautiful whole of many scattered clues until now undiscovered, ignored, misinterpreted, or – shamefully often – unacknowledged' – JILL TWEEDIE

WOMEN IN WESTERN POLITICAL THOUGHT
Susan Moller Okin

Through a detailed study of four political philosophers whose ideas on the rights of man have profoundly shaped our own – Plato, Aristotle, Rousseau and Mill – this book looks at why, despite gaining formal rights of citizenship, women still do not have full equality with men.

'An excellent book. . . her language is calm, clear, simple and strong, her feminist perspective a line of thought that guides her steadily along' – VIVIAN GORNICK, *Washington Post*

HALF THE SKY
An Introduction to Women's Studies
eds. The Bristol Women's Studies Group

An anthology of famous and lesser known texts from British, American and European sources providing a key interdisciplinary reader on women's lives and experiences.

'A wide ranging text which will interest the general reader as well as participants in women's studies courses. . . The wealth of source material quoted makes accessible a great deal of women's writing' – *Tribune*

FEMALE SEXUALITY
New Psychoanalytic Views
ed. Janine Chasseguet-Smirgel

A remarkable addition to the study of female sexual
identity which, while acknowledging the power of culture and
society in changing our lives, explores the profound influence of
instincts and the unconscious in our experiences of sex and love.

'Lucid and not too loaded with scientific terms. . . valuable
insights' – *Publisher's Weekly*

WOMEN IN SOCIETY (*to be published 1981*)
Interdisciplinary Essays in Women's Studies
eds. Cambridge Women's Studies Group

Combining original research with critical examination
of existing arguments, this authoritative book, based on the course
of the same name at Cambridge University, offers new
perspectives on themes central to the understanding of women's
place in society.

If you would like to know more about Virago books, write to us at 5 Wardour Street, London W1V 3HE for a full catalogue.

Please send a stamped addressed envelope

Book Tokens

Give them
the pleasure of choosing
Book Tokens can be bought
and exchanged at most
bookshops